MEDIEVAL TREASURES FROM HILDESHEIM

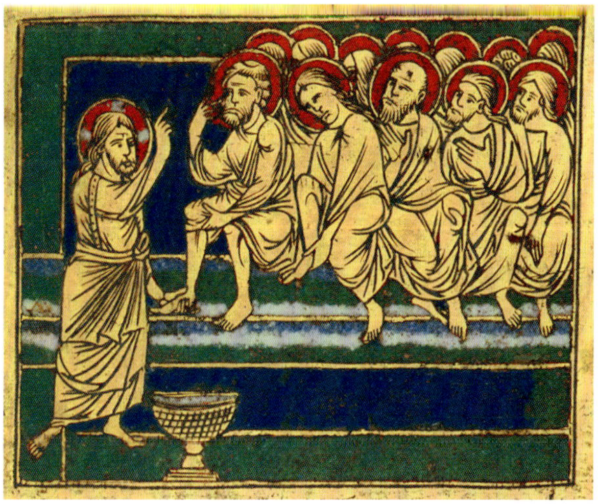

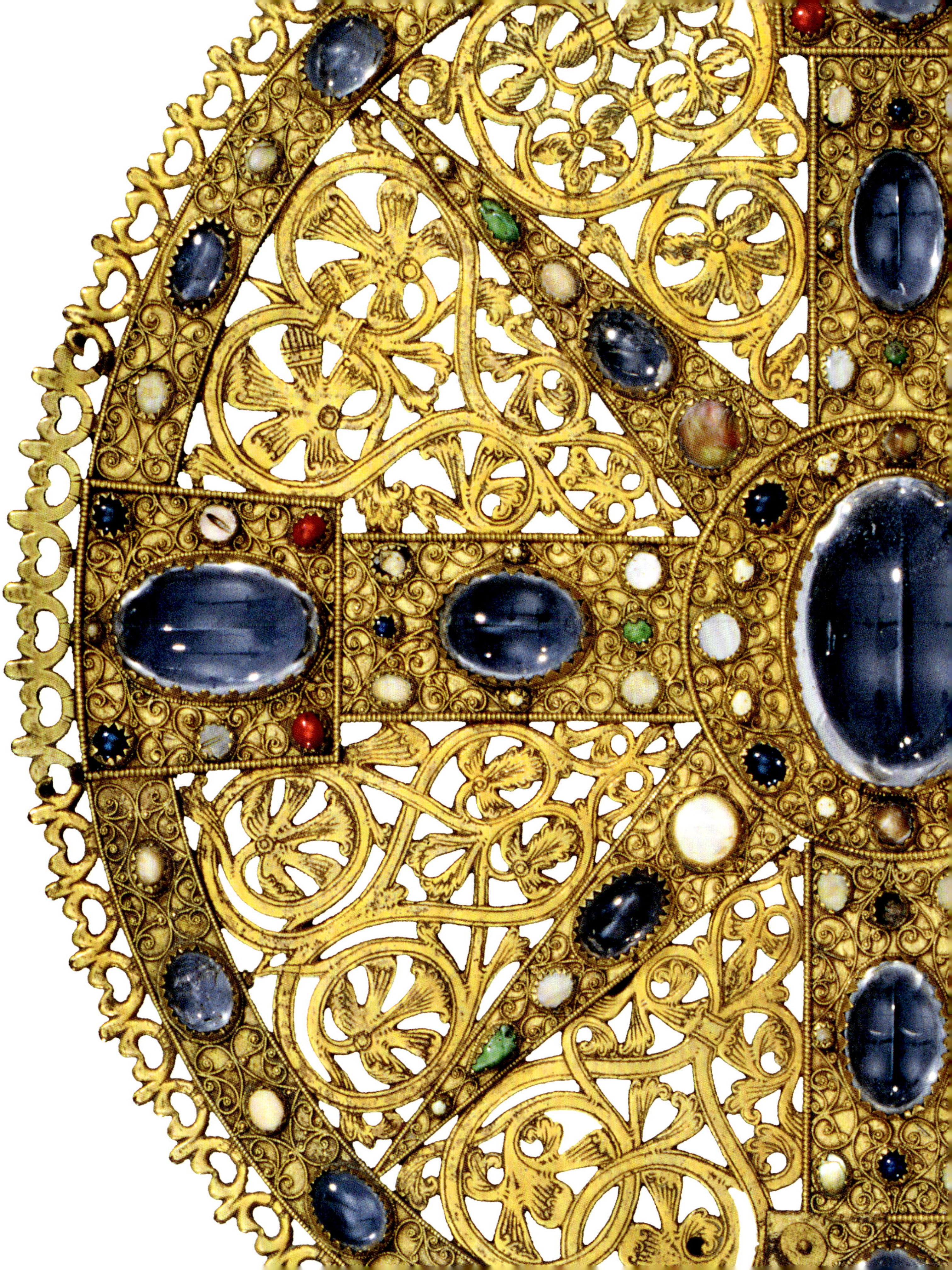

MEDIEVAL TREASURES FROM HILDESHEIM

Edited by Peter Barnet, Michael Brandt, and Gerhard Lutz

THE METROPOLITAN MUSEUM OF ART, NEW YORK

DISTRIBUTED BY YALE UNIVERSITY PRESS, NEW HAVEN AND LONDON

This catalogue is published in conjunction with "Medieval Treasures from Hildesheim," on view at The Metropolitan Museum of Art, New York, from September 17, 2013, through January 5, 2014.

The exhibition is made possible by the Michel David-Weill Fund.
This publication is made possible by The Andrew W. Mellon Foundation.

Published by The Metropolitan Museum of Art, New York
Mark Polizzotti, Publisher and Editor in Chief
Gwen Roginsky, Associate Publisher and General Manager of Publications
Peter Antony, Chief Production Manager
Michael Sittenfeld, Managing Editor
Robert Weisberg, Senior Project Manager

Edited by Nancy E. Cohen
Designed by Carl W. Scarbrough
Production by Sally Van Devanter
Bibliography edited by Jean Wagner and Sophia Wagner-Serrano
Translations from German by Russell Stockman
Translation from French by Jane Marie Todd

Typeset in Quadraat and Quadraat Sans
Printed on 150 gsm Gardamatte
Separations by Professional Graphics, Inc., Rockford, Illinois
Printed and bound by Graphicom S.r.l., Verona, Italy

COVER ILLUSTRATIONS: *front,* Crosier of Abbot Erkanbald, cat. 12; *back,* The Baptism of Christ, detail from Baptismal Font, cat. 38

P. i: Enamel Plaque (detail), cat. 27; P. ii: Liturgical Fan (detail), cat. 17; P. v: Bernward's Candlesticks (detail), cat. 11; P. 1: Enamel Plaque (detail), cat. 27; P. 128: Reliquary of Saint Oswald (detail), cat. 31; P. 132: Engraved sketch from reverse of Enamel Plaque, cat. 27

First printing

The Metropolitan Museum of Art
1000 Fifth Avenue
New York, New York 10028
metmuseum.org

Distributed by
Yale University Press, New Haven and London
yalebooks.com/art
yalebooks.co.uk

Cataloging-in-Publication Data is available from the Library of Congress.
ISBN 978-1-58839-497-2 (The Metropolitan Museum of Art)
ISBN 978-0-300-19699-3 (Yale University Press)

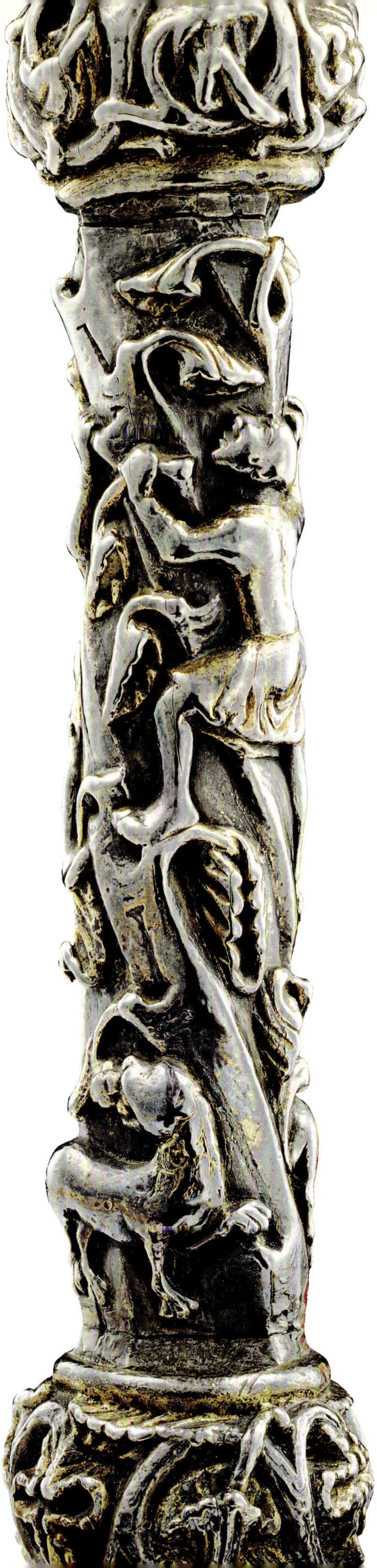

CONTENTS

Director's Foreword *Thomas P. Campbell* vi

Dean of Hildesheim Cathedral's Foreword *Hans Georg Koitz* vii

Acknowledgments viii

Contributing Authors x

Hildesheim: Center of Medieval Art
Martina Giese, Gerhard Lutz, and Harald Wolter-von dem Knesebeck 3

Works from Medieval Hildesheim 21

Bibliography 129

Index 133

Photography Credits 138

Director's Foreword

Writing enthusiastically in 1931, on the occasion of the American museum tour of the medieval Guelph Treasure, William M. Milliken, director of the Cleveland Museum of Art, declared, "It is as if the cathedrals of Hildesheim or Bamberg, Mainz or Limburg had been transported to our shore." Now, more than eighty years later, The Metropolitan Museum of Art is proud to welcome approximately fifty of the great medieval treasures from Hildesheim for the first such exhibition in America.

The Metropolitan's collection of medieval art is preeminent in the United States and indeed is one of the greatest collections of its kind in the world. Its nucleus was formed by J. Pierpont Morgan's extraordinary medieval collection, which came to the Museum in 1917. The Department of Medieval Art was created in 1933 and includes works from the early Middle Ages and Byzantium as well as Western European Romanesque and Gothic art. The Cloisters, our branch devoted to the art and architecture of medieval Europe, opened to the public in northern Manhattan in 1938 and celebrates its seventy-fifth anniversary this year.

The Metropolitan has a long history of important loan exhibitions of medieval works of art, including those devoted to such great treasuries as the royal abbey of Saint-Denis (1981), the Vatican (1983), San Marco in Venice (1985), and Basel Cathedral (2001). The works on loan from Hildesheim, however, stand out even in that rich context. The Ottonian illuminated manuscripts and silver works included in the present exhibition are arguably the greatest such objects ever shown in the United States. The twelfth-century reliquaries and the cast bronze works of the early thirteenth century are likewise among the finest to survive from the Middle Ages.

This catalogue is the first book on Hildesheim to appear in English, and I am grateful to Peter Barnet, Michel David-Weill Curator in Charge of the Museum's Department of Medieval Art and The Cloisters, and his coeditors, Michael Brandt, director of the Hildesheim Cathedral Museum, and Gerhard Lutz, curator there, for bringing this notable exhibition and its important publication to the Museum's audience. Furthermore, I extend my deep thanks to the Michel David-Weill Fund for its endowment support of the exhibition, and The Andrew W. Mellon Foundation for making this catalogue possible.

THOMAS P. CAMPBELL

DIRECTOR, THE METROPOLITAN MUSEUM OF ART

Dean of Hildesheim Cathedral's Foreword

More than a thousand years have passed since the founding of St. Mary's Cathedral in Hildesheim, Germany, the first church to be built in a diocese that would become one of the leading ecclesiastical and cultural centers of the Middle Ages. Thanks to the commissions and acquisitions of generations of clergy associated with Hildesheim, the cathedral and its museum today own one of the oldest, most extensive, and highest-quality collections of medieval treasures in Europe: reliquaries, portable altars, crosses, illuminated manuscripts, chalices, and other works of precious metals and gemstones.

These artworks uniquely have been preserved for centuries in the place for which they were created. That was a leading reason why UNESCO designated Hildesheim's St. Mary's Cathedral and St. Michael's Church as World Heritage Sites in 1985, recognizing them as monuments of medieval art with exceptionally rich treasures. Yet, unlike most museum holdings, the objects are not merely exhibits; they continue to serve their original liturgical purpose and are prominently featured in church services on feast days.

For many years the collection was housed adjacent to the cathedral choir in a crowded room. In the nineteenth century the trove significantly expanded through donations and acquisitions of art from the monasteries and other institutions in the diocese that were secularized in 1803. That effort was led by Hildesheim's Bishop Eduard J. Wedekin (1796–1870), who personally collected much of the newly available art and initiated a cathedral museum that would properly preserve the treasures in perpetuity.

The cathedral was all but destroyed in World War II, and exhibition space was limited until 1978, when the museum reopened with an expanded facility. Both the museum and the cathedral are now undergoing another major renovation, undertaken in connection with a significant milestone: In 2015 the bishopric of Hildesheim will celebrate its twelve-hundred-year jubilee. In addition to effecting necessary structural repairs, the renovation campaign will make it possible to appreciate the historical fabric of the cathedral in a new way. The museum is also to be enlarged, so that it can better display its vast collection.

The museum's closure during the renovations provides a rare opportunity to display many of these treasures in new venues. New York's Metropolitan Museum of Art, one of the world's great comprehensive museums, already preserves a number of objects that originated in Hildesheim. It gives me great pleasure to be able to present our treasures to the North American public in such a context before their return to Hildesheim. This book, published in conjunction with the exhibition, will bring them to an even wider audience. The first comprehensive overview of the collection to be published in English, it includes not only the extraordinary works in the exhibition but also Hildesheim's famous monumental bronzes – a set of doors and a triumphal column – that cannot travel owing to their size.

I am pleased to introduce you to these works of art here and warmly invite you to admire them in their original home once the cathedral and museum are reopened.

HANS GEORG KOITZ

AUXILIARY BISHOP EMERITUS

DEAN OF HILDESHEIM CATHEDRAL

Acknowledgments

This exhibition and catalogue would not have been possible without the support of many. We would like first to thank the other lending institutions in Hildesheim, in addition to the Dom-Museum: the cathedral church of Hildesheim and its dean, Hans Georg Koitz; the parish of the Holy Cross and Father Wolfgang Osthaus; and the cathedral library and its director, Jochen Bepler.

At The Metropolitan Museum of Art, Thomas P. Campbell, Director, has provided strong support from the outset, as have Emily Kernan Rafferty, President; Jennifer Russell, Associate Director for Exhibitions; and Carrie Rebora Barratt, Associate Director for Collections and Administration. Martha Deese and Maria E. Fillas in the Director's Office have also been helpful.

Colleagues in the Department of Medieval Art and The Cloisters, including Barbara D. Boehm, Helen C. Evans (Mary and Michael Jaharis Curator of Byzantine Art), Melanie Holcomb, Charles T. Little, Timothy B. Husband, Nancy Wu, Christine E. Brennan, Thomas C. Vinton, R. Theo Margelony, Christine D. McDermott, and Andrew Winslow, have all been generous with assistance. Thanks also to the department's interns Hannah Korn, Sarah Griffin, and Vittoria Vignone. Luke Syson, Iris and B. Gerald Cantor Curator in Charge of the Department of European Sculpture and Decorative Arts, and his predecessor, Ian Wardropper, have been valued colleagues and graciously agreed to allow the exhibition to be installed in the department's Wrightsman Exhibition Gallery.

The Museum's conservation departments have made great contributions to the exhibition. Lawrence Becker, Sherman Fairchild Conservator in Charge of the Department of Objects Conservation, and conservators Pete Dandridge and Jack Soultanian, Jr., of his staff deserve many thanks. In Paper Conservation thanks go to Marjorie Shelley, Sherman Fairchild Conservator in Charge, and conservator Yana Van Dyke. In Hildesheim, conservator Uwe Schuchardt prepared the objects for the exhibition.

We owe much appreciation to Sharon H. Cott, Senior Vice President, Secretary, and General Counsel, and to Kirstie M. Howard and Lee White Galvis in her office. Harold Holzer, Senior Vice President for External Affairs, and Karin Grafstrom, Market Research Manager, have offered useful advice. Nina McN. Diefenbach, Vice President for Development and Membership, and Sarah Higby, Deputy Chief Development Officer for Corporate Programs, have also contributed to the project. We also are grateful to Elyse Topalian, Vice President for Communications, and Egle Žygas, Senior Press Officer. Aileen Chuk, Chief Registrar, and Nina S. Maruca, Senior Associate Registrar, have helped extensively with loans.

Peggy Fogelman, Frederick P. and Sandra P. Rose Chairman of Education, deserves many thanks for her interest in the exhibition. Members of her staff who have been involved are Joseph Loh and Jennifer Mock. We also thank Missy McHugh, Chief Adviser to the President, and Limor Tomer, General Manager of Concerts and Lectures, and her staff. We are grateful to Kenneth Soehner, Arthur K. Watson Chief Librarian, and to all his staff for the resources they were able to provide for this project.

In Design, Linda Sylling, Manager for Special Exhibitions, Gallery Installations, and Design, and Patricia A. Gilkison, Associate Manager, were essential in coordinating the project. Michael Langley conceived the outstanding exhibition design, and Mortimer Lebigre provided the handsome graphics. Clint Ross Coller and Richard Lichte provided the effective lighting design.

Many others helped make the installation possible. We would like to recognize those in the Buildings Department under Tom Scally, Buildings General Manager, who were integral to the process. Taylor Miller, who manages exhibitions, and the staffs of the various shops provided essential support. We also appreciate the security provided by John Barelli, Chief Security Officer, and the maintenance of the galleries under Gordon Hairston.

The catalogue authors (see Contributing Authors) have been generous in their advice regarding the exhibition. We would also like to recognize insights provided by Christina Nielsen, Assistant Curator at the Art Institute of Chicago; Holger Klein, Professor of Art History at Columbia University; and Michele Marincola, Professor of Conservation at the Institute of Fine Arts, New York University.

Enormous thanks are due the Museum's exceptional editorial staff for their work on this catalogue. Mark Polizzotti, Publisher and Editor in Chief, ensured that the publication met the Museum's usual high standards. The efforts of Michael Sittenfeld, Managing Editor; Elizabeth Zechella, Editor; Gwen Roginsky, Associate Publisher and General Manager; and Peter Antony, Chief Production Manager, are much appreciated. The outstanding editor was Nancy E. Cohen. Production Managers Jennifer Van Dalsen and Sally Van Devanter were instrumental in assisting with the images for the book, and Sally was responsible for coordinating its production. Jean Wagner and Sophia Wagner-Serrano painstakingly edited the bibliography and selected references. Russell Stockman ably translated text from German, and Jane Marie Todd translated from French. We thank Carl W. Scarbrough for the book's elegant design.

Additional photography was provided by Antje Voigt, by arrangement of Lothar Lambacher and Julien Chapuis (Staatliche Museen zu Berlin); Ansgar Hoffmann (Schlangen); and Erika Dufour, courtesy of the Art Institute of Chicago.

Thanks also go to German Consul General Busso von Alvensleben and Jakob von Wagner, Cultural Attaché, for their advice.

The participation of all those mentioned above and many others made "Medieval Treasures from Hildesheim" a reality, and we thank everyone involved in the project.

PETER BARNET
MICHEL DAVID-WEILL CURATOR IN CHARGE,
DEPARTMENT OF MEDIEVAL ART
AND THE CLOISTERS

MICHAEL BRANDT
DIRECTOR, HILDESHEIM CATHEDRAL MUSEUM

GERHARD LUTZ
CURATOR, HILDESHEIM CATHEDRAL MUSEUM

CONTRIBUTING AUTHORS

PETER BARNET, Michel David-Weill Curator in Charge, Department of Medieval Art and The Cloisters, The Metropolitan Museum of Art

BARBARA DRAKE BOEHM, Curator, Department of Medieval Art and The Cloisters, The Metropolitan Museum of Art

CHRISTINE DESCATOIRE, Curator, Musée de Cluny–Musée National du Moyen Âge, Paris

HELEN C. EVANS, Mary and Michael Jaharis Curator of Byzantine Art, Department of Medieval Art and The Cloisters, The Metropolitan Museum of Art

MARTINA GIESE, Assistant Professor, University of Düsseldorf, Germany

CLAUDIA HÖHL, Curator, Hildesheim Cathedral Museum

MELANIE HOLCOMB, Curator, Department of Medieval Art and The Cloisters, The Metropolitan Museum of Art

TIMOTHY B. HUSBAND, Curator, Department of Medieval Art and The Cloisters, The Metropolitan Museum of Art

CHARLES T. LITTLE, Curator, Department of Medieval Art and The Cloisters, The Metropolitan Museum of Art

GERHARD LUTZ, Curator, Hildesheim Cathedral Museum

HARALD WOLTER-VON DEM KNESEBECK, Professor, Department of Art History, University of Bonn

MEDIEVAL TREASURES FROM HILDESHEIM

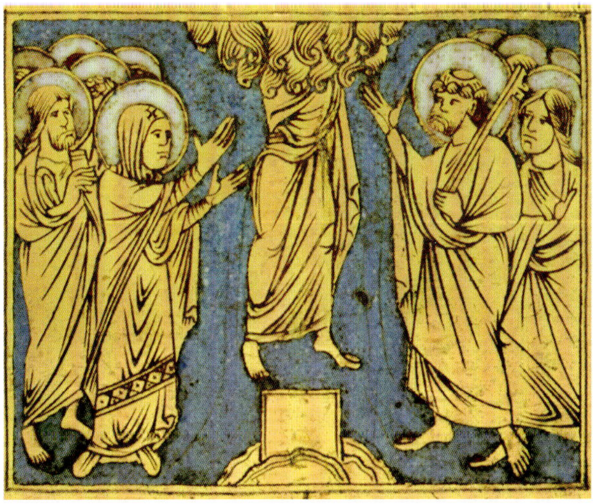

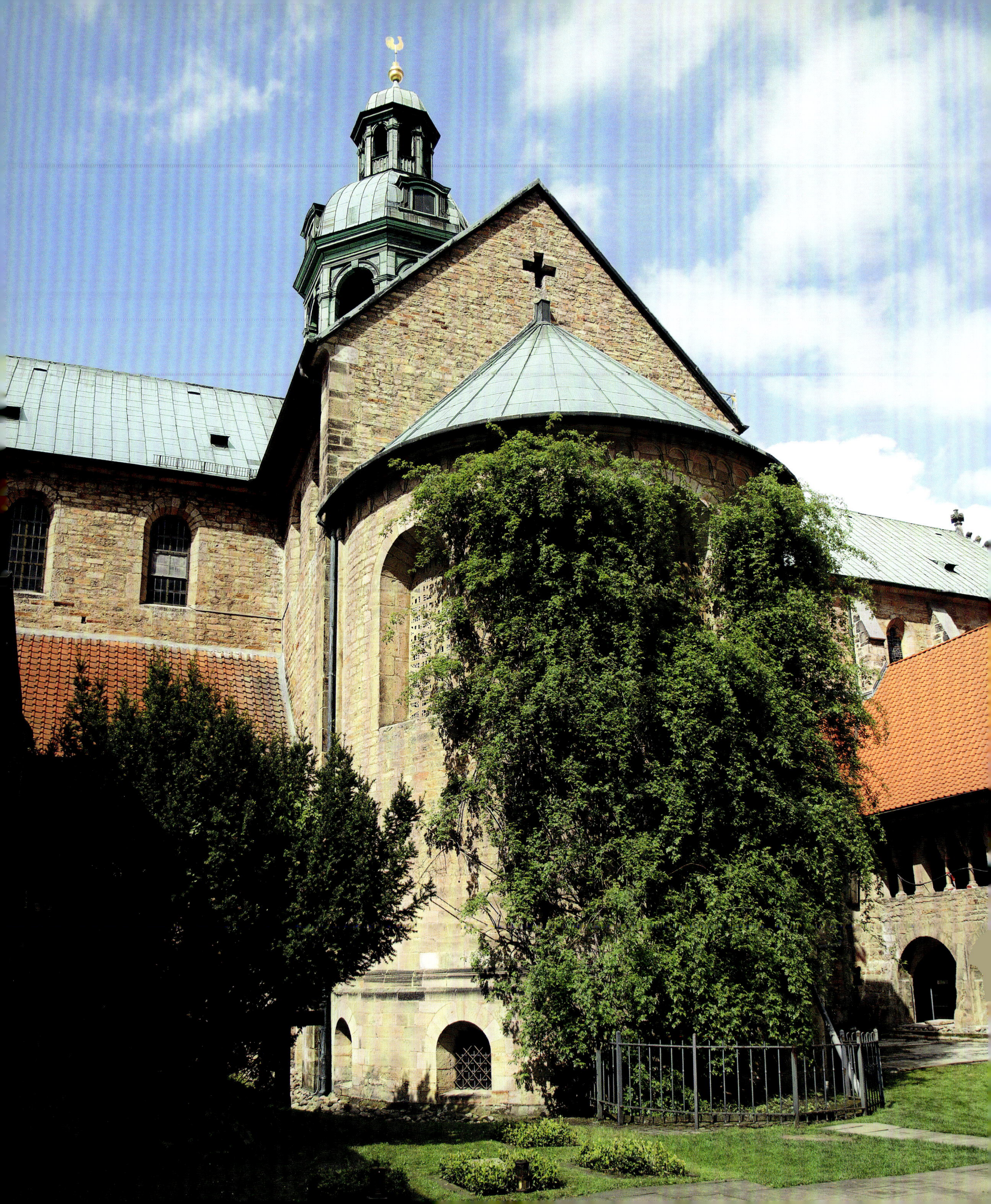

Hildesheim: Center of Medieval Art

MARTINA GIESE, GERHARD LUTZ, AND HARALD WOLTER-VON DEM KNESEBECK

Hildesheim, in Lower Saxony, is one of the oldest cities in northern Germany and was among the leading ecclesiastical and cultural centers of the Middle Ages, yet its origins are only sketchily documented. The pagan Saxons, after extended fighting, had finally been subdued by the emperor Charlemagne (747/48–814), who then energetically promoted Christian missionizing and established several bishoprics in the region. In 815 Charlemagne's son and successor, Louis the Pious (778–840), founded the bishopric of Hildesheim and installed its first bishop, Gunthar (reigned 815–34).

The late eleventh-century *Fundatio ecclesiæ Hildensemensis* (Founding of the Hildesheim Church) relates in detail the legend of the institution's early years. It recounts how Louis the Pious took a break during a hunt to order a reading of the Mass. His chaplain hung a reliquary of the Virgin on the branch of a tree – said to be the rosebush that still grows by the church's apse (fig. 1) – and forgot to retrieve it when the hunting party moved on. The relics were found the next day but miraculously could not be removed from the tree. Louis interpreted this as a divine revelation of the spot where a bishopric should be established. He had an altar erected there and, above it, a chapel in honor of the Virgin. The miraculous foundation reliquary, the Shrine of Our Lady (fig. 2), has been preserved in the cathedral treasure to this day.

From a historical point of view, this narrative explains both how Hildesheim Cathedral's site was chosen and why it came to be consecrated to the Virgin. Bishop Altfried (reigned 851–75) built the first cathedral on the site, which was well positioned on a hill near the Innerste River. Over the ensuing centuries his successors – all of whom are known by name – energetically expanded Hildesheim into a major religious center with numerous monasteries, churches, and a renowned school. The reputation of its cathedral chapter and school was such that Hildesheim produced no fewer than forty-four bishops and archbishops, who served in dioceses from Cologne to Magdeburg and from Schleswig to Salzburg and Brixen, between 918 and 1167.

Hildesheim flourished, gaining power and prosperity, as a new dynastic structure emerged in the tenth century. The Ottonians, a Saxon noble family, succeeded the Carolingians, assuming the German kingship in 919 and rule of a reconfigured empire (encompassing what are now Germany, Switzerland, and northern and central Italy but excluding France) in 962. The Ottonian era (919–1024) spurred a cultural revival, as sovereigns and bishops, seeking the prestige of the Roman and Byzantine empires, vigorously supported the production of art, especially illuminated manuscripts and their jeweled covers, fine metalwork, and other luxury church furnishings.

Under the Ottonian kings Hildesheim was elevated to the dynasty's home bishopric, and worthy churchmen in the kings' confidence were appointed to head it. Their proximity to the monarchy brought Hildesheim's bishops numerous privileges, including the right to mint coinage, and special sway. For example, on a journey to Italy in the king's retinue, Bishop Othwin (reigned 954–84) took advantage of his royal protection to seize a number of relics in a nighttime coup. On his return to Hildesheim in 963, this salutary treasure was ceremoniously deposited in the cathedral. It included a relic of Saint Epiphanius of Pavia, who subsequently joined the Virgin as one of the cathedral's chief patrons.

The bishops' power extended into civic affairs; they ruled the area as its ultimate secular as well as religious authorities.

OPPOSITE: FIG. 1 *St. Mary's Cathedral, Hildesheim, with rosebush growing by the apse*

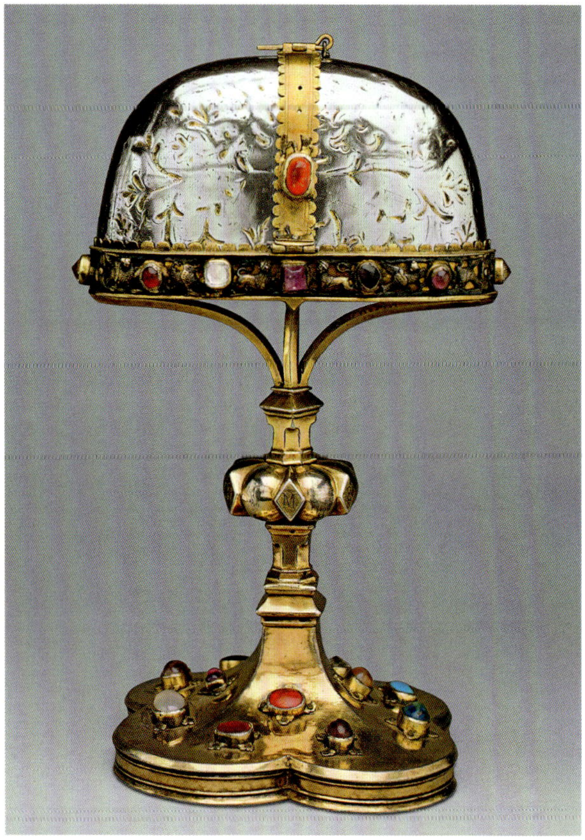

FIG. 2 *Foundation Reliquary. Relic capsule: Workshop at the Carolingian Court, Aachen, early 9th century; base: Hildesheim, late 14th century. Silver with precious stones (added to capsule in Hildesheim ca. 1210–20), H. 11¼ in. (28.6 cm) with base. Dom-Museum Hildesheim (DS 1)*

OPPOSITE: FIG. 3 *Transept of St. Mary's Cathedral, looking west into the nave, with Hezilo Chandelier. Chandelier: German (Hildesheim), 1061. Copper with vernis brun, Diam. ca. 19 ft. 8 in. (ca. 6 m)*

It was due to their considerable influence – notably that of Bishop Bernward (reigned 993–1022), one of the Middle Ages' greatest patrons of the arts – that medieval Hildesheim came to produce and accumulate such a vast quantity of art. By richly endowing their see in Lower Saxony with monasteries, each of which in turn commissioned a wealth of church furnishings, they ensured the success of Hildesheim's workshops, whose production was highly regarded at the time and today claims eminence in the art history of the Middle Ages.

As a newly established bishopric in Saxony, only recently converted to Christianity, Hildesheim looked to the bishoprics in the western territories of the Frankish Empire (essentially present-day France and Belgium and the centers along the Rhine); it depended on talent as well as cultural stimuli from the West, which had rich traditions of ecclesiastical art. The bishopric of Reims, in northeast France, was considered the mother of the Hildesheim church and shared with it the patronage of the Virgin; Hildesheim's first bishop, Gunthar, is thought to have been sent from Reims. Monks from Corbie, in northern France, arrived in Saxony soon thereafter, founding a monastery in 822 in Corvey (derived from the Latin Corbeia nova, the "new Corbie"). Hildesheim also had close links to Cologne, from which St. Michael's first monks would be summoned in the early eleventh century.

The objects from the Carolingian era (ninth century) surviving in Hildesheim reflect that wide-ranging network. For example, the reliquary known as the Shrine of Our Lady (see fig. 2), which was mentioned in the founding legend, was probably fashioned in Aachen during Charlemagne's lifetime. The same is true of the so-called Small Bernward Gospel (cat. 1). Written in northeastern France in the last third of the ninth century and simply decorated, it was so highly valued in Hildesheim that a century later Bishop Bernward had it rebound, prominently brandishing his bishop's monogram on the back cover. The rare fragments of Carolingian plaster sculpture still in Hildesheim Cathedral – two much-damaged tympanums in high relief above the entrances to the crypt of Bishop Altfried's cathedral – were based not only on Carolingian stucco figures from the westwork (monumental west-facing entrance) of the monastery church at Corvey but ultimately on earlier examples in the small church of Sta. Maria in Valle in Cividale (Friuli, northern Italy).

Altfried's cathedral, consecrated in 872, was built around the architectural nucleus of Louis the Pious's Mary Chapel. Its plan was characteristic of major cathedrals and abbey churches of the later Carolingian period, with three aisles, a continuous transept, and an annular crypt. In 1046 the cathedral burned virtually to the ground. Bishop Azelin (reigned 1044–54) and his successor, Hezilo (reigned 1054–79), erected a new structure on the foundations of Altfried's cathedral, retaining the crypt; it was consecrated in 1061. The cathedral was repeatedly expanded and remodeled over the next centuries. After being heavily damaged in World War II, it was rebuilt and consecrated in 1960. The reconstructed exterior primarily reflects the late medieval version of the building; the interior, which maintains the three-aisle structure, expresses a postwar interpretation of medieval

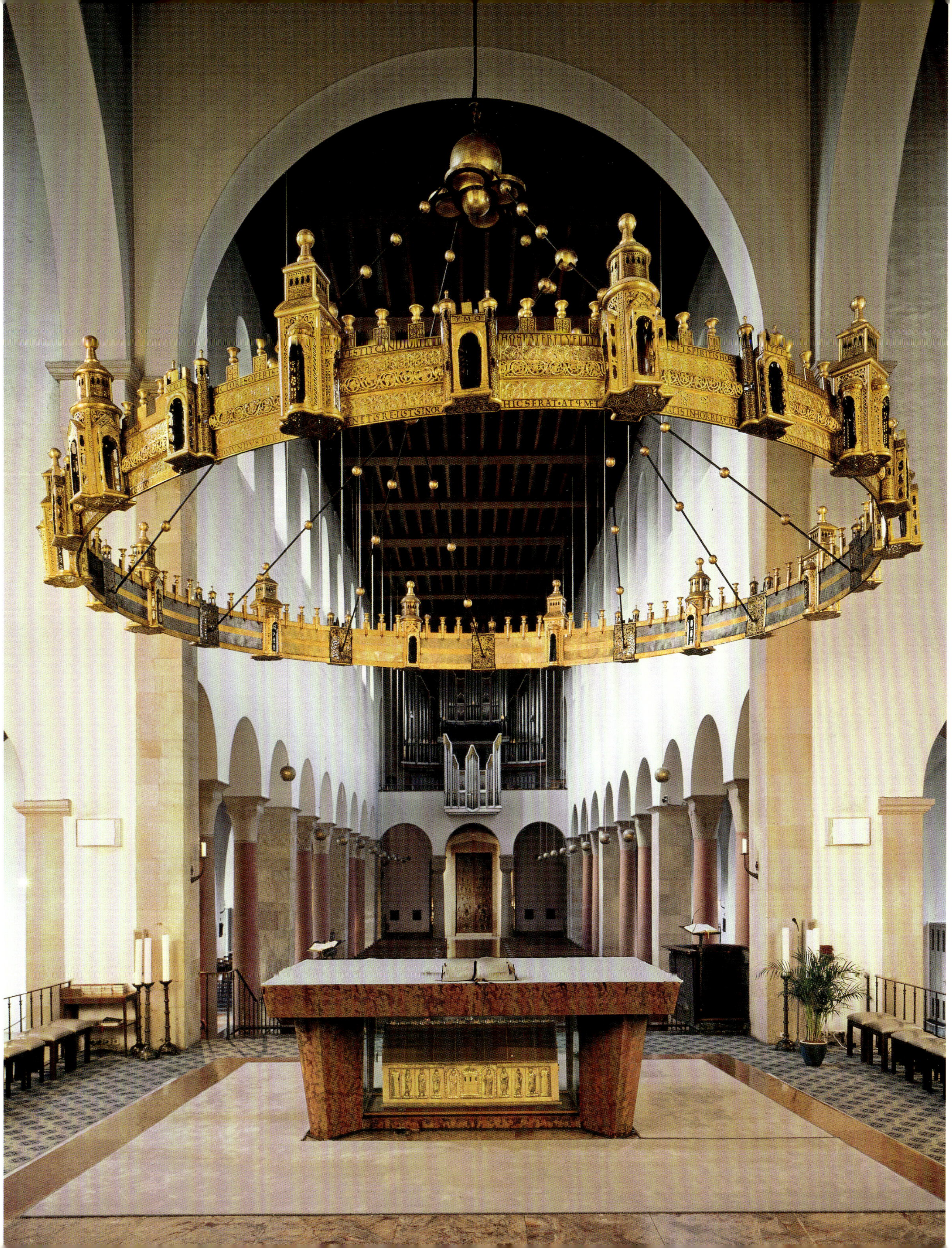

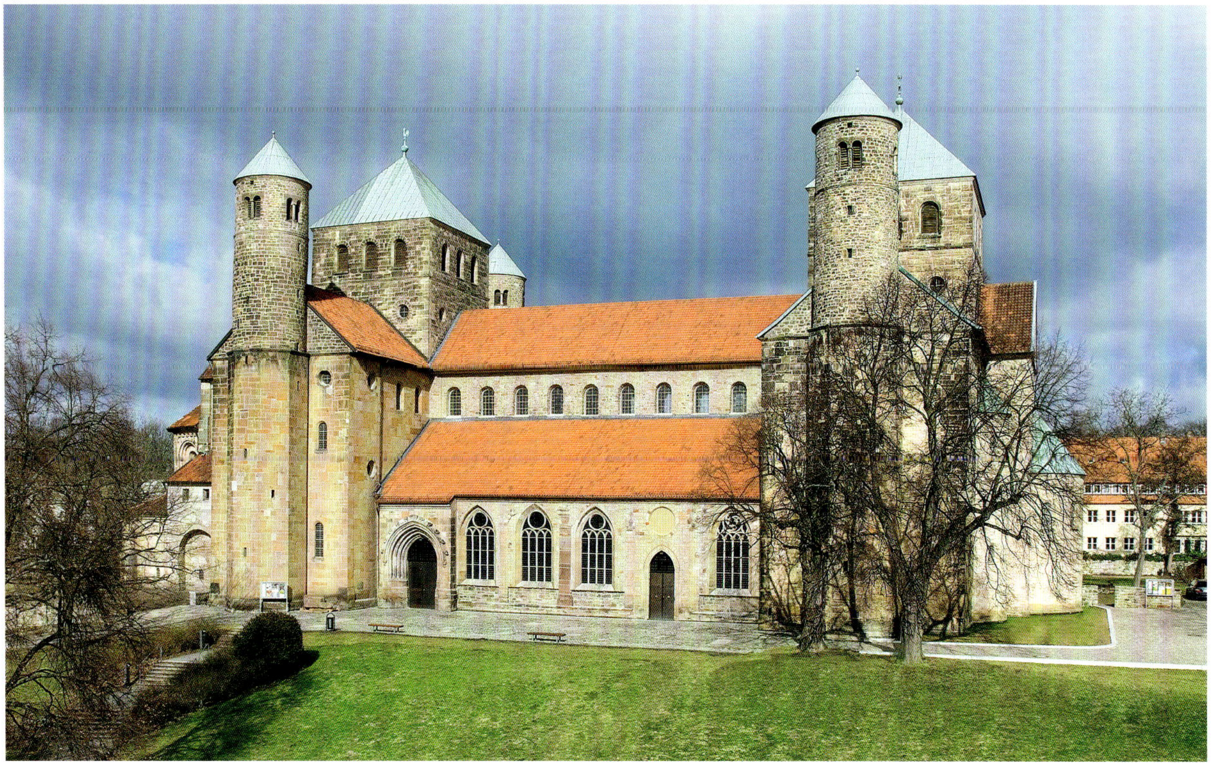

FIG. 4 *Abbey church of St. Michael, Hildesheim, begun 1010*

architecture, with plain white walls evoking the simplicity of the Bauhaus (fig. 3). In 2010 the church undertook another major renovation, which will be completed in 2014.

Despite all the reconstruction, renovation, and damage over the years, Hildesheim Cathedral still preserves its original furnishings in unparalleled quantity and variety. One of the outstanding examples is the wheel-shape Hezilo Chandelier (see fig. 3), which dates to 1061 and will be returned to its permanent position, suspended above the middle of the nave, following the cathedral's restoration. Measuring almost twenty feet in diameter, it represents the Heavenly Jerusalem; the golden city walls with their twelve gates and twelve watchtowers form the chandelier's ring. The Hezilo Chandelier and the slightly earlier Thietmar Chandelier, also made for the cathedral, are two of only four such wheel-shaped chandeliers to survive from the Middle Ages. Each was likely donated by the reigning bishop for which it is named. (Bishop Thietmar served from 1038 to 1044.)

While many of Hildesheim's bishops endowed its institutions with extraordinary works of art, no donor was more prolific or had a more significant impact on Hildesheim's production than Bernward, thirteenth bishop of Hildesheim. During his almost thirty-year episcopate he directed the construction of St. Michael's Monastery and Abbey Church as well as numerous other churches and buildings in the diocese, and he sponsored some of the most important works of Ottonian art.

Bernward was himself a member of the Saxon nobility – thus enjoying both personal wealth and an unusually close relationship with the ruling house – and was educated in the renowned Hildesheim cathedral school. He served as a tutor and adviser to the future emperor Otto III (980–1002) and as a member of the royal chancellery before assuming the bishop's throne in Hildesheim in 993. Thanks to his royal contacts he managed to acquire the sumptuous Byzantine ivories that adorned his manuscripts (cats. 1, 32) and traveled widely for his time. He visited pilgrimage sites in France in search of relics and journeyed as far south as Rome.

Historians' fascination with Bernward, unbroken to this day, is nurtured by an uncommonly rich trove of surviving

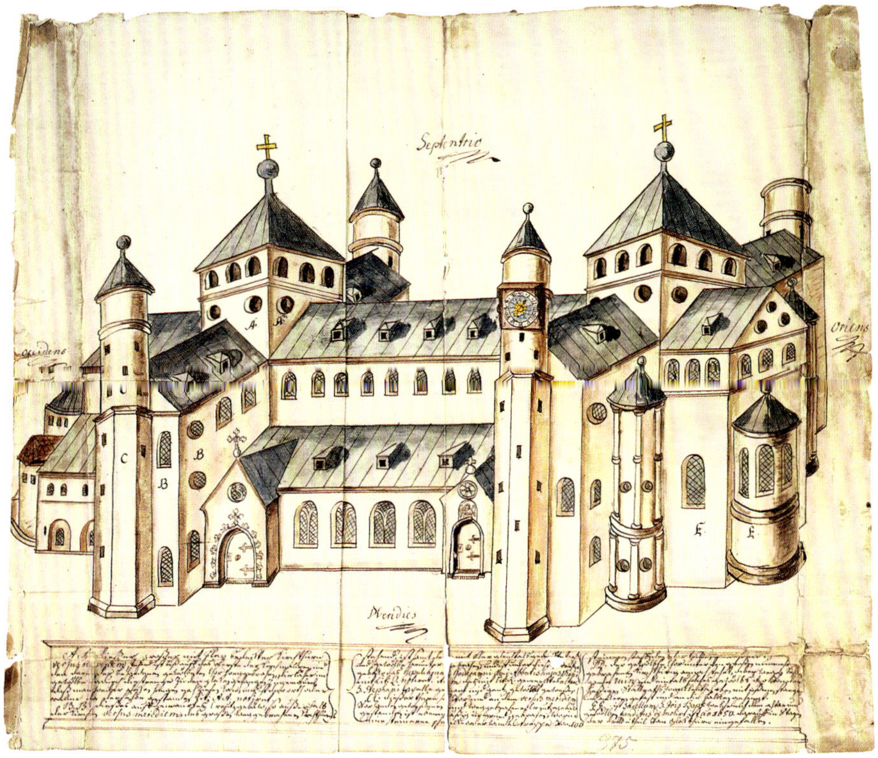

FIG. 5 St. Michael's Church. German (Hildesheim), 1650. Colored drawing, 15¾ × 19¾ in. (40 × 50 cm). Dom-Museum Hildesheim (1978-13)

artifacts and documents, notably a biography (*Vita Bernwardi*) written by his close confidant, Thangmar of Hildesheim. Thangmar lauds Bernward's profound commitment to his church and describes his artistic activities in great detail. A copy of his text served as one of the exhibits in the successful effort to achieve Bernward's canonization in Rome in 1192–93; a first such attempt had failed some forty years earlier, in 1150.

The most prominent example of Bernward's legacy is St. Michael's Church, the best-preserved major Ottonian structure in Europe (fig. 4). When he laid its cornerstone in 1010, it was the first significant ecclesiastical institution to be built in Hildesheim after the cathedral, the one that marked the city's expansion into a leading religious center, and the first Benedictine monastery in the entire diocese. Although it was rebuilt and embellished, much of the original structure was preserved through the centuries (fig. 5), perhaps because Bernward's sainthood and supposed involvement as an architect and artist gave St. Michael's itself the status of a relic. (It did not escape World War II unscathed, but more of its Ottonian architecture survived than at other churches.)

Recent archaeological findings are revising a long-held understanding of the original building, but Bernward seems to have designed a coherent plan for St. Michael's that thoughtfully combined elements of church architecture seen locally and on his travels. For example, departing from the typical orientation to the east, the main choir was situated in the west, as it was at Old St. Peter's Basilica and other major churches in Rome. Some of St. Michael's features subsequently became characteristic of Saxon architecture, such as the nave arcade's alternating pattern of two pillars followed by a column (fig. 6) and the modular plan, whereby the square of the transept crossing defines a unit of measurement upon which most of the building's proportions are based.

An extensive refurbishment campaign began after the monastery's first attempt to canonize its founder in 1150. The choir and crypt were rebuilt in the last quarter of the twelfth century; that work included the addition, about 1193, of a choir screen with stucco reliefs of saints, including Bernward, who had finally been canonized by then (fig. 7). The embellishment of Bernward's church temporarily ended about 1230–40 with the

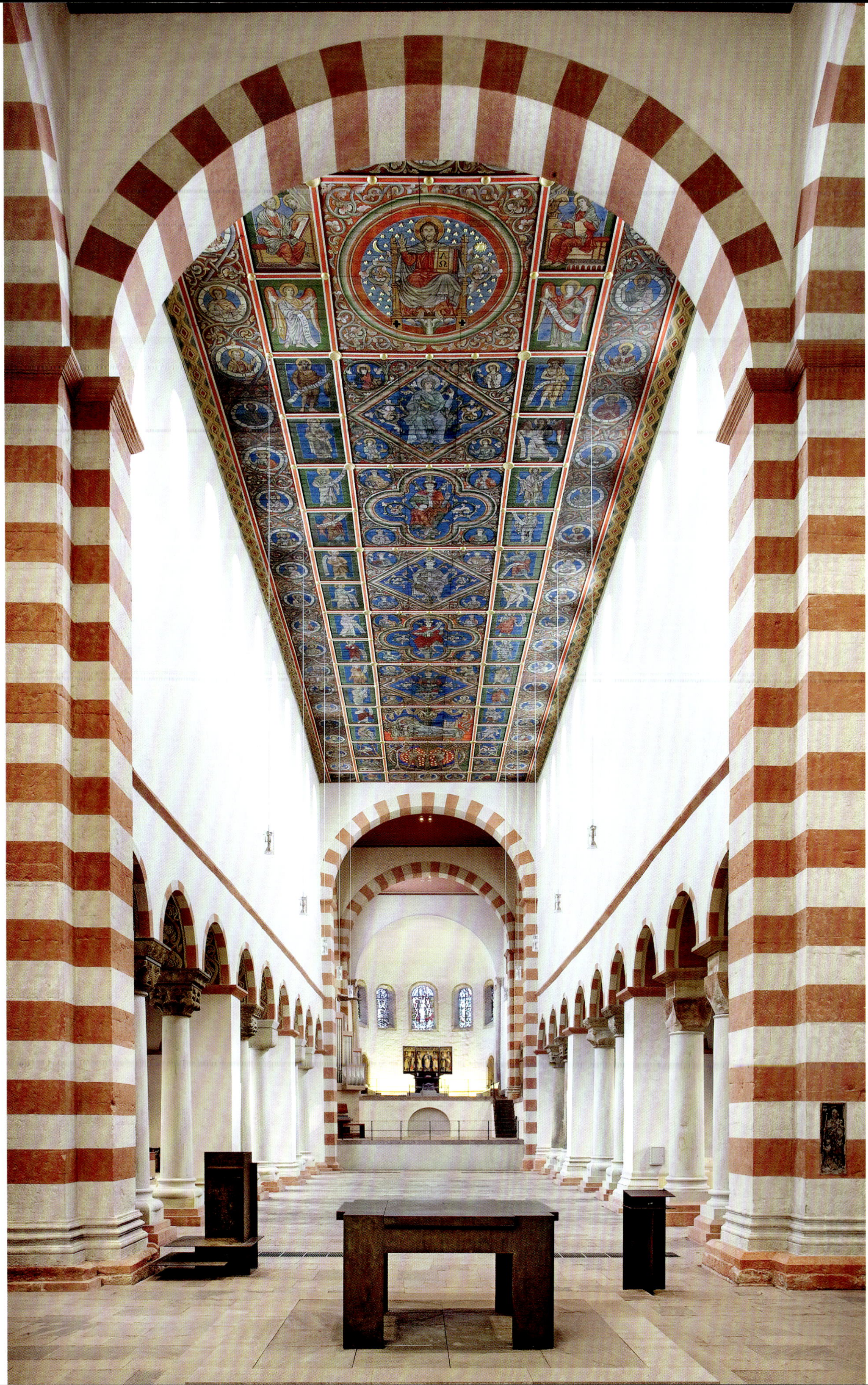

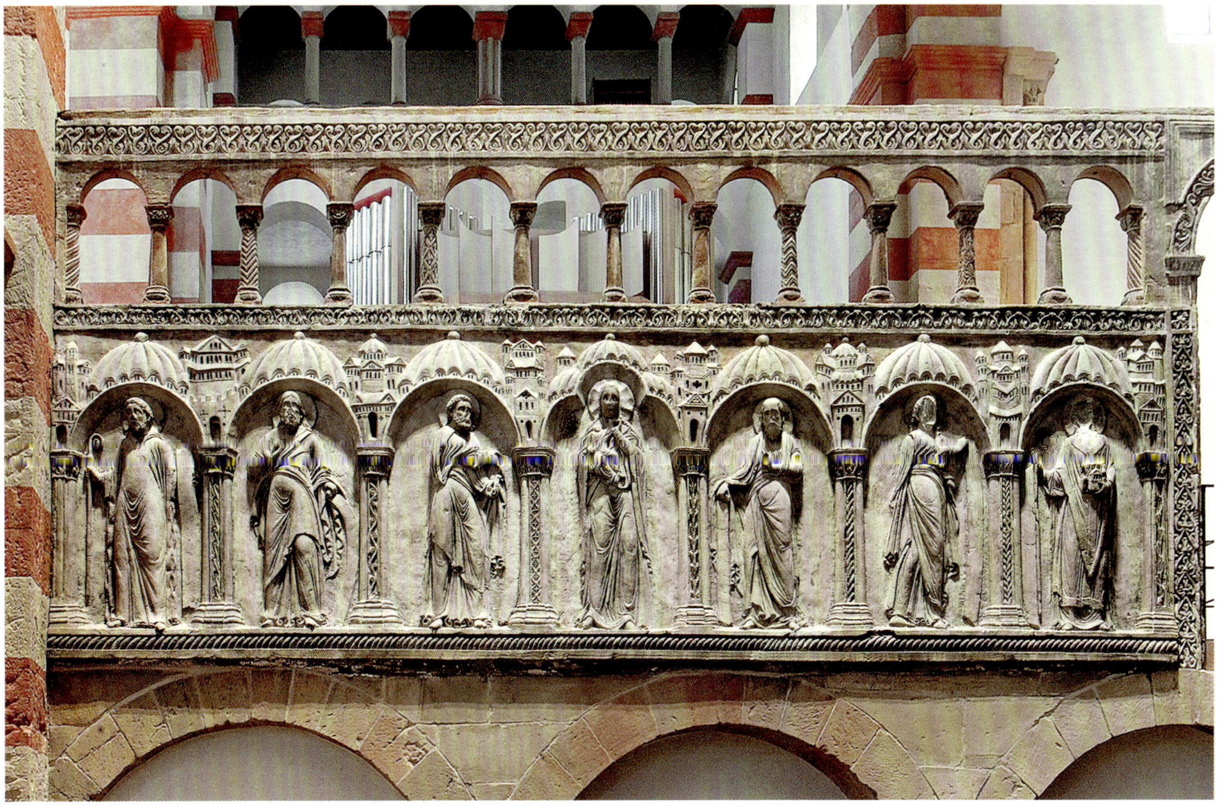

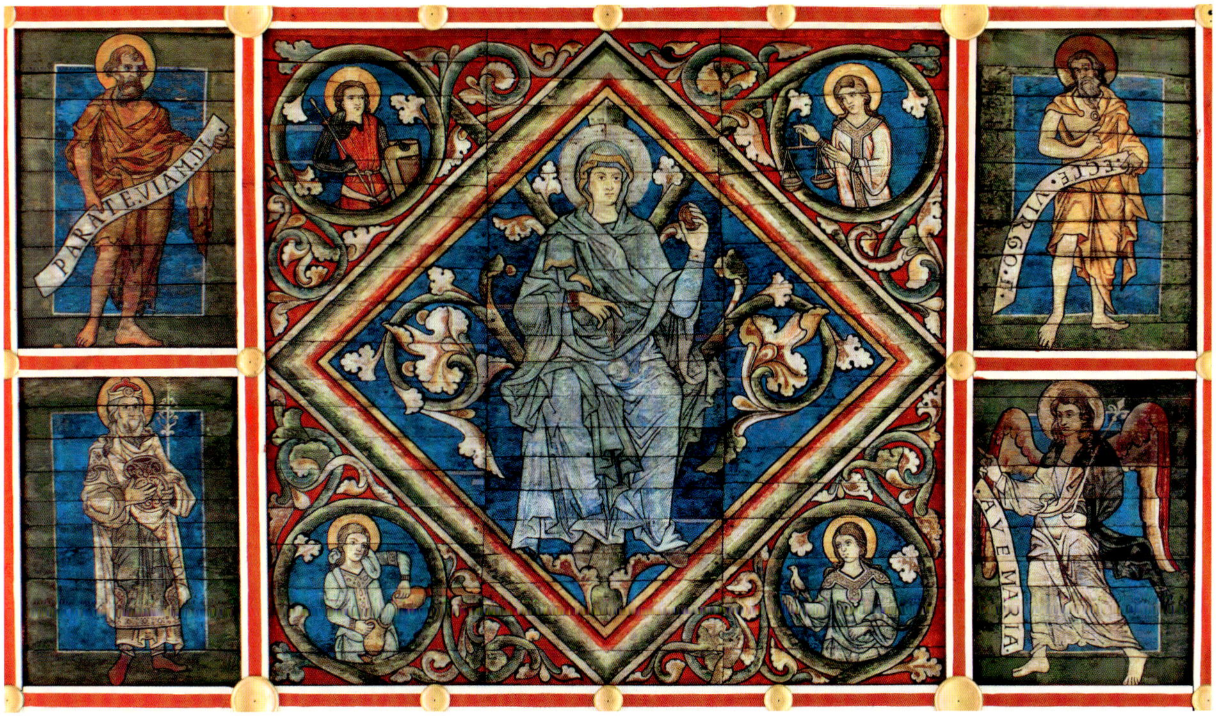

OPPOSITE: FIG. 6 *Nave of St. Michael's Church, looking west. Wooden ceiling (Tree of Jesse): German (Hildesheim), ca. 1230–40. Paint on oak boards, 91 ft. 2⅜ in. × 28 ft. 6⅝ in. (27.8 × 8.7 m)*

TOP: FIG. 7 *St. Michael's Choir Screen. German (Hildesheim), ca. 1193. Stucco, ca. 10 ft. 2 in. × 25 ft. 5½ in. (ca. 3.1 × 7.76 m); H. of figures ca. 50 in. (ca. 127 cm)*

ABOVE: FIG. 8 *The Virgin Mary, detail from the Tree of Jesse, St. Michael's Church*

construction of a painted wooden ceiling in the nave, exceptionally beautiful and one of only two from the Middle Ages to survive. Built of thirteen hundred oak planks, its complex pictoral program is based on the Tree of Jesse: Seven central panels depicting Christ's family tree are bordered by rectangular fields and medallions showing Evangelists and prophets, collectively conveying a message of salvation (fig. 8; see fig. 6).

In founding and furnishing St. Michael's, Bernward was creating his burial place and a memorial to himself so as to "merit heaven," as he put it, by way of an "architecture of credits," that is, worldly goods. Bernward's pious donation may have been intended to ensure his eternal salvation, but it unquestionably contributed to his fame here on Earth. The Benedictine monks of St. Michael's commemorated its founder in liturgy without interruption until secularization in 1803, and his elaborate tomb survives in its crypt to this day. It has an unusual design, with a stone coffin set beneath a stone slab (fig. 9); both bear reliefs and inscriptions in which Bernward describes himself as a humble servant awaiting his final judge, a message prompting the monks who visited the crypt daily to pray continually for his soul.

Although Bernward clearly saw to his reputation's immortality, he seems to have commissioned few portraits of himself. The only assured one is the dedicatory miniature in the Precious Gospels (fig. 10), in which he is pictured at the foot of the Mary Altar in the crypt of St. Michael's, at precisely the spot where he ultimately would be interred; the Virgin and Child are enthroned on the facing page (fig. 11). Bernward did, however, leave behind an abundance of inscriptions as testimony of his patronage, piety, and erudition. Some include

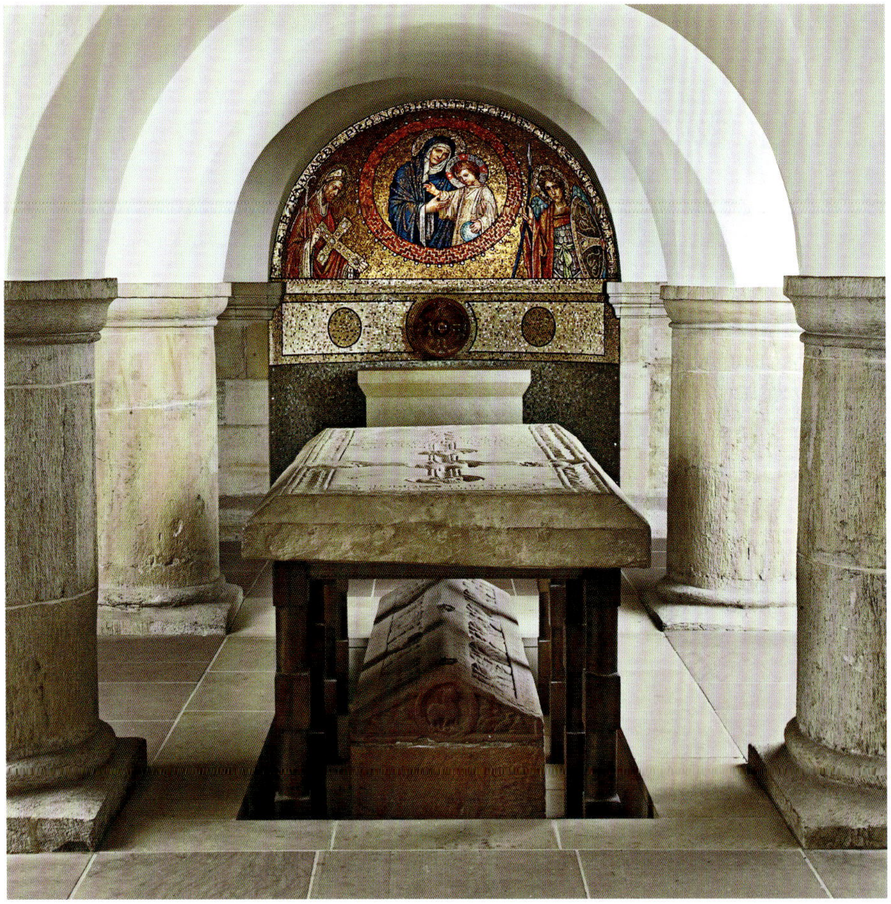

FIG. 9 *Bernward's Tomb, crypt of* St. Michael's Church, Hildesheim. German (Hildesheim), *ca.* 1022. Stone, *coffin* 24 × 85 1/8 × 22 5/8 in. (60.7 × 216 × 57.5 cm)

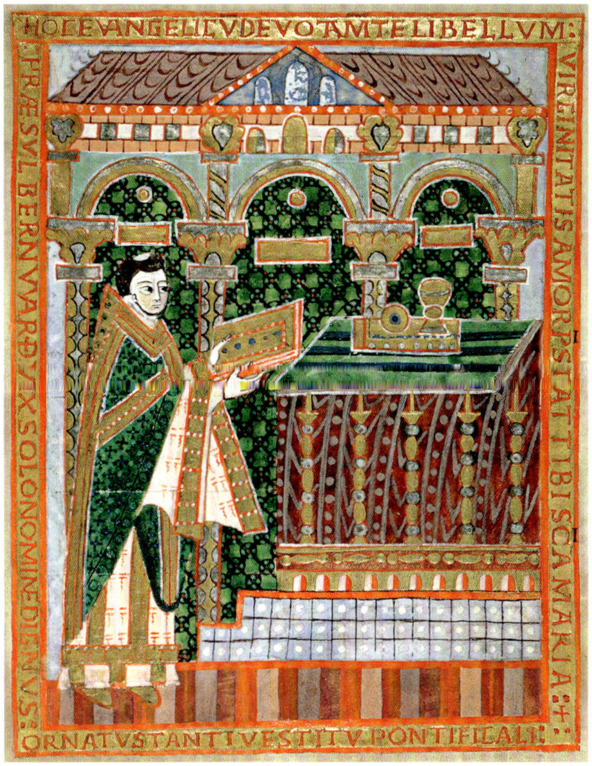

FIG. 10 *Precious Gospels, fol. 16v. German (Hildesheim), ca. 1015. Tempera, gold, and silver on parchment, 11 × 7⅞ in. (28 × 20 cm). Dom-Museum Hildesheim (DS 18). See also cat. 32*

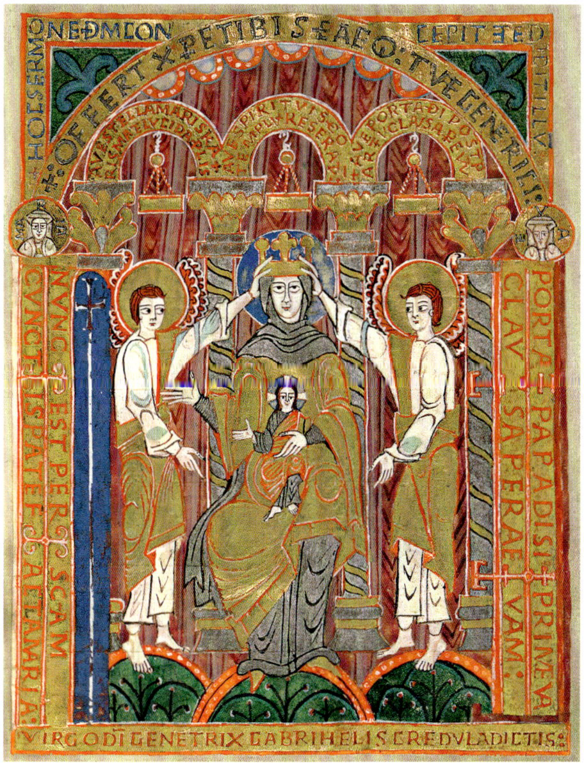

FIG. 11 *Precious Gospels, fol. 17r. German (Hildesheim), ca. 1015. Tempera, gold, and silver on parchment, 11 × 7⅞ in. (28 × 20 cm). Dom-Museum Hildesheim (DS 18). See also cat. 32*

only his name and official title, which were stamped even on the cathedral's roof tiles, a revival of Roman tradition; others are complex and sometimes cryptic texts, such as those on his gilded silver candlesticks (cat. 11).

Bernward was ambitious in his commissions, as were other members of the imperial episcopate of the time. He was one of the first, along with Cologne's Archbishop Gero (969–76) and Mainz's Archbishop Willigis (975–1011), to commission large sculptures in wood and bronze. The so-called Golden Madonna (cat. 7) and the Ringelheim Crucifix (cat. 8), which are linked to Bernward, were among the earliest examples of fully three-dimensional sculpture in this period, and both he and Willigis commissioned monumental bronze doors that were each made in one piece, in a single casting – a technical feat at that or any time. Willigis, Bernward's metropolitan (provincial bishop) and former mentor, proclaimed in an inscription that his bronze door (ca. 1000) was the first of its kind since the door Charlemagne had commissioned for his palace in Aachen, some two hundred years earlier, but like Charlemagne's it was largely unembellished.

Bernward's Doors (figs. 12, 13, 14), completed about 1015, far surpassed it. They were the first since late antiquity to be decorated with a pictorial program and to be cast using the lost-wax technique. Producing a sculptural bronze of such monumental size – more than fifteen feet high – was a technological breakthrough for the Middle Ages and a milestone in the history of art.

The doors depict eight scenes from the Old Testament on the left and eight from the New Testament on the right. The artists based the reliefs on illuminations in a Carolingian Bible from Tours, superbly transforming the scenes into three dimensions. They modeled expressive human figures in high relief, framing them in spare, low-relief settings of trees and buildings, to enhance the doors' narrative power. The doors' paired panels read as a kind of picture poem about sin and salvation: The scene of Eve nursing Cain is opposite the

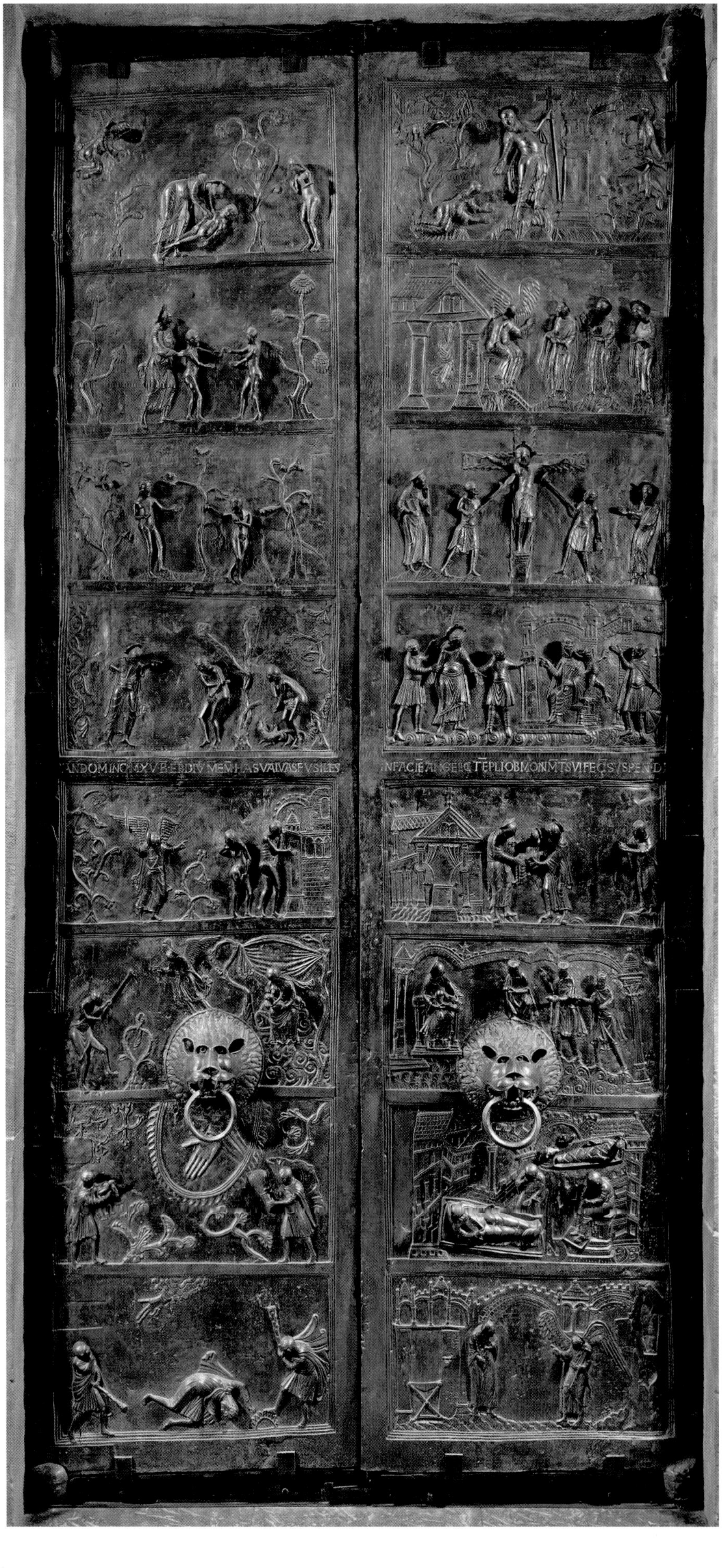

FIG. 12 *Bernward's Doors, Hildesheim Cathedral. German (Hildesheim), ca. 1015. Bronze, 15 ft. 6 in. × 89 in. (472 × 226 cm)*

OPPOSITE, TOP: FIG. 13 *Creation of Man, detail from Bernward's Doors*

OPPOSITE, BOTTOM: FIG. 14 *Detail from Bernward's Doors. Scenes clockwise from top left: Life under the Curse; The Adoration of the Magi; The Nativity; The Sacrifice of Cain and Abel*

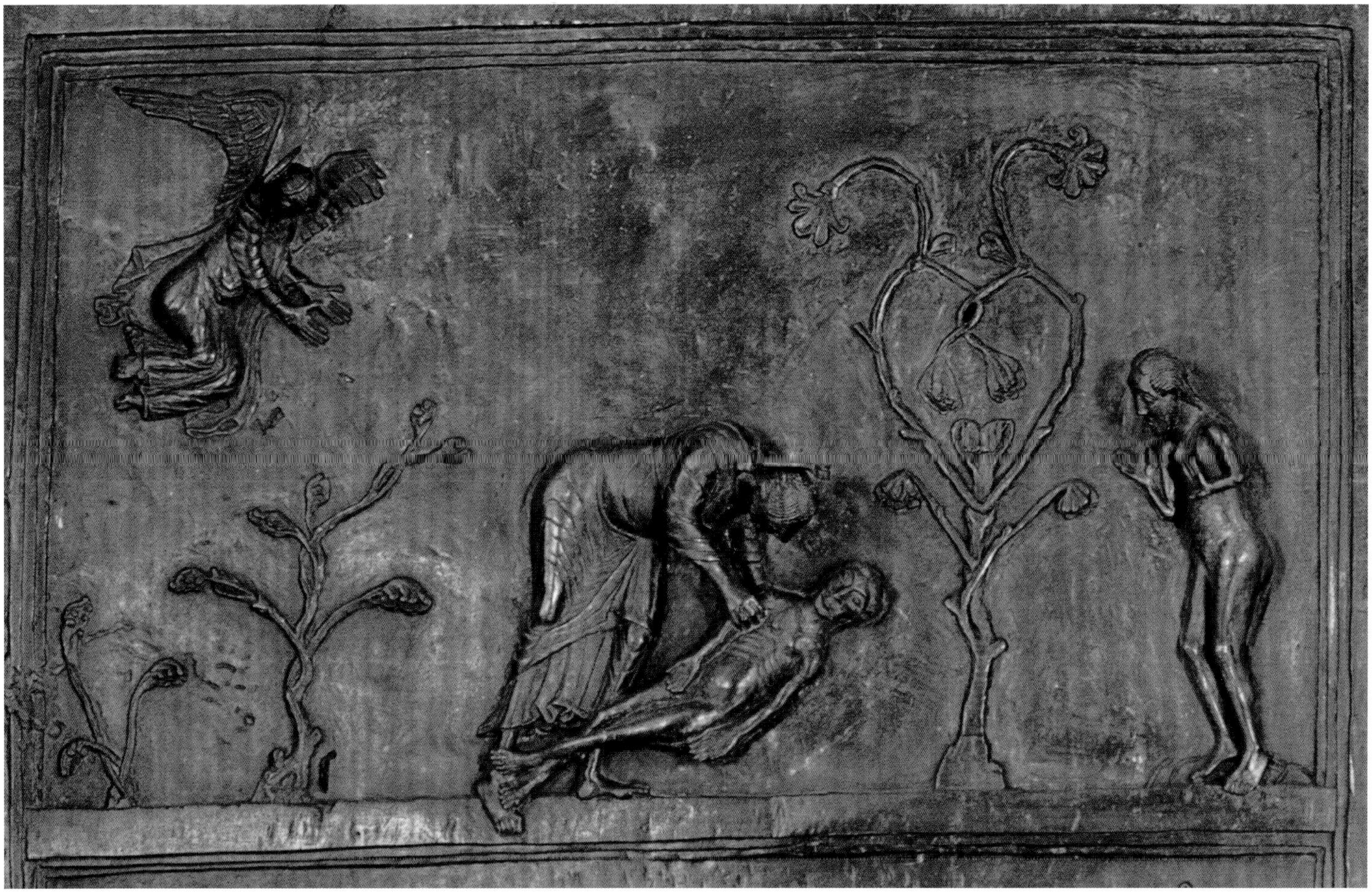

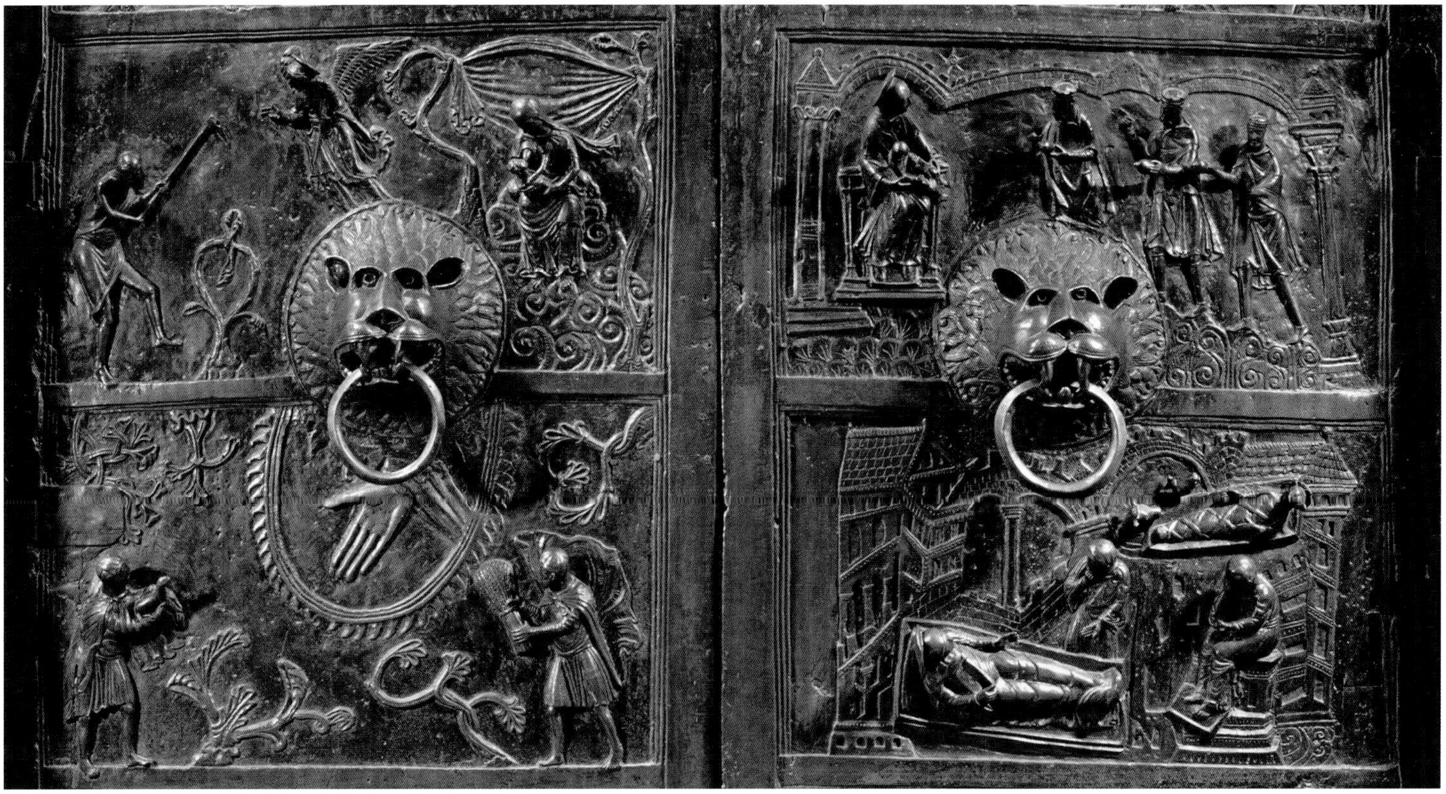

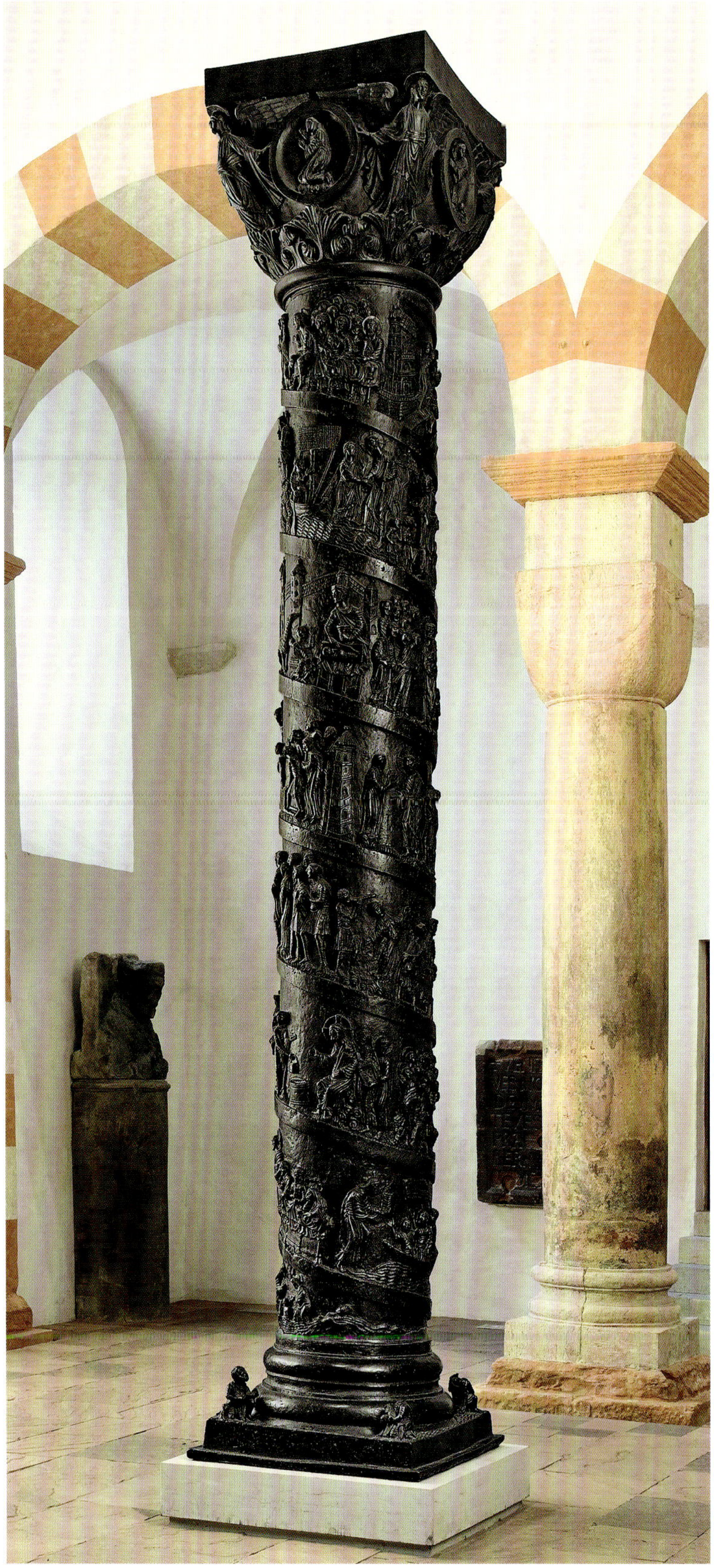

Adoration of the Magi before the Virgin and Child; the Temptation in the Garden is juxtaposed with the Crucifixion.

Bernward's extensive travels in the service of the Ottonian court, especially to Rome, provided ongoing stimulation for his commissions. The bronze doors may have been inspired by those of Old St. Peter's Basilica, and the pierced-metal Madonna and Child on the back of the Precious Gospels (cat. 32) by Roman icons.

Bernward's second monumental bronze, the first triumphal column since antiquity, also followed Roman precedent; it was patterned after the columns of Hadrian and Trajan. The column – more than twelve feet high – formerly stood in St. Michael's but today is in the cathedral (figs. 15, 16, 17). Instead of a pictorial program focused on military triumphs, the scenes spiraling around Bernward's Column depict twenty-four episodes from the life of Christ. As on Trajan's Column, the story reads from bottom to top, beginning with Jesus's baptism in the River Jordan and ending with the Entry into Jerusalem. Like Bernward's Doors, the column is a technical and artistic masterpiece.

Bernward could not have envisioned, much less brought about, his large bronzes or many works of fine metalsmithing, such as his exquisite silver cross (cat. 10), had he not been able to rely on talented local craftsmen and the rich natural resources nearby. Large ore deposits on Rammelsberg Mountain in the Harz range, a leading mining center since the tenth century, made raw materials easily available and gave rise to a tradition of metalworking expertise that reached its first peak during Bernward's era.

Bernward clearly knew how to engage excellent artists, especially in the fields of sculpture, bronze casting, and goldsmithing, yet he personally is credited for many of the works he commissioned – and which he may well have designed. Indeed, scholars refer to Bernward as "sapiens architectus" (wise architect, a term drawn from I Corinthians 3:10) for his greatest commission, the monastery church of St. Michael. Except for the calligraphers and miniaturists of his manuscripts – notably Guntbald, a deacon from Regensburg, who worked on four manuscripts for Bernward (cats. 3, 4) – his artists largely remained anonymous. Even Bernward's most

FIG. 15 *Bernward's Column, pictured in a temporary location at St. Michael's before its return to Hildesheim Cathedral. German (Hildesheim), ca. 1015. Bronze, 12 ft. 5¼ in. × 22⅞ in. (3.79 m × 58 cm)*

technically demanding works, such as the bronze doors, are unsigned. The doors carry only the extremely abbreviated identification of the patron: "B . Ep." for B[ERNVVARDVS] . EP[ISCOPVS]. Such was not always the case: Berengar, who cast Archbishop Willigis's bronze door, listed his name immediately after those of Charlemagne and the archbishop.

Bernward's successor, Godehard (reigned 1022–38), was just as energetic a builder, patron, and founder of churches, including the monastery of St. Bartholomew (consecrated in 1034), a pilgrim's hospice in Hildesheim. He was equally learned, as well, but came from a markedly different background. Godehard was educated as a monk at the renowned Benedictine monastery of Niederaltaich, near the Danube River in Bavaria. He returned to Niederaltaich after travel and advanced study, quickly becoming its abbot before his elevation as bishop of Hildesheim.

In contrast to Bernward, who spent his career close to the royal court and commissioned great works to secure his own reputation and salvation, Godehard was known for his modesty and spirituality. He attained fame as a successful monastic reformer, even advocating for the relocation of St. Michael's monks to a remote spot almost ten miles south of Hildesheim, presumably because it would be more conducive to quiet contemplation. Whereas the cult of Bernward achieved little more than regional importance, Godehard, canonized in 1131, became one of the more prominent saints of the Middle Ages, venerated from Italy to Scandinavia. The St. Gotthard Pass, a major Alpine pass, is dedicated to him.

Hildesheim demonstrated early interest in documenting Godehard's exemplary sanctity for posterity. In addition to two biographies written not long after his death (in approximately 1038 and 1054–61), numerous medieval texts report Godehard's many miracles, which were said especially to occur at his tomb in the cathedral. With Godehard's canonization (followed by Bernward's, some sixty years later), Hildesheim was transformed into a pilgrimage destination. The spread of his cult had financial repercussions in Hildesheim. The cathedral canons had to bear the greater expense of hosting so many pilgrims, but in 1146 Bishop Bernhard (reigned 1130–53) allocated all the offerings placed on Godehard's tomb to the cathedral chapter because, as he stated in his charter, "through God's mercy and the virtues of this saint the Hildesheim church has become worthy of veneration among peoples who knew nothing of it before."

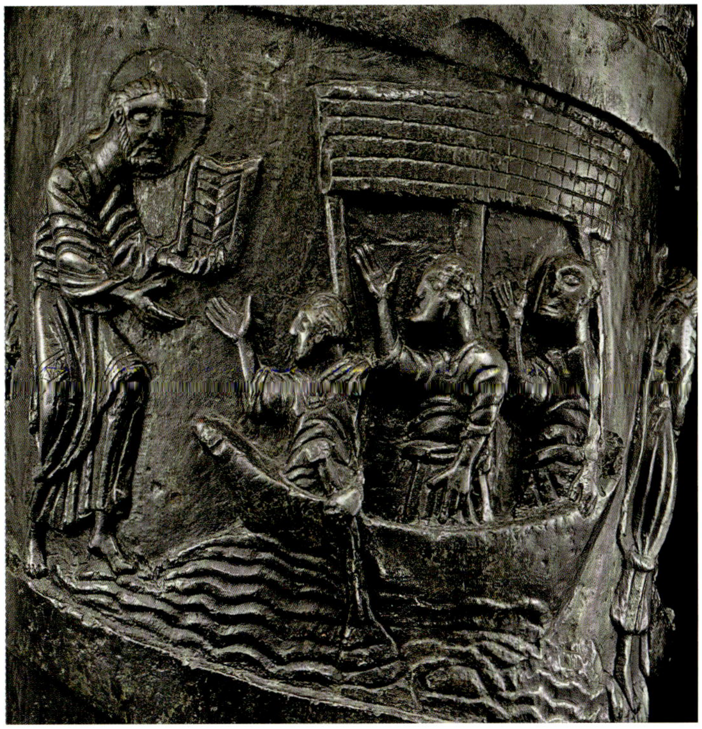

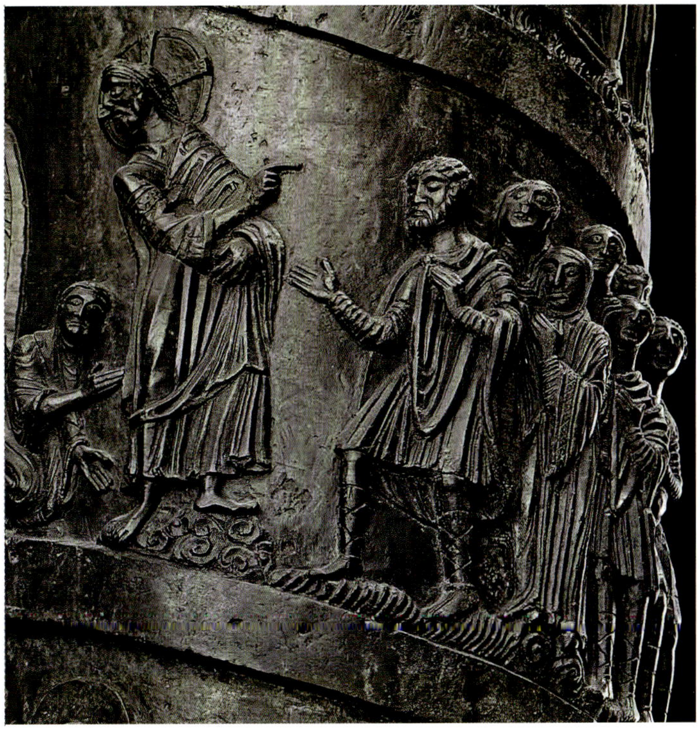

TOP: FIG. 16 *Christ Calling the Apostles James and John, detail from Bernward's Column*

ABOVE: FIG. 17 *Christ Healing the Bleeding Woman, detail from Bernward's Column*

Bishop Bernhard was instrumental in furthering the cult. Hardly had he secured Godehard's canonization before he founded a Benedictine monastery in Hildesheim in the new saint's honor, designating it as his own final resting place. The cornerstone for the three-aisle monastery church was laid in 1133, and the completed St. Godehard's was consecrated in 1172 (fig. 18). The surviving original structures include the sacristy, the chapter house, and a room that served as the library in the twelfth century. The church's plan, with its choir surrounded by an ambulatory with rounded chapels, was common for French monastic churches but highly unusual in twelfth-century Saxony. Bernhard, who had studied in Paris after his education at the Hildesheim cathedral school, surely encountered the form there and may have deemed it ideal for his monastery. Preserved in St. Godehard's treasury are two objects presumed to have belonged to the saint, his crosier (cat. 14) and his beaker (cat. 35).

Bernward had placed St. Michael's Monastery to the north of the cathedral; Bernhard chose for his own monastic foundation a site to the south of it. St. Bartholomew's lay to the east; to the west, beyond the city walls, was St. Maurice's, built as a chapel about 1025 by Bishop Godehard and founded as a monastery in 1055–68 by Bishop Hezilo, who is buried there. Thus the ring of religious foundations surrounding the cathedral was complete, extending about three-quarters of a mile from north to south and just over two miles from east to west. Radiating outward from the cathedral precinct, the Hildesheim see had become a sacred landscape in the form of a cross.

By the time Bernhard instigated his building activity in the twelfth century, Hildesheim had been recognized as a European center for metalwork for well over a century, but improvements in mining and the production of copper contributed to the further development of metalsmithing techniques in this period. Two extraordinary works of goldsmithing – the Godehard Shrine (fig. 19) and the Epiphanius Shrine – were created for Hildesheim Cathedral about 1130–40. Gilded silver caskets ornamented with filigree, portraits of saints and

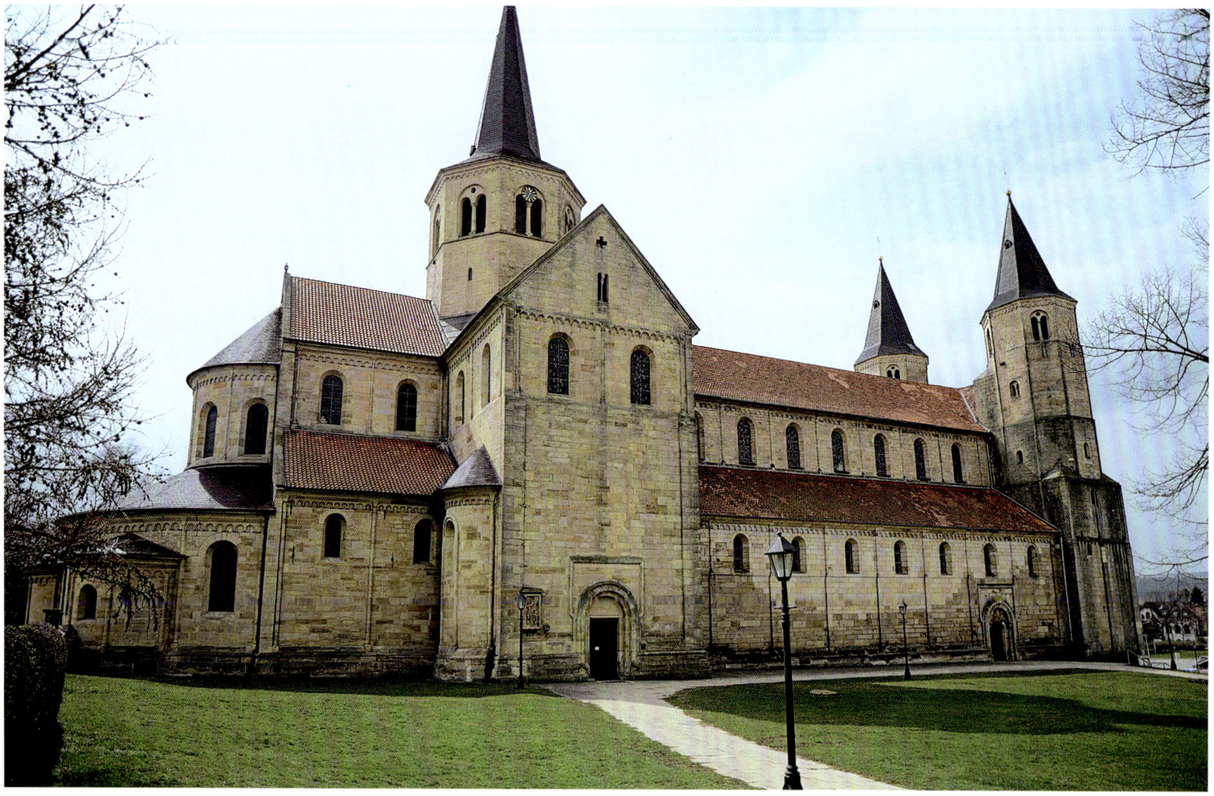

FIG. 18 St. Godehard's Church, Hildesheim, 1133–ca. 1172

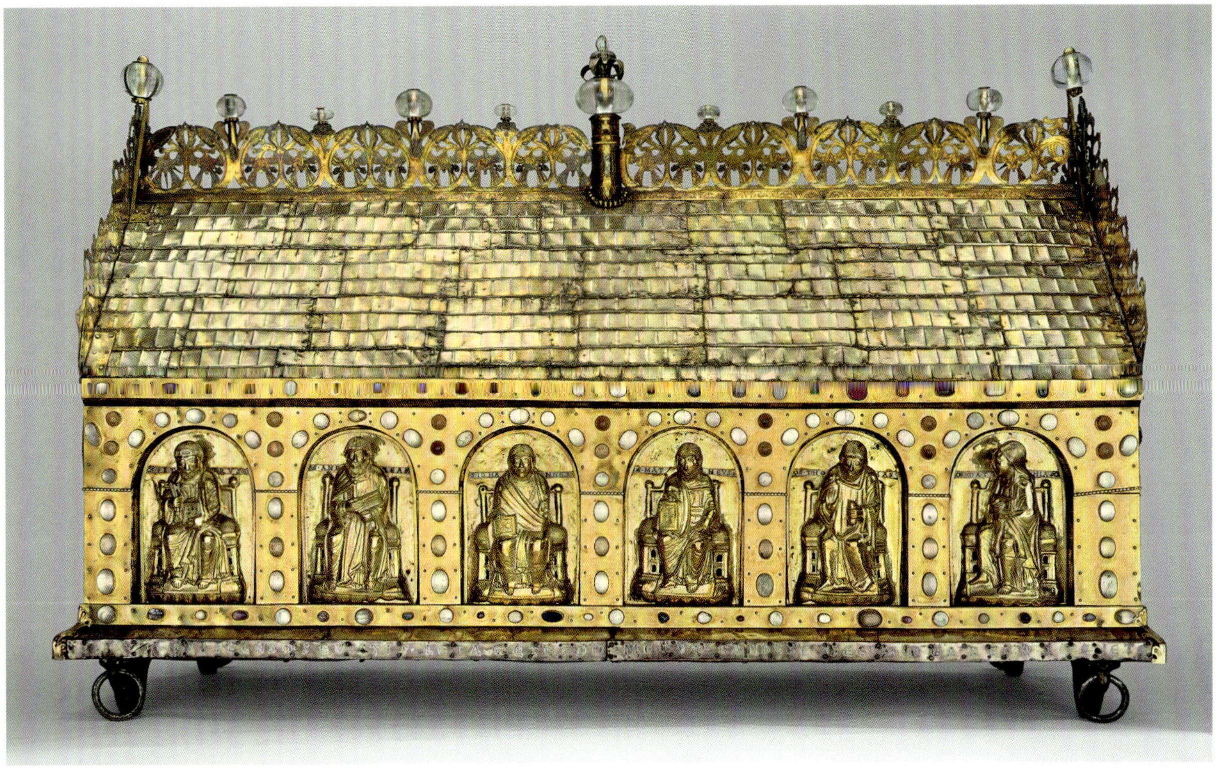

FIG. 19 *Godehard Shrine. German (Hildesheim), ca. 1130–40. Gilded silver and rock crystal, wood core, 25⅝ × 48⅛ × 20⅛ in. (65 × 122 × 51 cm). Hildesheim Cathedral*

other figures in high relief, and crests of pierced scrollwork, they are early examples of shrines for saints' relics in the form of a church. They were produced by a workshop affiliated with Hildesheim and about forty-five miles to the southwest, at the monastery at Helmarshausen on the Weser River.

Helmarshausen's metalsmithing workshop and equally celebrated scriptorium were established in the early twelfth century by the artist-monk Roger of Helmarshausen, a noted goldsmith who is thought to have arrived from Stavelot Abbey (Liège, Belgium) by way of Cologne. He is credited as the author of the *Schedula diversarum artium*, a detailed, three-volume description of the art techniques of the period, and was likely called to Helmarshausen to create a shrine for its recently acquired relics of the sainted Bishop Modoaldus of Trier. The Helmarshausen workshops also produced Hildesheim Cathedral's unique set of gilded liturgical fans (cats. 17, 18, 19) and are linked to two manuscripts created for St. Michael's after the first attempt to canonize Bernward, in 1150: the Ratmann Sacramentary (cat. 21) and the slightly later Stammheim Missal, now in Los Angeles (J. Paul Getty Museum, MS 64).

Workshops throughout Hildesheim were tremendously productive in the second half of the twelfth century, as can be seen by the great number of surviving smaller-scale works. Several gem-studded altar crosses date from this period. Legend has it that one of them, the sumptuously decorated Bernward Cross, which contains the relic of the Holy Cross that Bernward donated (fig. 20), is the work of Bernward himself; it is more likely related to the first attempt to have Bernward canonized, in 1150. Another cross, which is preserved in St. Godehard's treasury (cat. 36), incorporates enamel panels typical of Hildesheim's production in the late twelfth century. Among the other outstanding works employing this use of enamel is the cycle on the New Testament (cat. 27) that can be linked to an altar in the cathedral.

One of the major patrons of the arts in late twelfth-century Saxony was Henry the Lion (ca. 1130–1195), the powerful duke of Saxony and Bavaria. He kept Helmarshausen busy with such commissions as his magnificent gospel book from about 1188, which is preserved in near-mint condition in Wolfenbüttel, in Lower Saxony, and may also have made

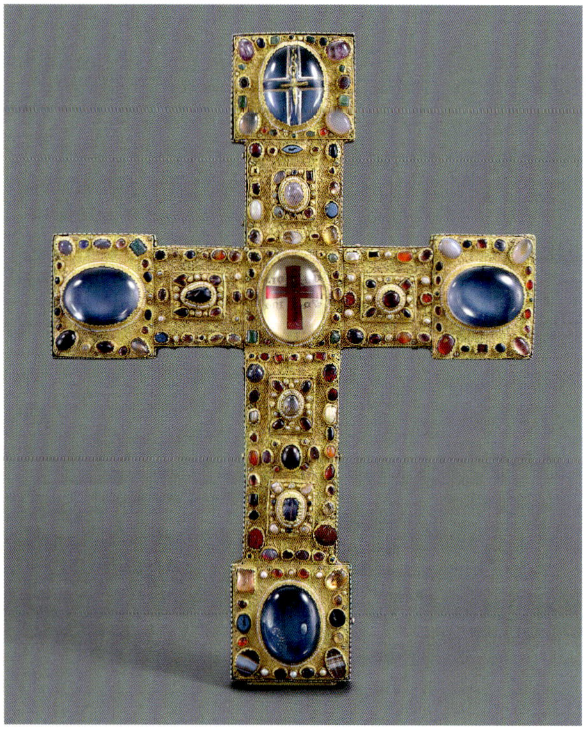

FIG. 20 *Bernward Cross. German (Hildesheim), ca. 1150. Oak, gold, silver, gilding, filigree, precious stones, and earlier small gold cross (German [Hildesheim], before 1022), 19 × 14⅝ in. (48 × 37 cm) without tang. Dom-Museum Hildesheim (DS L 109)*

donations to Hildesheim. A richly jeweled reliquary cross in the cathedral's treasury (cat. 30) has been linked to Henry the Lion, and his patronage is suspected on the cathedral's reliquary of the sainted King Oswald (cat. 31).

While individual bishops and royals are justly recognized as patrons, it can also be said that Hildesheim as a whole supported the arts. Home to one of the empire's leading cathedral schools from the tenth until the thirteenth century, it was a place of great learning and sophistication. Its numerous clerics' names and backgrounds have been insufficiently studied, but many came from the upper ranks of nobility; they were highly educated and culturally aware, thanks to extensive travel and far-flung relationships. For example, the cathedral chapter's canons maintained a prayer network, ensuring reciprocal prayers for salvation, with monasteries and chapters across Europe, and individual members journeyed as far as Jerusalem and Armenia. Acquisitions such as the pair of candlesticks from the Mosan region (cat. 22) and the reliquary cross with Slavonic inscriptions (cat. 46) testify to the Hildesheim clergy's wide-ranging connections and expansive horizons.

Since Hildesheim's elevation to an episcopal see in 815, its population apparently had grown rapidly, fostered by both the building activity sponsored by its bishops and its advantageous position at the intersection of various trading routes; it had developed into an active market town. The fortified cathedral can be considered the core of the city, bordered by the pre-urban settlement later known as Old Town (Altstadt). By the beginning of the thirteenth century two adjacent settlements had developed: Dammstadt, to the west, and Neustadt (New Town), to the east. Here, in the shadow of the religious institutions, lived the lay population, which was actively involved – first as craftsmen, then increasingly as patrons – in local art production.

The locals strove for independence from clerical rule and eventually, in 1249, obtained a city charter and the concomitant legal rights to elect representatives to a town council, erect a town hall, and issue charters. The seal of the city, made of silver and dating to about 1300, testifies to its citizens' wealth and aspirations for self-governance (fig. 21). Hildesheim was then one of the largest towns in northern Germany, with more than five thousand inhabitants. As it continued to grow in the thirteenth century, its art production also increased, doubtless more and more oriented toward export. Its high-quality works in bronze, especially aquamanilia (cat. 39), were widely sought after from as far as Scandinavia and Russia.

But as political power shifted from the clergy to the laity in the thirteenth century, bitter quarrels between the commune and the bishops became frequent. Ultimately the bishops were forced to move their residence outside the city, yet even as their influence waned the bishops battled with the neighboring nobility. Given the tensions, it is unsurprising that Hildesheim's churches only rarely acquired outstanding works of art in the late Middle Ages, from about 1300 to 1500.

One exception is the chalice with paten (cat. 47) in pure gold, which legend associated with the artist-bishop Bernward but was in fact commissioned by Bishop Gerhard vom Berge (reigned 1365–98). It was probably financed by the ransom of thirteen thousand silver marks that Gerhard received for his noble captives – including the duke of Braunschweig and the bishop of Halberstadt – following the landmark Battle of Dinklar in 1367. Gerhard is said to have prayed before the battle to Mary, the cathedral's patron, giving her the choice of a roof of gold or one of straw, suggesting that the Hildesheim bishopric would become impoverished should he be defeated. Though sorely outnumbered, with only six hundred men to his opponent's twenty-five hundred, Gerhard – armed with the cathedral's foundation reliquary of Our Lady – rode to victory over Braunschweig, averting that fate.

But over the ensuing six centuries Hildesheim confronted many more challenges to the preservation of its medieval treasures. After the Reformation and Hildesheim's adoption of Lutheranism in 1542, only a few religious institutions remained Catholic, including the cathedral and St. Godehard's. St. Michael's was divided: Benedictine monks remained in its cloister, and its crypt, Bernward's burial ground, stayed Catholic as well, but from that point on most of the abbey church served the Protestant parish. A ten-year dispute over the use and maintenance of the church building ensued, causing stalemate and decay. This deadlock ultimately proved felicitous, as it stymied city officials' repeated attempts to sell the church treasures they had carefully inventoried.

The next great threat to Hildesheim's treasures loomed in 1803, with the secularization of church properties; all the monasteries were dissolved and their treasures dispersed. In due course, however, this allowed the collection not only to survive but to expand. Bishop Eduard J. Wedekin (reigned 1850–70) ardently collected the diocese's artworks, which he bequeathed to the cathedral, and initiated a cathedral museum to preserve them. When Allied bombing leveled Hildesheim's medieval core in 1945, the treasures were safely hidden away. Today they constitute one of the world's most extensive and precious collections of early medieval objects, an incomparable group that, uniquely, has survived intact, sheltered in Hildesheim, for a millennium.

SELECTED REFERENCES: Lüntzel, *Geschichte der Diöcese und Stadt Hildesheim*, 1858; Goetting, *Die Hildesheimer Bischöfe von 815 bis 1221 (1227)*, 1984; Gosebruch and Steigerwald, *Bernwardinische Kunst*, 1988; *Der Schatz von St. Godehard*, 1988; *Kirchenkunst des Mittelalters*, 1989; *Bernward von Hildesheim und das Zeitalter der Ottonen*, 1993; *Das Kostbare Evangeliar des Heiligen Bernward*, 1993; Wolfson, *Der große Goldkelch Bischof Gerhards*, 1996; Binding, *Der früh- und hochmittelalterliche Bauherr*, 1998; *Ego sum Hildensemensis: Bischof, Domkapitel und Dom in Hildesheim*, 2000; Gallistl, *Epiphanius von Pavia*, 2000; *Abglanz des Himmels*, 2001; Grote and Kellner, *Die Bilderdecke der Hildesheimer Michaeliskirche*, 2002; Wulf, *Die Inschriften der Stadt Hildesheim*, 2003; Petersen, "Stadtentstehung im Schatten der Kirche," 2004; Jakobs, *Germania Pontificia*, vol. 5.2, *Provincia Maguntinensis*, part 6, *Dioceses Hildesheimensis et Halberstadensis*, 2005; Giese, *Die Textfassungen der Lebensbeschreibung Bischof Bernwards von Hildesheim*, 2006; Kruppa and Wilke, *Die Hildesheimer Bischöfe von 1221 bis 1398*, 2006; Wilschewski, *Die karolingischen Bischofssitze des sächsischen Stammesgebiets bis 1200*, 2007; *Bild und Bestie: Hildesheimer Bronzen der Stauferzeit*, 2008; Exner, *Das Guntbald-Evangeliar*, 2008; Segers-Glocke, *St. Michaelis in Hildesheim*, 2008; Brandt, *Bernwards Säule*, 2009; Höhl, *Das Taufbecken des Wilbernus*, 2009; Brandt, *Bernwards Tür*, 2010; *Schätze im Himmel – Bücher auf Erden*, 2010; Schulz-Mons, *Das Michaeliskloster in Hildesheim*, 2010; Dolle and Knochenhauer, *Niedersächsisches Klosterbuch*, 2012; Giese, "Die schriftliche Pflege des Bernward-Kultes," 2012; Lutz and Weyer, *1000 Jahre St. Michael in Hildesheim*, 2012.

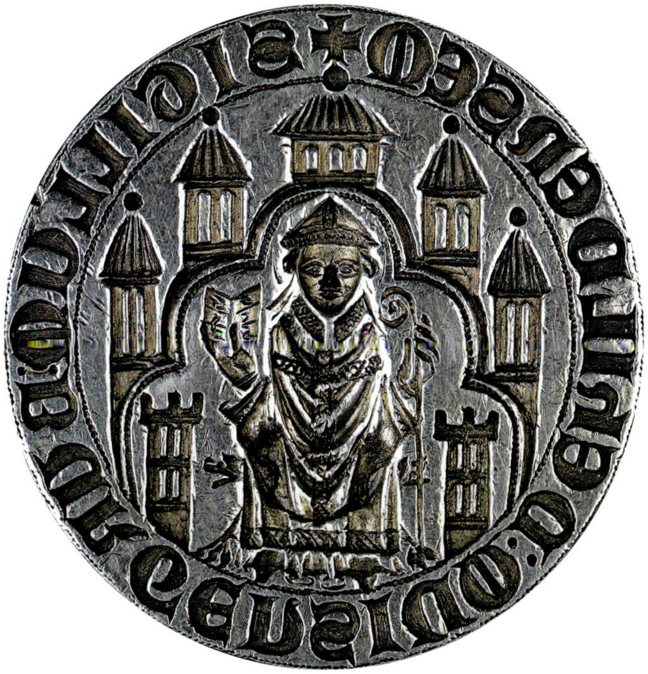

FIG. 21 Hildesheim City Seal. German (Hildesheim), ca. 1300. Silver, Diam. 3¼ in. (8.2 cm). Stadtarchiv Hildesheim (Best. 854, Nr. 1)

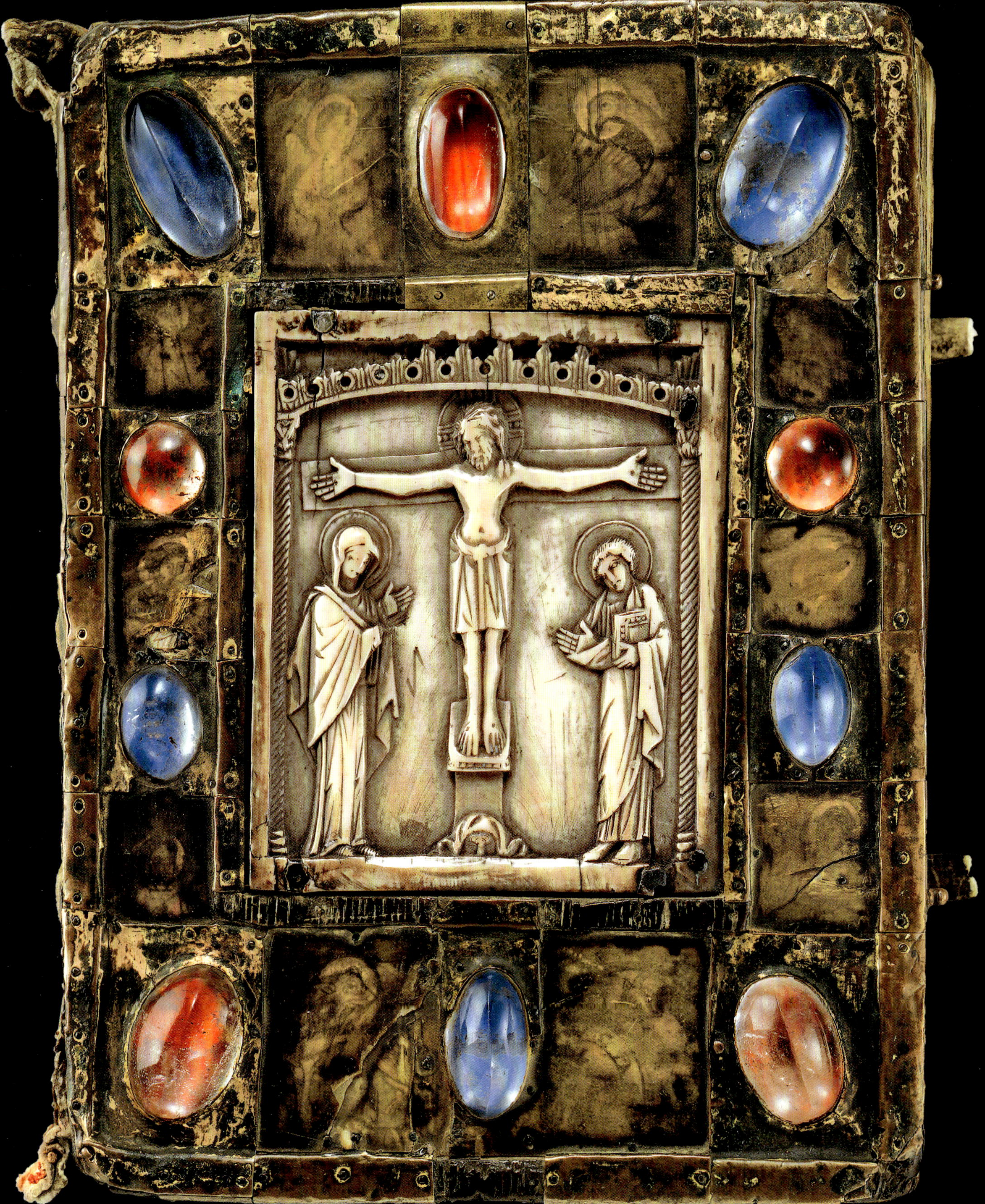

1 · Gospel Book (so-called Small Bernward Gospel)

FRONT COVER: *German (Hildesheim), second half of 12th century. Gilded copper, rock crystal, and paint on parchment under horn on oak; Byzantine ivory plaque*
MANUSCRIPT: *northeast France, last third of 9th century. Opaque paint, gold, and silver on parchment*
BINDING AND BACK COVER: *German (Hildesheim), ca. 1000. Leather, copper worked in* vernis brun *on oak*
Overall (book closed) 8 ⅞ × 6 ¾ in. (22.5 × 17 cm); 187 leaves
Only the covers are exhibited.
Dom-Museum Hildesheim (DS 13)

This small gospel book, an amalgam of precious objects assembled at several stages, attests to Bernward of Hildesheim's formidable stature as a collector, patron, and saint. The manuscript itself belonged to Bernward – a hundred-year-old treasure by the time he decided to ameliorate it with a new cover. Neither the fanciest nor the shabbiest of books, its decoration is limited to the canon tables and four large-scale ornamental initials (see following page). Though painted in red, green, and yellow, with occasional interlace and zoomorphic elements, the pages are notably spare and simple in design. Modern scholars localize it to northeastern France as a product of the Franco-Saxon school on the basis of those elements. There is evidence of a broad appreciation for such manuscripts among Ottonian patrons, and books associated with Hildesheim, such as the Hezilo Gospels (cat. 2), clearly drew inspiration from Franco-Saxon manuscripts.

Bernward's new cover likely included the Byzantine, mid-tenth-century, carved ivory plaque we see on the book today. The image of Jesus on the cross flanked by John and Mary was a fitting subject to adorn a gospel book, and the ivory would have flaunted Bernward's familiarity with and admiration for the powerful and distant Byzantine Empire. Before becoming bishop he had served as tutor to the future Holy Roman emperor Otto III, whose mother was the Byzantine princess Theophano (coregent for her son 983–91), and the Ottonian rulers maintained diplomacy and trade with Byzantium. In some ways more ostentatious than the plaque is the outsize and gilded monogram worked in *vernis brun* (by which a pattern is created by baking linseed oil on the surface of copper) that appears on the back cover (see p. 23). Here Bernward forcefully asserts his status as owner of the book and instigator of this multimedia art object.

A new, bejeweled frame, striking in the variety of materials it uses, was added in the twelfth century, probably in response to Bernward's canonization. Translucent (though now darkened) horn plates protect a series of painted miniatures, which show images of saints and the Four Evangelists. These alternate with rock crystal cabochons, embellished by an underlayer of alternating blue and red material. Those changes enhanced an already sumptuous object, one that would have been particularly appreciated for its direct and clear association with the new saint.

M.H.

SELECTED REFERENCES. Stähli, *Die Handschriften im Domschatz zu Hildesheim*, 1984, pp. 1–15; *Bernward von Hildesheim und das Zeitalter der Ottonen*, 1993, vol. 2, pp. 550–52, no. VIII-19 (Ulrich Kuder and Martina Pippal); *Abglanz des Himmels*, 2001, p. 183, no. 4.4 (Michael Brandt); Nees, "Aspects of Antiquarianism in the Art of Bernward," 2012, pp. 163–64.

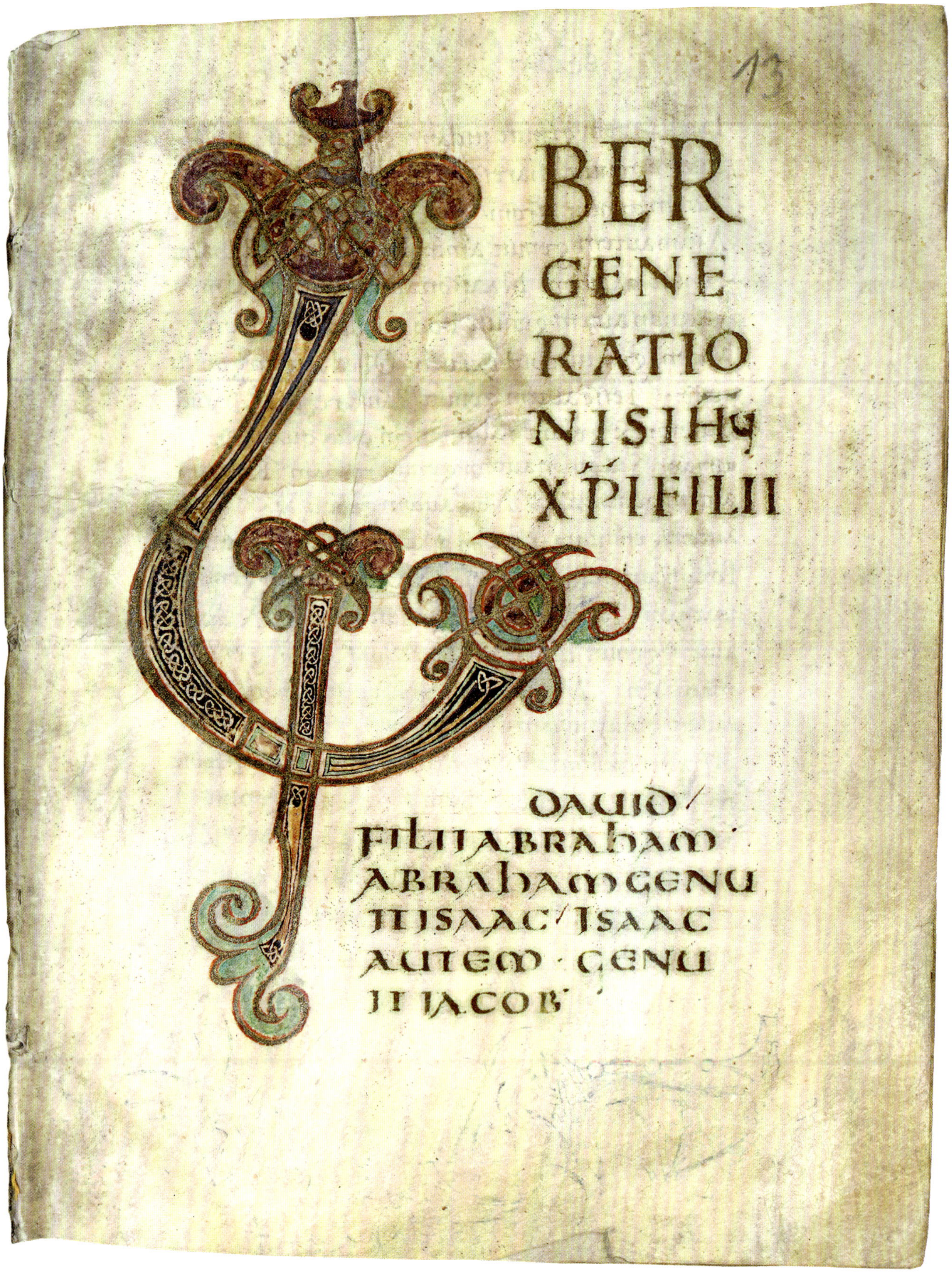
13
BER
GENE
RATIO
NISIHU
XPI FILII
DAUID
FILII ABRAHAM
ABRAHAM GENU
IT ISAAC ISAAC
AUTEM GENU
IT IACOB

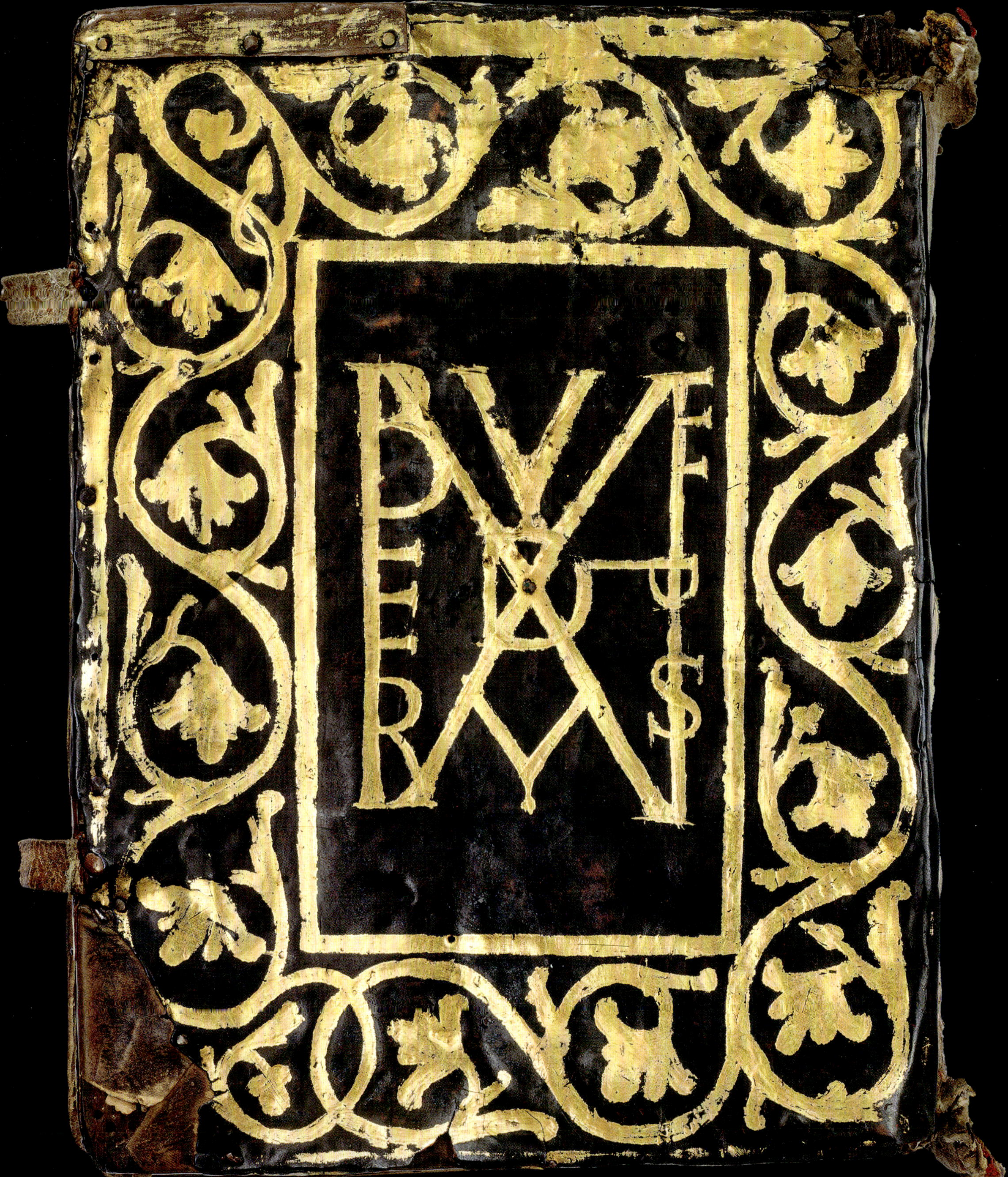

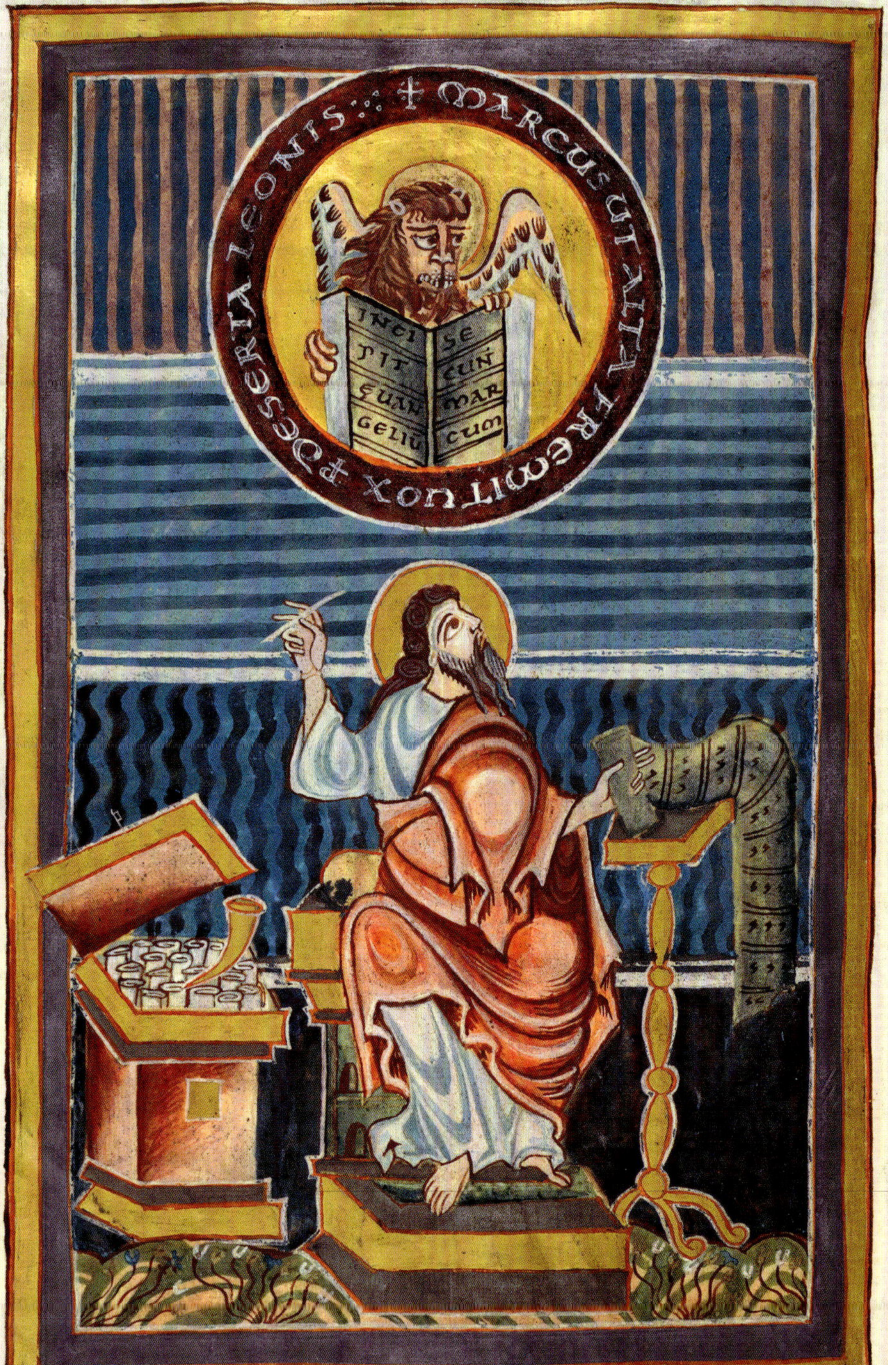

+ MARCUS UT ALTA FREMIT UOX ꝑ DESERTA LEONIS
INCI PIT EUAN GELIU
SE CUN MAR CUM

2 · Hezilo Gospels

German (Hildesheim[?]), 975–1050
Opaque paint, gold, and silver on parchment
Each folio 11 ⅞ × 9 ⅛ in. (30 × 23 cm); 214 leaves
Dom-Museum Hildesheim (DS 34)

We have no way to know which discerning patron commissioned this opulent gospel book. In the mid-nineteenth century the manuscript was linked to Hezilo, bishop of Hildesheim from 1054 to 1079. In the absence of documentary or other concrete evidence, style serves as the principal determinant for the manuscript's date and hence patron. On those grounds, few scholars today would argue that it was painted as late as Hezilo's tenure; indeed, many are comfortable linking it more closely to Bishop Bernward (reigned 993–1022).

The manuscript follows a decorative program perfected by Carolingian artists and much favored by their Ottonian successors. Each of the four books of the Gospels is introduced by several full-page illuminations, which include a lively portrait of each Evangelist immersed in the task and tools of writing and accompanied by the symbols associated with him (opposite). In many gospel books of this type, particularly those of the Franco-Saxon school from northeast France or Tours, the portraits include excerpts from the *Carmen Paschale*, a poem about the Bible written by the fifth-century poet Sedulius. In the Hezilo Gospels the Sedulius verses appear in the frame of the roundel containing the Evangelist symbols. In some manuscripts the ornamental preamble to each Evangelist's book can extend to as many as four pages; here it is limited to a two-page spread, where the paired images are coordinated through patterns, colors, compositions, and especially by matching frames to make evident the tight relationship between each book's text and its author (see following pages).

The abundance of easily identifiable furniture – writing desk, inkstand, chair, and storage chest – in each Evangelist portrait seems at odds with the abstract space each inhabits, a peculiar zone of multicolored geometric schemes and decorative patterns that recalls the striking backdrops of scenes in the Precious Gospels (see Introduction, figs. 10, 11). Presumably this feature, along with the Evangelists' strongly similar poses, fueled the scholarly debate over whether this manuscript or the Precious Gospels came first and which influenced the other. With our current knowledge, it is an impossible question. We are left to appreciate their respective strengths: the decorative profusion of the Precious Gospels and the Hezilo Gospels' elegant structure.

M.H.

SELECTED REFERENCES: Stähli, *Die Handschriften im Domschatz zu Hildesheim*, 1984, pp. xvi–xvii, 99–115; *Bernward von Hildesheim und das Zeitalter der Ottonen*, 1993, vol. 2, pp. 512–14, no. VII-34 (Ulrich Kuder); *Buch und Bild*, 1999, pp. 60–66, no. 7 (Ulrich Knapp).

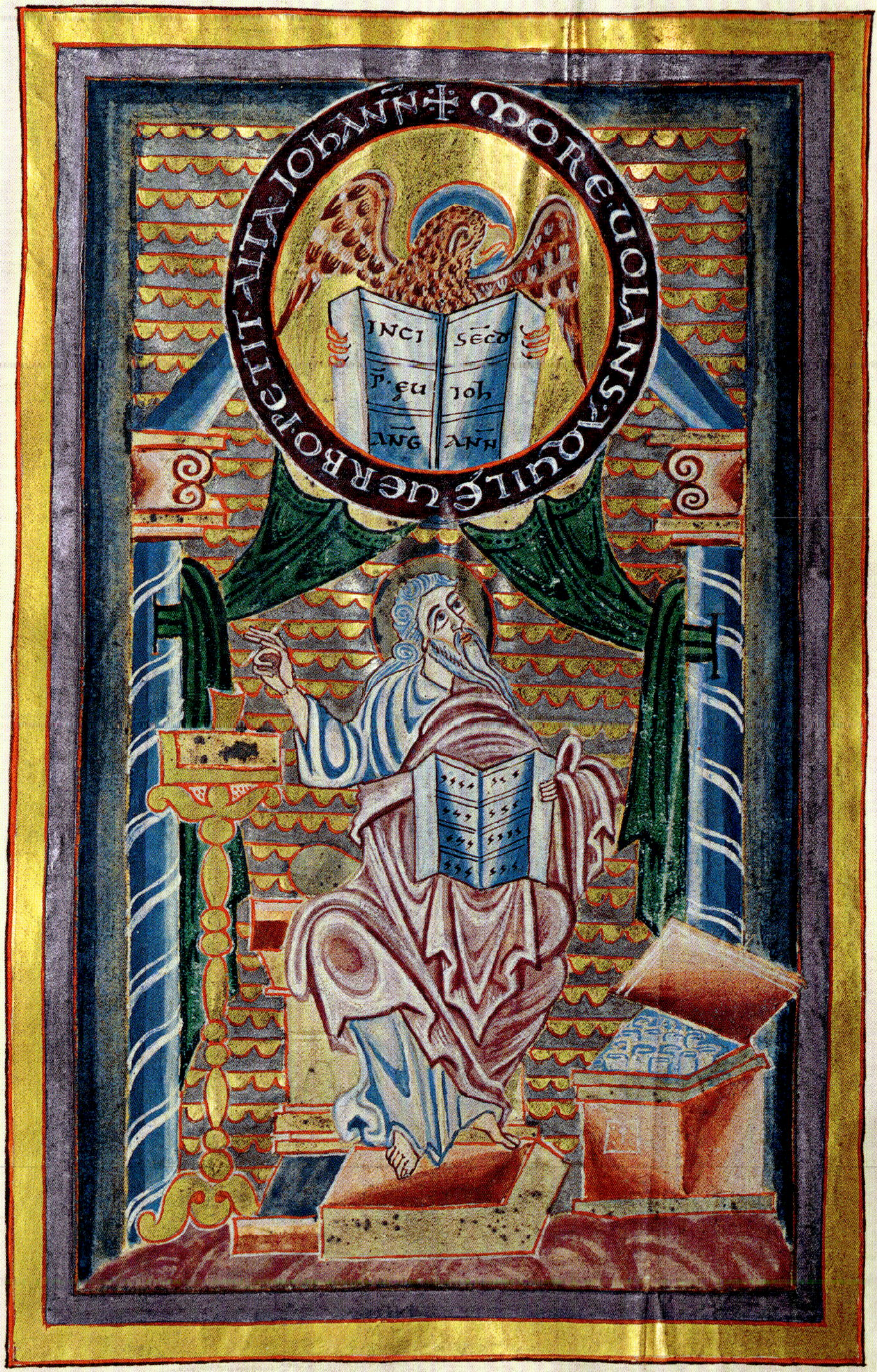
IOHANN ✠ MORE UOLANS AQUILE UERBO PETIT ALTA
INCI SECD
P. EU IOH
ANG ANH

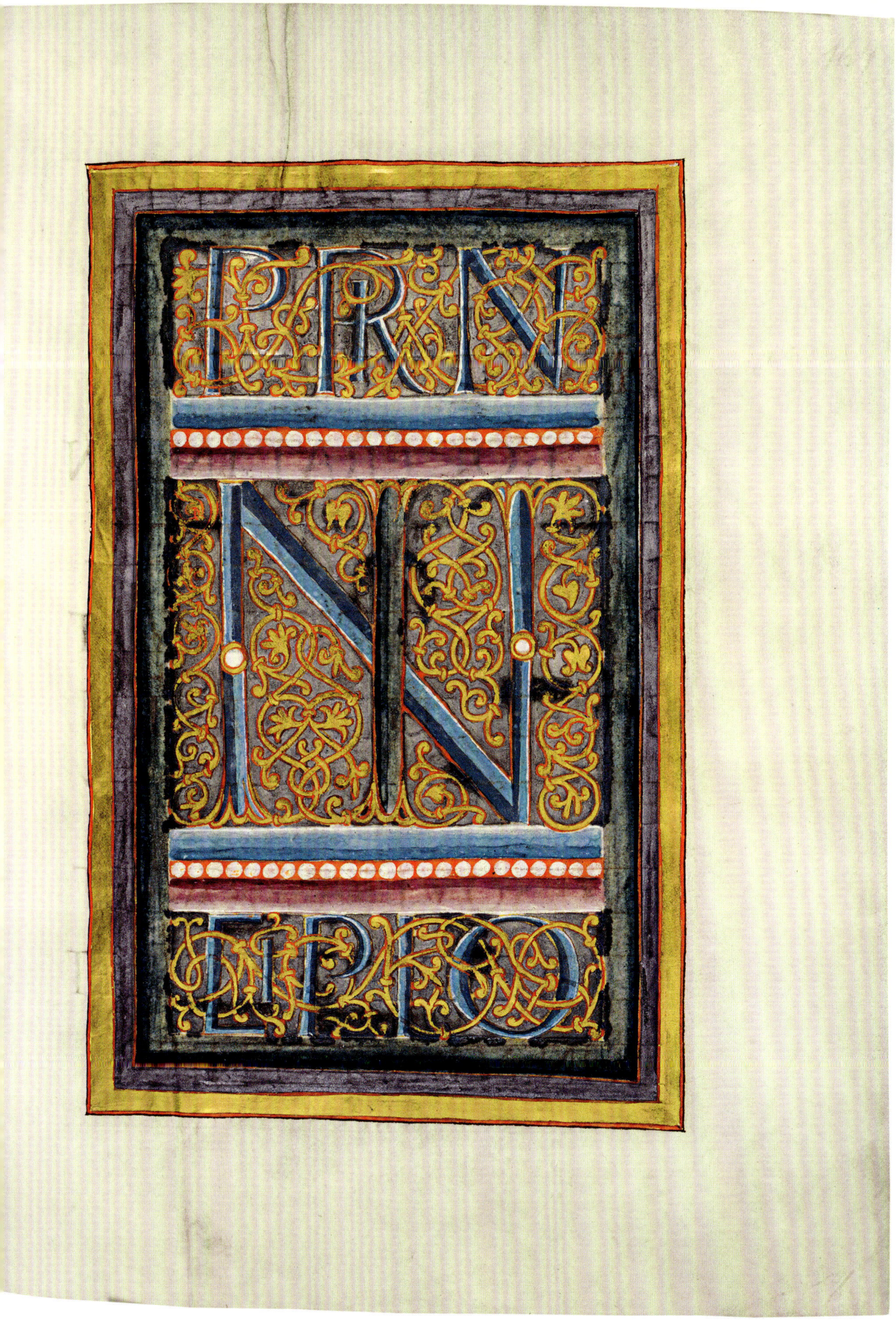

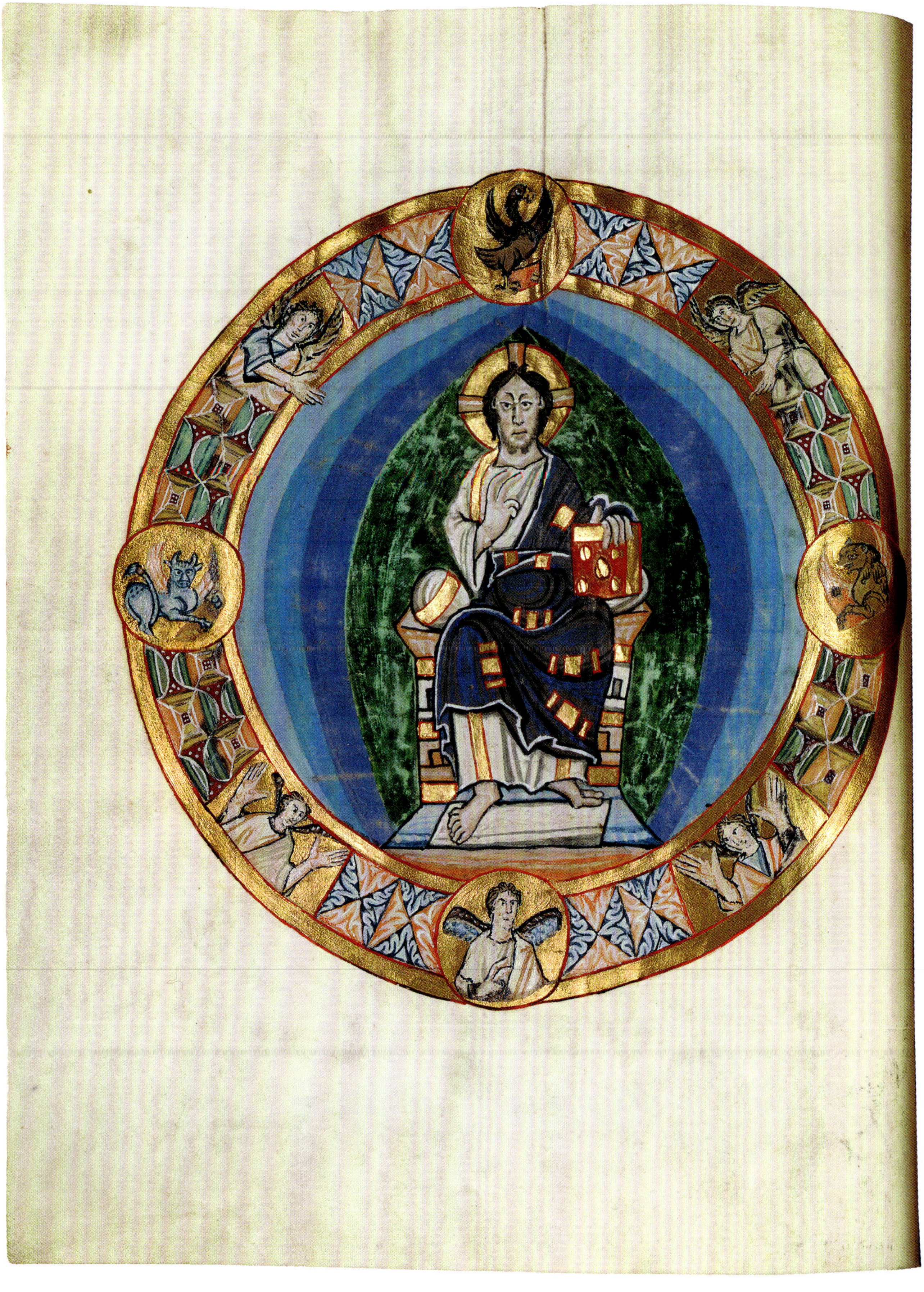

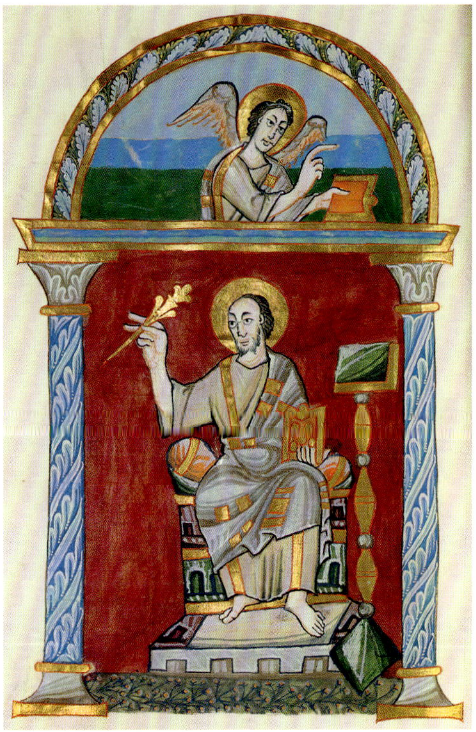

3 · Guntbald Gospels

German (Hildesheim), 1011
Opaque paint and gold on parchment
Each folio 11 ½ × 9 ⅛ in. (29 × 23 cm); 272 leaves
Dom-Museum Hildesheim (DS 33)

This gospel book is one of several produced in the Carolingian and Ottonian periods that look to the Lorsch Gospels, one of the most luxurious manuscripts associated with Charlemagne, for their model. All of those manuscripts include a set of Evangelists' portraits, strikingly similar in the figures' gestures and poses, the architectural settings in which they sit, and the presentation of the symbol that accompanies each. Many also devote space to a distinctive full-page image of Christ in Majesty – the enthroned God blessing, book in hand, and surrounded by symbols of the Four Evangelists. In the Lorsch Gospels (now in the Batthyáneum Library, Alba Iulia, Romania, and the Vatican Library, Rome), as in the copies, the Evangelist symbols occupy a framing roundel ornamented with decorative patterns.

The Guntbald Gospels contains all of these elements, including Christ in Majesty (fol. 21v, opposite). As richly decorated as it is, with its full-page Evangelist portraits (such as fol. 20v, above right), painted canon tables, and initial pages saturated with color and accented with silver and gold, it is nonetheless easy to characterize the Hildesheim manuscript as simply a lesser version of the Lorsch Gospels. It lacks the bold palette, compositional verve, and lavish piling on of decorative patterns that make the original so noteworthy. But precisely because every manuscript is handmade and no copy an exact one, a comparison between the model and the copy that keeps in mind that the book was likely ordered by Bishop Bernward of Hildesheim, one of the most important patrons of his day, can offer insight into the priorities and aesthetic preferences of Ottonian painters and patrons.

The Guntbald Gospels has eliminated the excess of the original to give pride of place to the figures themselves. Dark contours define the individual Evangelists, who are presented against simple fields of rich, contrasting color without extraneous architecture. Gone are the exuberant garments and the careening furniture of the Lorsch model. The Hildesheim artist achieves a sober, deliberate elegance. The figures are stable, centered on the page, the whole more symmetrical than not.

The scribe, Guntbald, left a colophon at the end of the book, stating that he produced the book under Bernward's episcopate at Hildesheim in the year 1011. Another inscription, perhaps in Bernward's own hand, tells us that he commissioned the book and gave it to the abbey of St. Michael. Analysis of the script suggests that Guntbald also wrote a pericope book, now in Nuremberg, as well as a psalter, now in Wolfenbüttel. Assuming he also wrote the Guntbald Sacramentary (cat. 4), it would appear that Guntbald was responsible for supplying Bernward with the four most important books needed to celebrate Mass. At least three of the four were part of the collection of St. Michael's at some time, which suggests they may have been part of the stock of books Bernward commissioned and acquired to equip the abbey he was building.

M.H.

SELECTED REFERENCES: Stähli, *Die Handschriften im Domschatz zu Hildesheim*, 1984, pp. 75–98; Exner, *Das Guntbald-Evangeliar*, 2008.

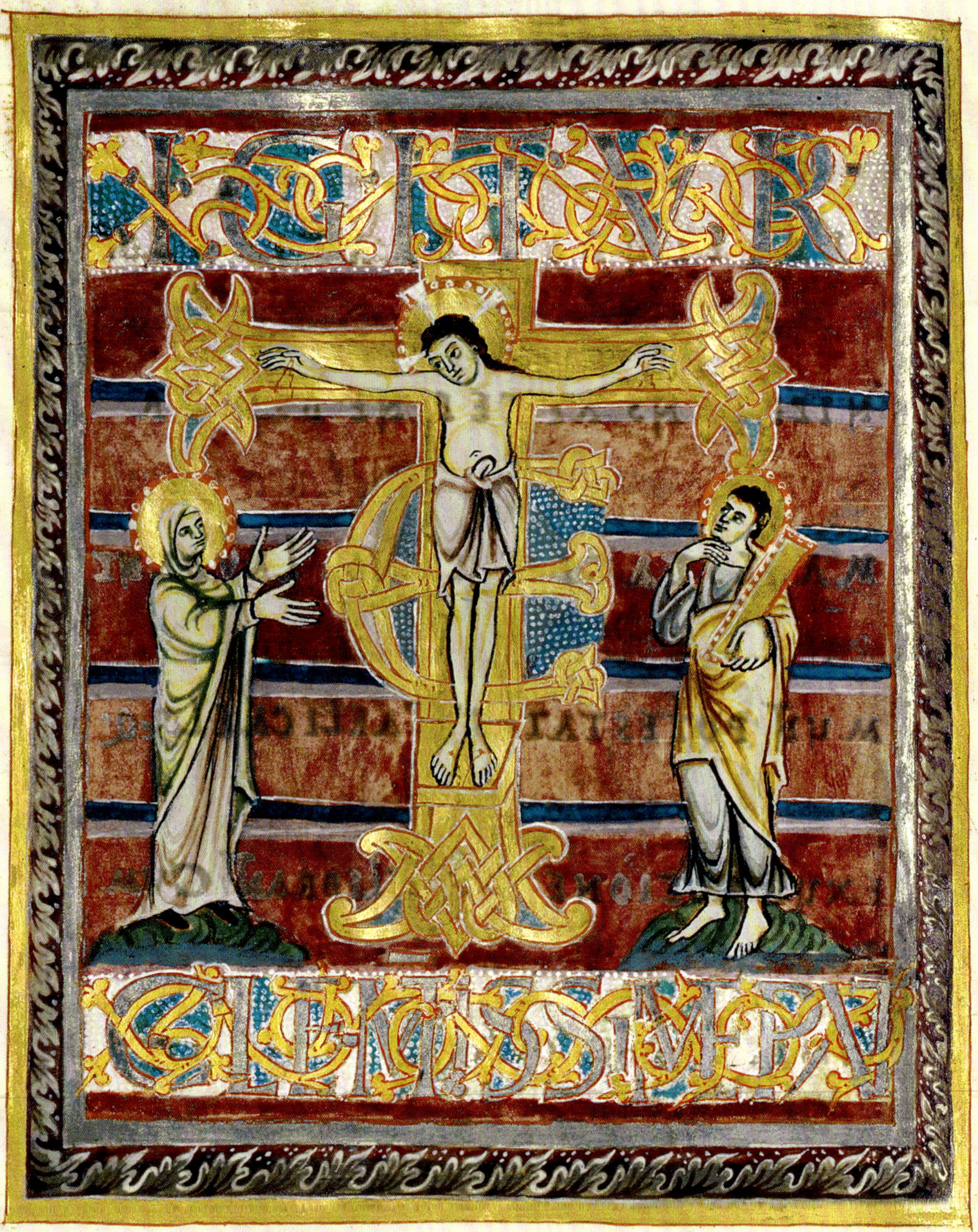

4 · Guntbald Sacramentary

German (Hildesheim), 1014–22
Opaque paint, gold, and silver on parchment
Each folio 12 × 7⅞ in. (30.5 × 20 cm); 245 leaves
Dom-Museum Hildesheim (DS 19)

This splendid sacramentary, a celebrant's guide to the Mass, confirms that the finest Ottonian manuscript illuminators were masters of the ornamental letter. The text is highlighted throughout by decorated initials, most of them intricate entanglements of gold and silver set against fields of saturated color. In addition, nine full pages are entirely given over to artful elaborations of the written word.

Many of the full-page illuminations introduce the different orations for the principal christological feasts of the liturgical year, but the highest concentration appears at the beginning of the manuscript, with the invariable Preface and Canon of the Mass. In an extraordinary sequence of pages, the celebrant's recitations receive lavish treatment. On one page (fol. 2bv, following page) the text almost disappears in a thicket of intertwining vines set against a confetti-strewn backdrop. On another (fol. 3r, shown on p. 33), alternating rows of silver and gold capitals shimmer against a purple backdrop that simulates luxurious Byzantine silk. The Canon itself is introduced by a large T (for *Te Igitur*, the first words of the first prayer) that has been transformed into a resplendent cross on which hangs the crucified Christ (fol. 3v, opposite). This page – the only one in the book with figural decoration – calls to mind the *Te Igitur* page in a luxury sacramentary made for Charles the Bald in the ninth century (Bibliothèque Nationale de France, Paris, lat. 1141). It too uses the letter "T" as an occasion to depict Jesus on the cross; the Hildesheim artist extends the narrative conceit of its model by adding Mary and John as participants in the scene.

Though we do not know the artist responsible for the illuminations, the scribe is generally thought to be Guntbald, who transcribed the Guntbald Gospels (cat. 3). At the end of the book appears a notice, similar to that found in the Guntbald Gospels, indicating that Deacon Guntbald produced the book at Bernward's behest in the year 1014 – seemingly concrete information undercut by the fact that it was written by a different and somewhat later hand than that found in the rest of the book.

M.H.

SELECTED REFERENCES: Stähli, *Die Handschriften im Domschatz zu Hildesheim*, 1984, pp. 51–69; *Buch und Bild*, 1999, pp. 67–73, no. 8 (Ulrich Knapp).

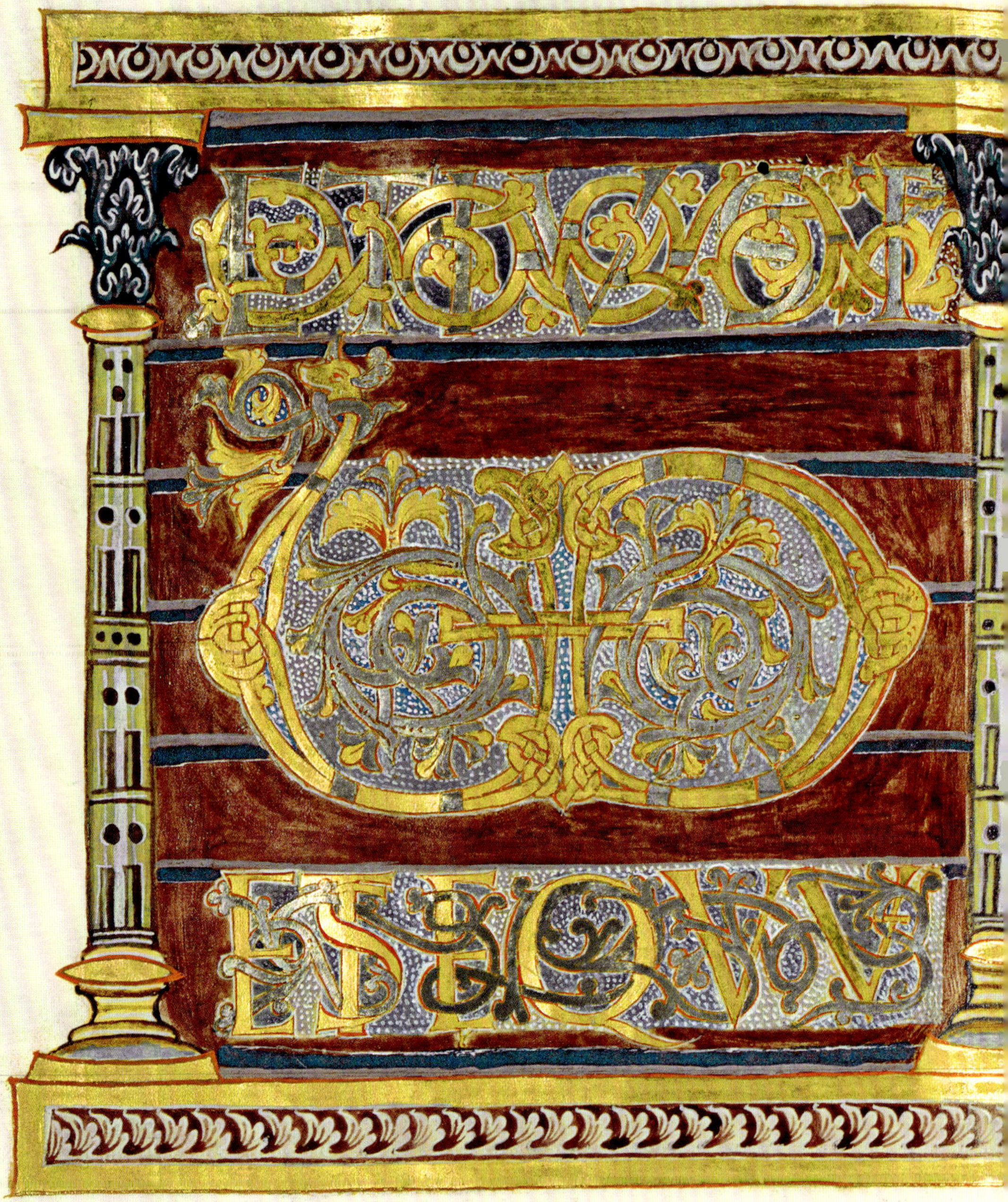

ET SALUTARE · NOS TIBI SEM
PER · ET UBIQ; GRATIAS AGE
RE · DN̄E SANCTAE PATER OM
NIPOTENS AETERNE DS̄ · PER
XP̄M DN̄M NR̄M · PER QUEM
MAIESTATEM TUAM LAUDANT
ANGLI · ADORANT DOMINATION̄ · TRE
MUNT POTESTATES · CAELI CAELORUMQ;
UIRTUTES · AC BEATA SERAPHIN̄ · SOCIA
EXULTATIONE CONCELEBRANT · CUM
QUIB; ET NR̄AS UOCES · UT ADMITTI
IUBEAS DEPRECAMUR · SUPPLICI
CONFESSIONE DICENTES · SC̄S ·

et resurrectione eius non tam pro
phetiam quam historiam scribi
mus. Aliter enim audita aliter
uisa narrantur. Quod melius in
tellegimus melius et proferimus.
Audi igitur emule. obtrectator
ausculta. Non damno non re
prehendo lxx sed confidenter
cunctis illis aplos profero. Per
istorum os mihi xps sonat quos
ante prophetas inter spiritalia
carismata positos lego. In quibus
ultimum pene gradum interpretes
tenent. quid liuore torqueris.
quid imperitorum animos contra me
concitas. Sicubi tibi in translati
one uideor errare. interroga he
breos diuersarum urbium magistros
consule. Quod illi habent de xpo
tui codices non habent. Aliud est
si contra se post ea ab aptis usurpata
testimonia probauerunt. et emen
datiora sunt exemplaria latina
quam greca. quam hebrea. Uerum
hec contra inuidos. Nunc te precor
desiderii carissime. ut qui tantum
opus me subire fecisti. et a genesi
exordium capere. orationibus iu
ues quo possim eodem spu quo scrip
ti sunt libri in latinum eos trans
ferre sermonem.

EXPLICIT PROLOGUS.

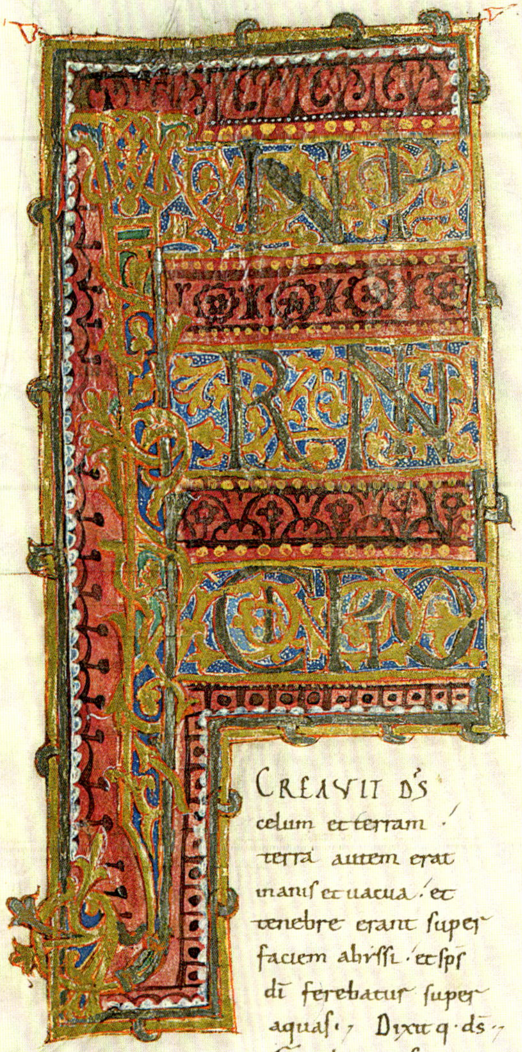

CREAVIT DS
celum et terram.
terra autem erat
inanis et uacua. et
tenebre erant super
faciem abyssi. et sps
di ferebatur super
aquas. Dixitque ds.
Fiat lux. et facta
est lux. Et uidit ds lucem quod
esset bona. et diuisit lucem a tene
bris. Appellauitque lucem diem. et te
nebras noctem. factumque est ues
pere et mane. dies unus. Dixit quoque
ds. Fiat firmamentum in medio a
quarum. et diuidat aquas ab aquis.
Et fecit ds firmamentum. diuisitque
aquas que erant sub firmamento.
ab his que erant super firmamentum.
Et factum est ita. Uocauitque ds fir
mamentum celum. et factum est
uespere et mane. dies secds. Dixit
uero ds. Congregentur aque
quae sub celo sunt in locum unum.

5 · Leaves from the Bernward Bible

German (Hildesheim), early 11th century
Opaque paint, gold, and silver on parchment
Each folio 18 × 13⅝ in. (45.5 × 34.5 cm); 486 leaves (when bound)
The book is currently disbound as it undergoes conservation.
Dom-Museum Hildesheim (DS 61)

Complete Bibles, containing all the canonical books from both the Old and the New Testaments, appear to have been relatively rare before the end of the eleventh century. The requirements of ritual and study at the time must have contributed to a preponderance of books containing only the Bible's most useful excerpts: gospel books, pericope books, psalters, and commentaries. The Bernward Bible is the sole Ottonian example of a complete Bible to survive from the tenth and early eleventh centuries.

Ottonian illumination is as much a calligraphic art as a narrative one, and this book offers a compendium of virtuoso letter forms. With the exception of a single full-page illumination, all of its decoration appears as the initials that begin the prefatory material and each biblical book. The lavish opening page of the Book of Genesis (fol. 5r, opposite) is typical: Against a puce and blue background, outsize letters in gold and silver, densely interwoven with gold vines, spell out "In principio" (In the beginning). No interstice goes to waste, as speckled passages of blue and green fill in the smallest gaps. The curiously spare rendering of the canon tables (fol. 396v, following page), presented as the simplest of ruled drawings, provides a restrained counterpoint to the opulence of the initials.

The only painted human figures appear on the dedication page (fol. 1r, shown on p. 37), a single sheet inserted at the beginning of the book. Within an interior space dominated by an enormous golden altar cross, a young man with pen in hand presents a book to a haloed woman, an act notably blessed by the hand of God. Were it not for the man's halo, we would assume the picture to show Bishop Bernward, whom his biographer tells us was a scribe, offering his Bible to the Virgin in a manner akin to that seen in Bernward's Precious Gospels (see Introduction, fig. 10). The initials in the Bible resemble those in the Guntbald Sacramentary (cat. 4), which Bernward likely commissioned, and he seems the probable patron of so imposing a volume. Whomever it depicts, the frontispiece displays the same sumptuous layering of pattern and solid, gold and rich color, that we see in the initials.

M.H.

SELECTED REFERENCES: Stähli, *Die Handschriften im Domschatz zu Hildesheim*, 1984, pp. 147–66; *Buch und Bild*, 1999, pp. 32–37, no. 1 (Elisabeth Scholz).

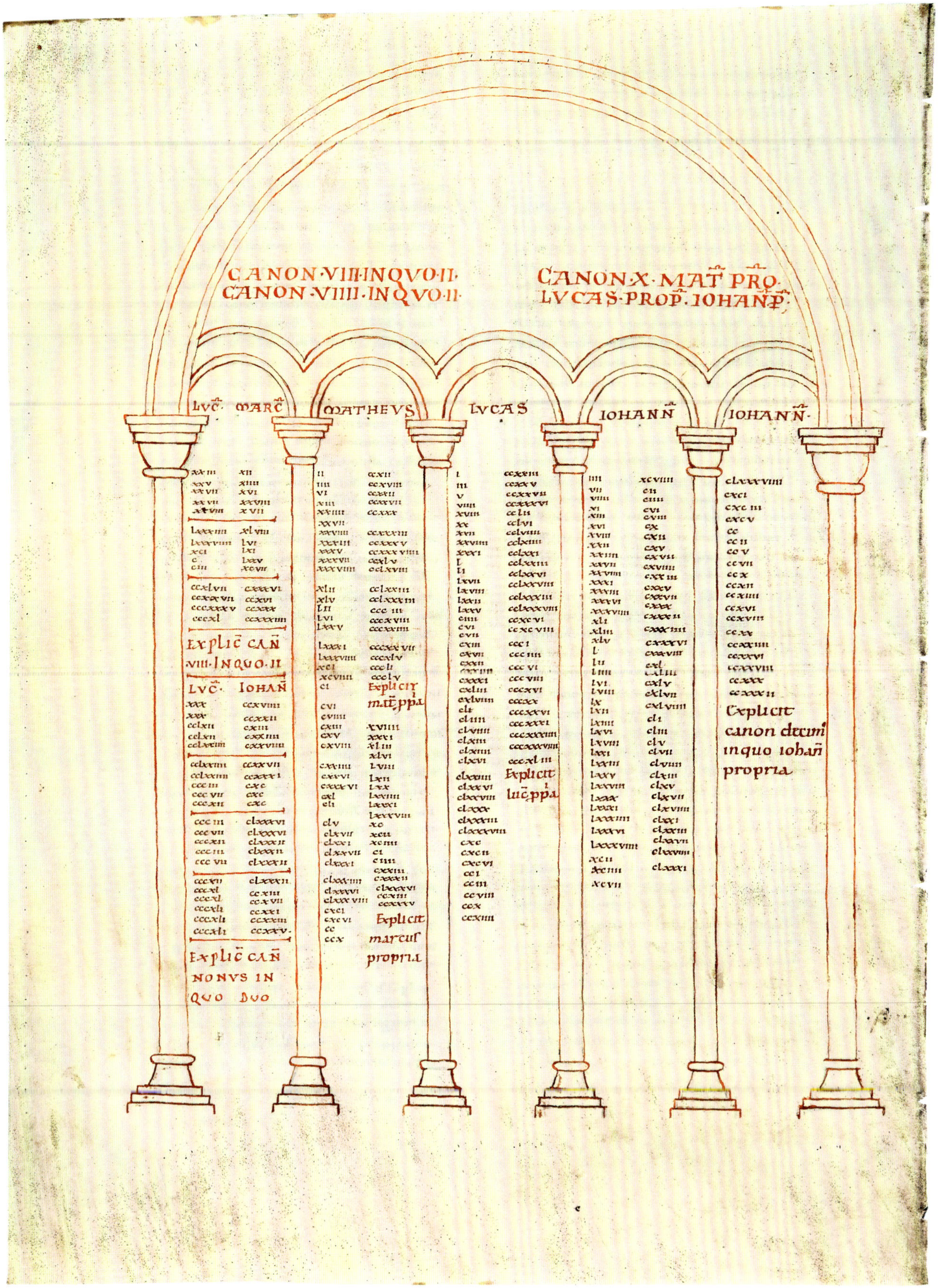
CANON·VIII·IN QVO·II·
CANON·VIIII·IN QVO·II·
CANON·X·MAT PRO
LVCAS·PROP·IOHAN P
LVC MARC
MATHEVS
LVCAS
IOHANN
IOHANN
EXPLIC CAN VIII·IN QVO·II
LVC IOHAN
EXPLIC CAN NONVS IN QVO DVO
Explicit mat ppa
Explicit marcus propria
Explicit luc ppa
Explicit canon decimi inquo iohan propria

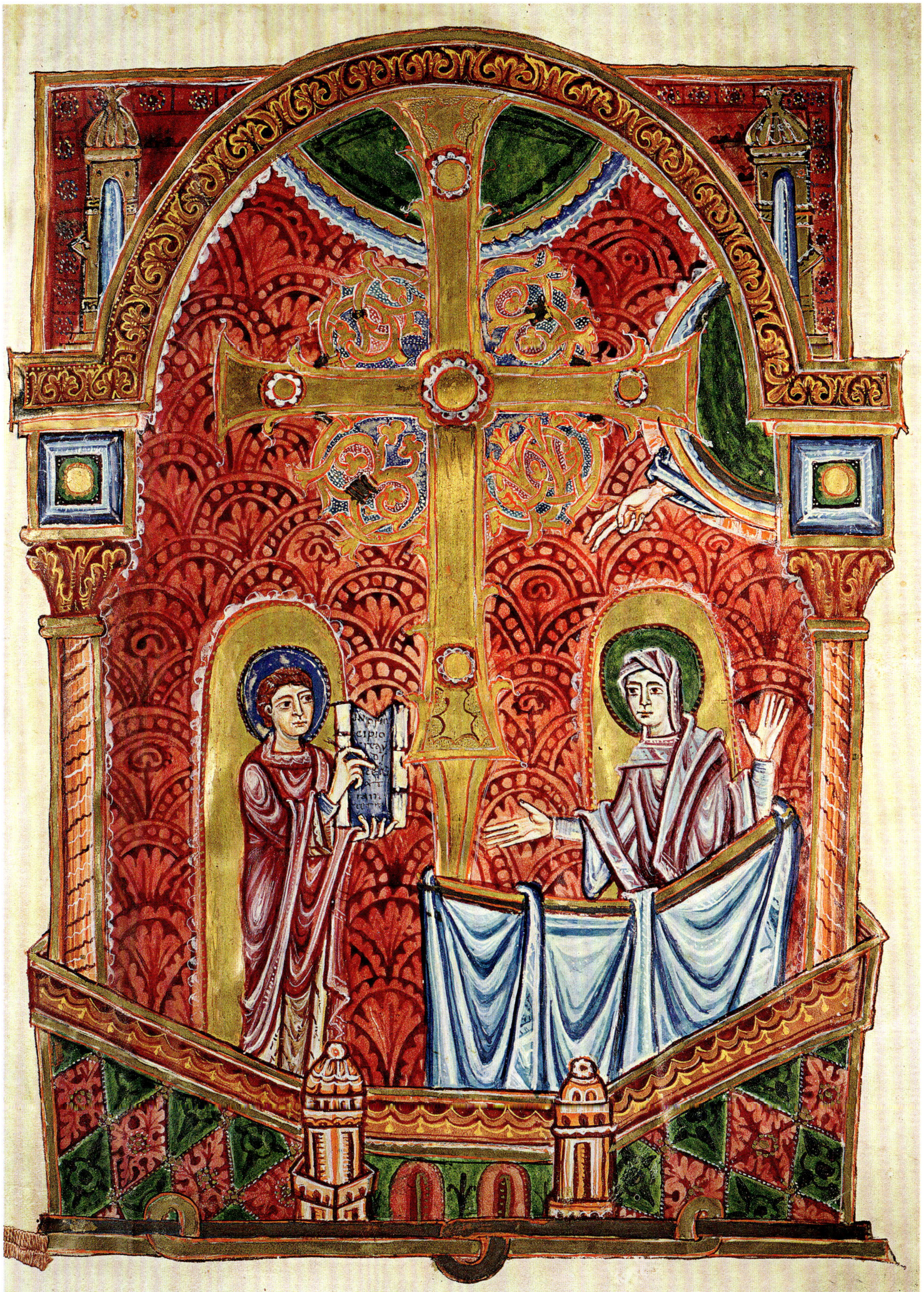

6 · Gospel Lectionary and Collectar

German (Reichenau), ca. 1010–30
Tempera and gold on vellum
Overall 8 ¾ × 6 ½ in. (22 × 16.5 cm); 96 leaves
Dombibliothek Hildesheim (Hs. 688)

Lavishly decorated liturgical manuscripts were often specially commissioned and donated by emperors. This sumptuously illustrated codex incorporates a lectionary (a book of readings from the Old and New Testaments for use during the Mass) and a collectar (a book of prayers for the canonical hours or before the Epistle of the Mass). It includes illuminations of five principal feast days – Christmas (depicting the Nativity and the Annunciation to the Shepherds), Maundy Thursday (Christ Washing the Feet of the Apostles), Easter (Holy Women at the Holy Sepulcher; Christ in Limbo), and the two shown here: the Ascension of the Virgin and All Saints Day.

The All Saints Day illuminations are among the most impressive, their composition, set against a shimmering gold ground, seeming to reflect the arrangement and grandeur of monumental wall decoration of the period. The double-page spread (opposite) shows an apocalyptic vision, with clergymen and nuns adoring the Lamb of God (fol. 83v) and a Last Judgment, where Christ in Majesty crowns them in the company of musicians, among them King David with his harp (fol. 84r). Heaven and Earth are here united, as in Psalm 96: "Sing to the Lord, all the earth. . . . Let the heavens rejoice, and let the earth be glad."

The female figures wear wimples, indicating that the codex was created for an order of nuns. It was probably intended for Sophia, the sister of Emperor Otto II, who was abbess (1002–39) of the convent of Gandersheim, near Hildesheim. At that time Gandersheim was the subject of a jurisdictional dispute between the bishop of Hildesheim and the archbishop of Mainz; the codex went to Hildesheim only in the eighteenth century, presumably from Gandersheim.

Another resplendent double-page image (shown on pp. 40–41), for the Ascension of the Virgin, depicts the Dormition (Mary upon her deathbed) and the Assumption or Glorification of the Virgin (Mary's body and soul reunited and borne to heaven) – a pairing with few precedents. The Dormition (fol. 76v) is based upon a Byzantine prototype – perhaps not a painted image but an ivory icon of this popular subject, one of the main feasts of the Orthodox Church – in which Christ standing by the bier receives the soul of the Virgin, shown as a child. Several contemporary Byzantine icons depicting this theme had come to the West and were incorporated into deluxe Ottonian book covers, such as the Gospels of Otto III (Bayerische Staatsbibliothek, Munich, Clm 4453).

The Assumption on the facing page (fol. 77r) depicts angels bearing to heaven the Virgin's soul (shown as a bust in orans, with arms outstretched in prayer) and the hand of God drawing her upward by a distinctive flaming red cross – rare imagery for this subject.

Stylistically and technically the illuminations are associated with the famous monastery of Reichenau, near Lake Constance, one of the principal centers of manuscript production about 1000. As further evidence that the manuscript was produced there, the page following the Assumption illumination includes a Reichenau variant of prayers for the spiritual rather than bodily assumption of Mary's soul to heaven.

C.T.L.

SELECTED REFERENCES: *Bernward von Hildesheim und das Zeitalter der Ottonen*, 1993, vol. 2, pp. 479–82, no. VII-23 (Ulrich Kuder); Kahsnitz, "Coronas aureas in capite," 1997; Mayr-Harting, *Ottonian Book Illumination*, 1999, pp. 150–52; *Kaiser Heinrich II.*, 2002, pp. 284–87, no. 121 (Gude Suckale-Redlefsen); Engel and Gallistl, "Die Reichenauer Handschriften," 2009.

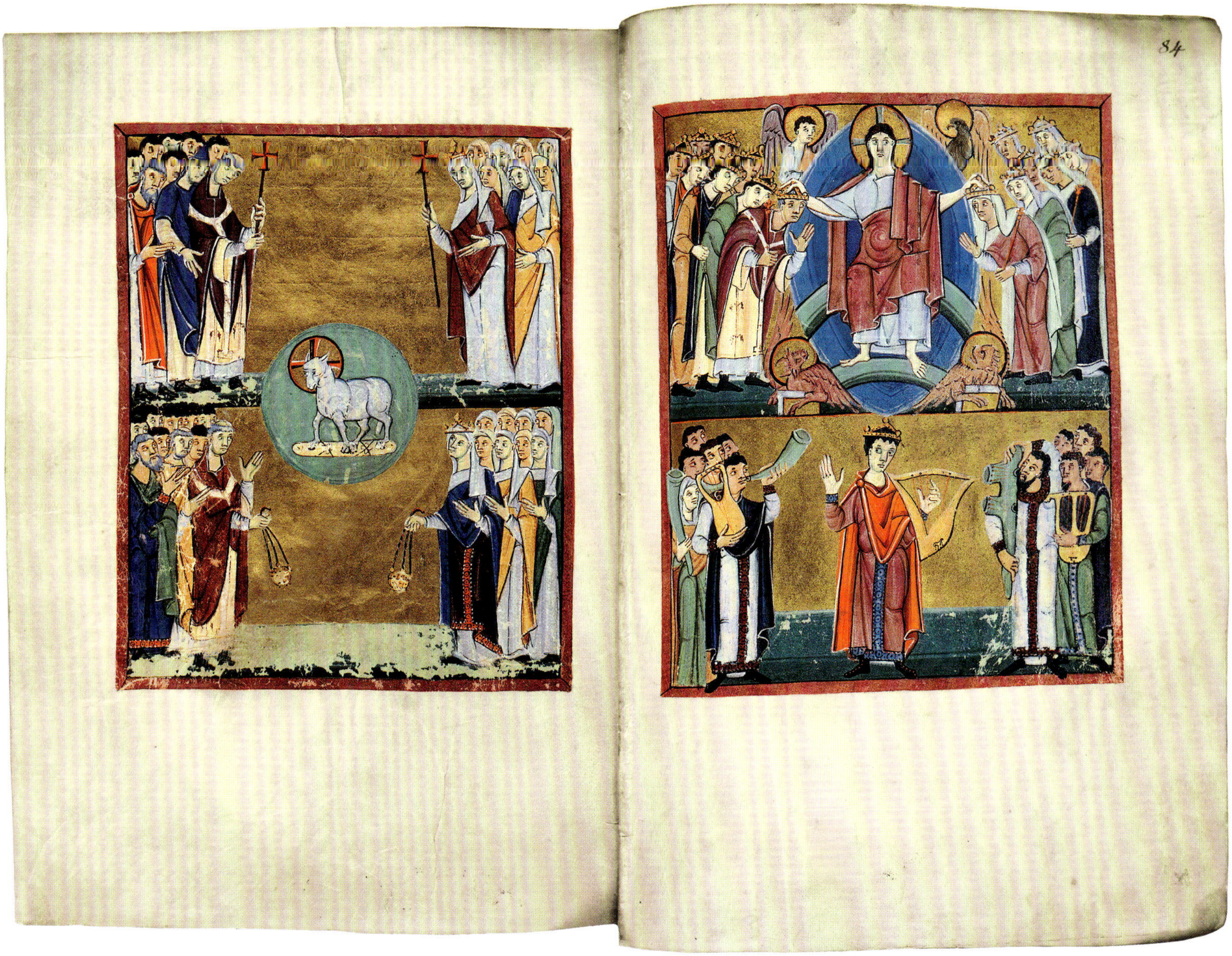
84

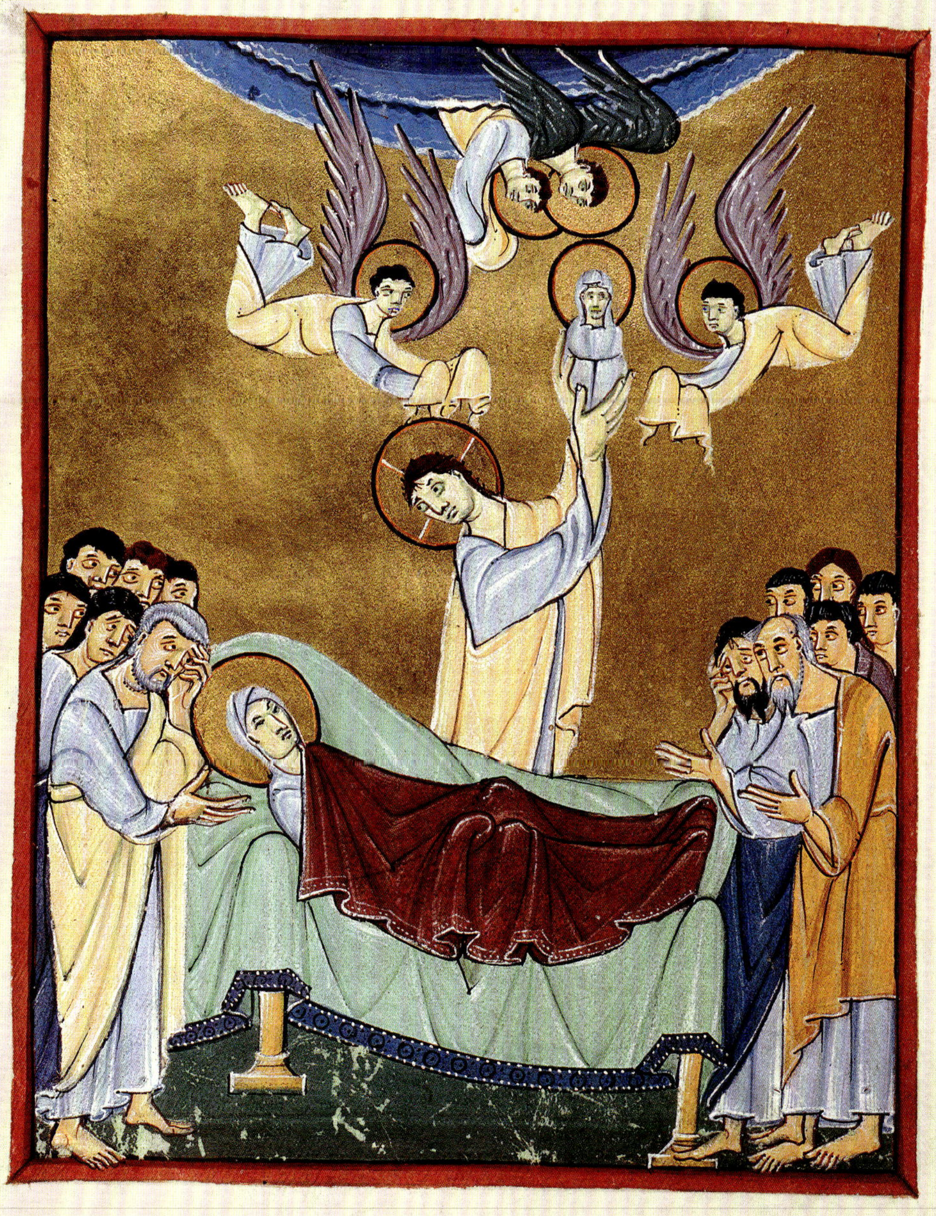

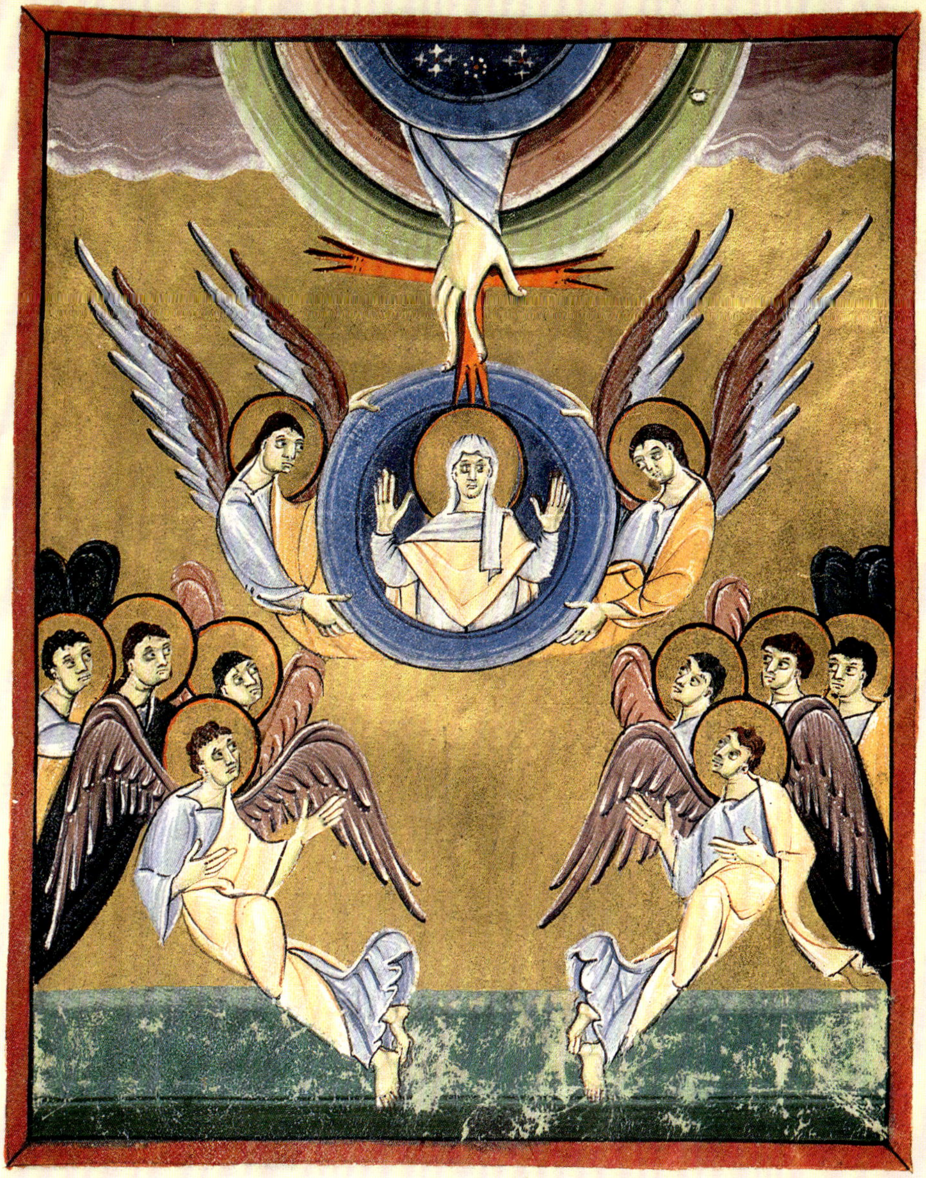

7 · Virgin and Child Enthroned (so-called Golden Madonna)

German (Hildesheim), before 1022
Gold sheet on linden wood core, filigree, and precious and semiprecious stones
22 3/8 × 10 1/8 × 10 in. (56.6 × 25.5 × 25.2 cm)
Dom-Museum Hildesheim (DS 82)

One of the oldest three-dimensional sculptures in the medieval Latin West, this shimmering golden Madonna sits at the beginning of a tradition of worship specially venerating the Mother of God. Her gleaming physical splendor, its brilliance a clear reference to heavenly glory, conveys that she is the Queen of Heaven personified. Such cult figures, often termed the "Throne of Wisdom," were considered powerful intermediaries between this world and heaven. Many functioned also as containers for relics, but there is no evidence that this one did; the panel on the back of the hollow figure seems intended only to alleviate the splitting of the wood.

Over time the statue has suffered considerably, but it is nevertheless one of the most important images of the *Maestà* (the Virgin in Majesty, shown enthroned with the Christ Child) from the early Middle Ages. Oriented frontally, with formal bearing and the Child sitting upright on her lap, she is conceived fully in the round, the form of the figure and the elegant drapery patterns beautifully rendered.

Figures like this developed a cult role as monastic centers began celebrating not only Mary's biblical presence and liturgical function but also her miraculous powers. Some sources describe miracles even in the making of such statues. For example, when the artist-monk Tuotilo was making a figure of Mary for the city of Metz about 900, Mary herself was said to have made the gold leaf for it. The Hildesheim figure, used in liturgical processions on feast days, was honored, touched, and adored. According to an early thirteenth-century source, parts of her gold clothing were stolen; consequently, large sections had to be renewed, including the elegant filigree bands on the arms and mantle, which are set with semiprecious stones.

That work, from about 1220–30, is the major restoration to the original object still visible today. Another restoration was conducted in 1664, and some of the gold covering is a later replacement. Due to the deterioration of the linden wood core, the gold sheeting was removed and reattached during further restorations in 1950.

During the thirteenth century the statue was located on the high altar of the eastern apse of Hildesheim Cathedral, along with the Saint Oswald Reliquary (cat. 31). There, offerings of jewelry accumulated over time, underscoring Mary's role as a cult figure. According to the 1438 cathedral inventory, more than a hundred brooches, pins, rings, and chains adorned the statue, left as gifts and votive offerings.

Bishop Bernward is the likely patron, but that supposition cannot be proven, though stylistic links to the art he sponsored make it plausible. Indeed, the Virgin in Majesty in Bernward's Precious Gospels (see Introduction, fig. 11) echoes the form of this statue, including the cowl to cover her head and shoulder. An ivory statuette may well have provided the model; a strikingly similar contemporary work that may have been carved in Cologne, Trier, Mainz, or another Rhineland ecclesiastical center exists in Mainz (Altertumsmuseum, 0/1517).

C.T.L.

SSELECTED REFERENCES: Forsyth, *Throne of Wisdom*, 1972, pp. 121–24; *Kirchenkunst des Mittelalters*, 1989, pp. 37–84, no. 4; Beer, "Orte und Wege," 2010; Kingsley, "Picturing the Treasury," 2011; Pawlik, *Das Bildwerk als Reliquiar*, 2013, pp. 234–44, no. 17.

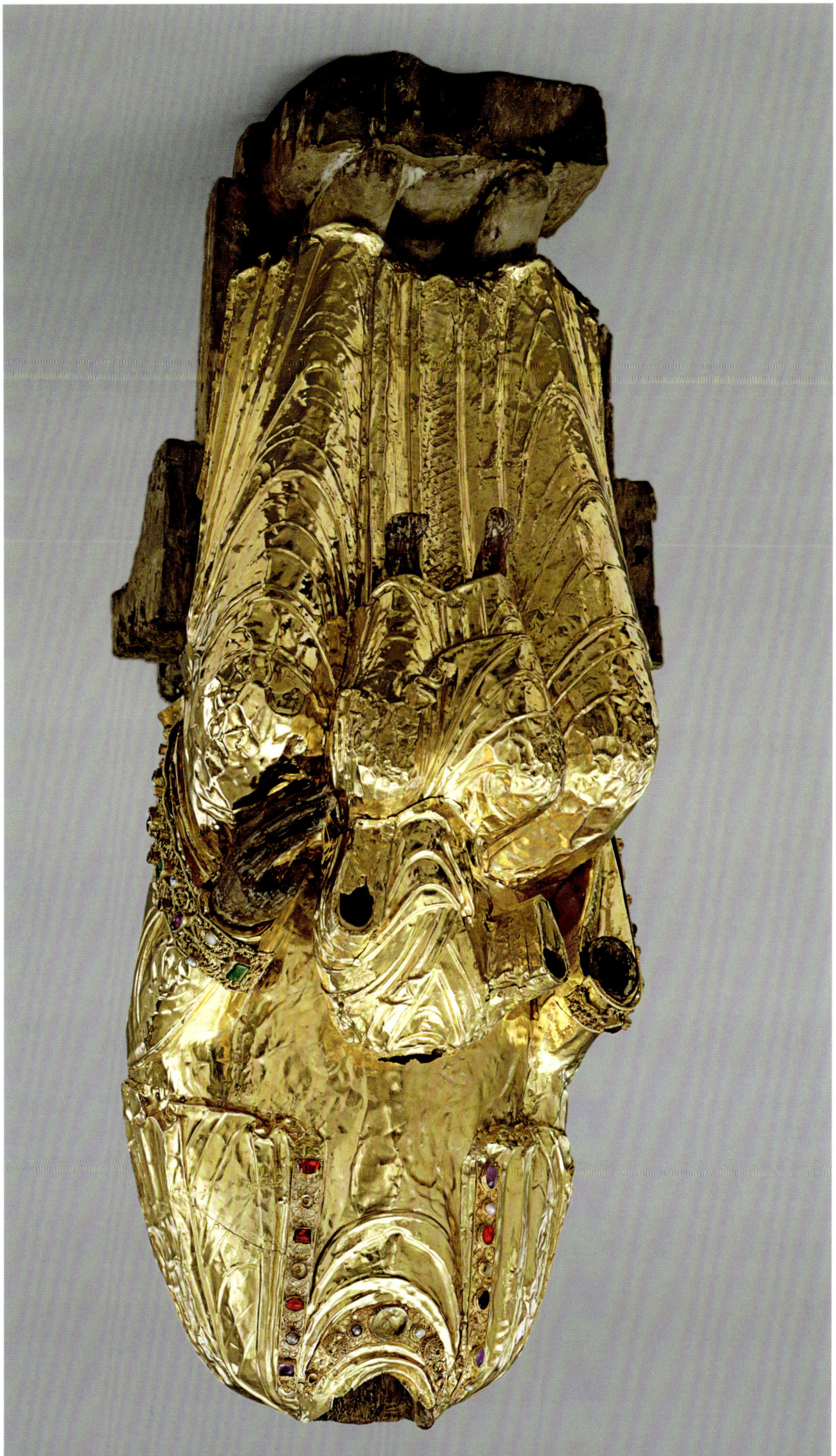

8 · Ringelheim Crucifix

German (Hildesheim), ca. 1000/before 1022
Linden wood (corpus) and oak (arms)
Overall 63⅞ × 63⅜ × 9⅞ in. (162 × 161 × 25 cm)
Dom-Museum Hildesheim, on loan from the church of
Sts. Abdon and Sennen, Salzgitter-Ringelheim (L 1993-8)

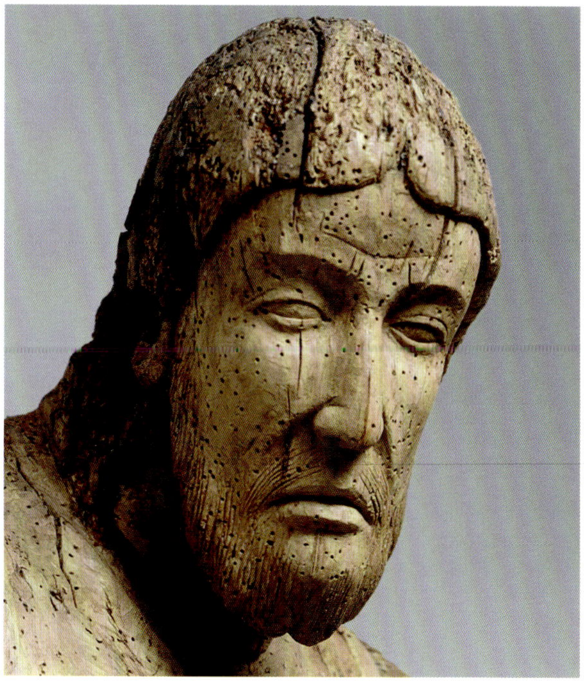

This elegantly carved and poignant crucifix is one of the key monumental wood sculptures from the Ottonian era to survive. More standing against than hanging on a cross (now lost), the imposing, near-lifesize figure conveys not physical suffering but quiet triumph.

The torso, legs, and head are constructed of one piece of linden wood; the outstretched arms (twelfth-century replacements) are a single piece of oak. The feet also were replaced in the twelfth century, perhaps due to damage from candles burning below. The subtle rotation of the body and the head is without precedent in surviving early medieval monumental crucifixes and helps convey the plasticity of the figure. With a gentle orientation toward the right, Christ stands upon a suppedaneum (a crucifix's foot support), knees slightly bent, his loincloth tied in the front with an overall soft modeling. The head is exceptionally sensitive, even in its present state, with the surface of the hair lost; the open eyes signify Christ triumphant over death. A similar representation of Christ is on an ivory panel made in about 1000 for Archbishop Adalbero II of Metz (Metz Museums, 3550). The wooden figure's power must have been enhanced by polychromy, long ago lost.

This magnificent crucifix was in the convent of Ringelheim, in the Harz Mountains, near Hildesheim, when the convent was turned over to Augustinian monks in the twelfth century. It is thought to have been commissioned by Hildesheim's Bishop Bernward for Ringelheim in honor of his sister, Judith, the convent's abbess, who died about 1012–20. It may have been created upon Judith's becoming abbess, the date of which is unknown, or in her memory, but certainly before Bernward's death in 1022.

During conservation treatment in 1949–52 relics were discovered within a cavity inside the top of the head. They included two stones in a leather pouch, accompanied by a parchment indicating they were from the Holy Sepulcher, in Jerusalem, and marked B[ernwardus] + ep[iscopus], which can mean only Bishop Bernward. Two bone relics were also found, wrapped in silk, with a parchment indicating they were relics of the early Christian saints Cosmas and Damian. Presumably the relics came from Hildesheim's earlier, Carolingian cathedral treasury or were acquired by Bernward when he traveled to Rome in 1001.

Some other monumental crucifixes had – or were thought to have had – reliquary functions, enhancing their status as devotional objects. The famous Gero Crucifix in Cologne Cathedral, which was carved before 990, was said to have had a similar cavity in the head, caused by a split in the wood. According to the contemporary account by Thietmar of Merseburg (975–1018), the fissure miraculously sealed after a piece of sacramental host was inserted into it. However, a 1976 technical study revealed no physical evidence to support the legend, underscoring the "miraculous" nature of the story.

By the thirteenth century lifesize crucifixes were placed on top of the choir screens, but there is no evidence of how this monumental figure was positioned two centuries earlier. It may have been situated near an altar dedicated to the cross.

C.T.L.

SELECTED REFERENCES: *Kirchenkunst des Mittelalters*, 1989, pp. 85–106, no. 5; *Bernward von Hildesheim und das Zeitalter der Ottonen*, 1993, vol. 2, pp. 496–500, no. VII-31 (Rainer Kahsnitz); Pawlik, *Das Bildwerk als Reliquiar*, 2013, pp. 229–34, no. 16; Lutz, Cambareri, and Fozi, *Striking Images*, forthcoming.

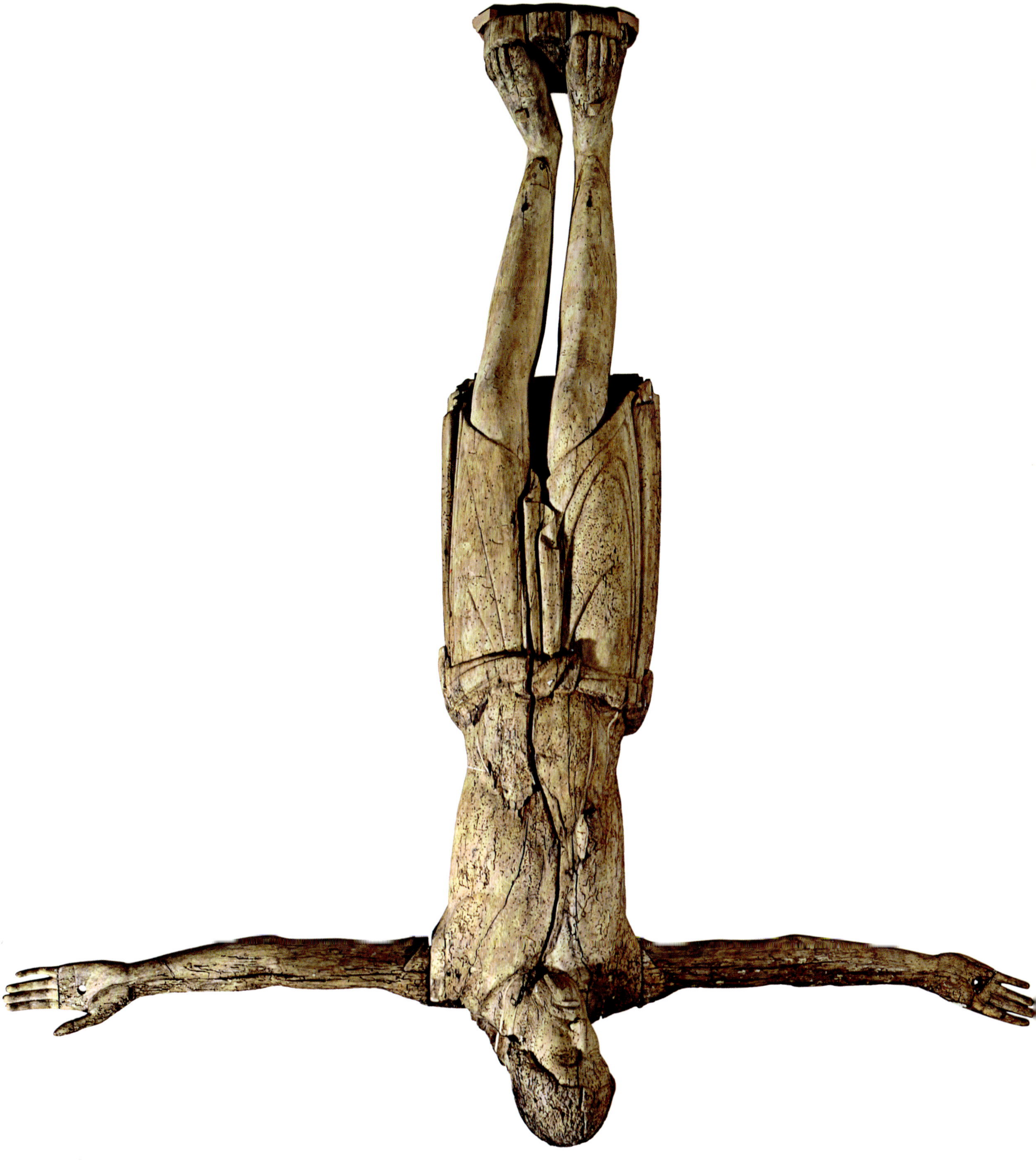

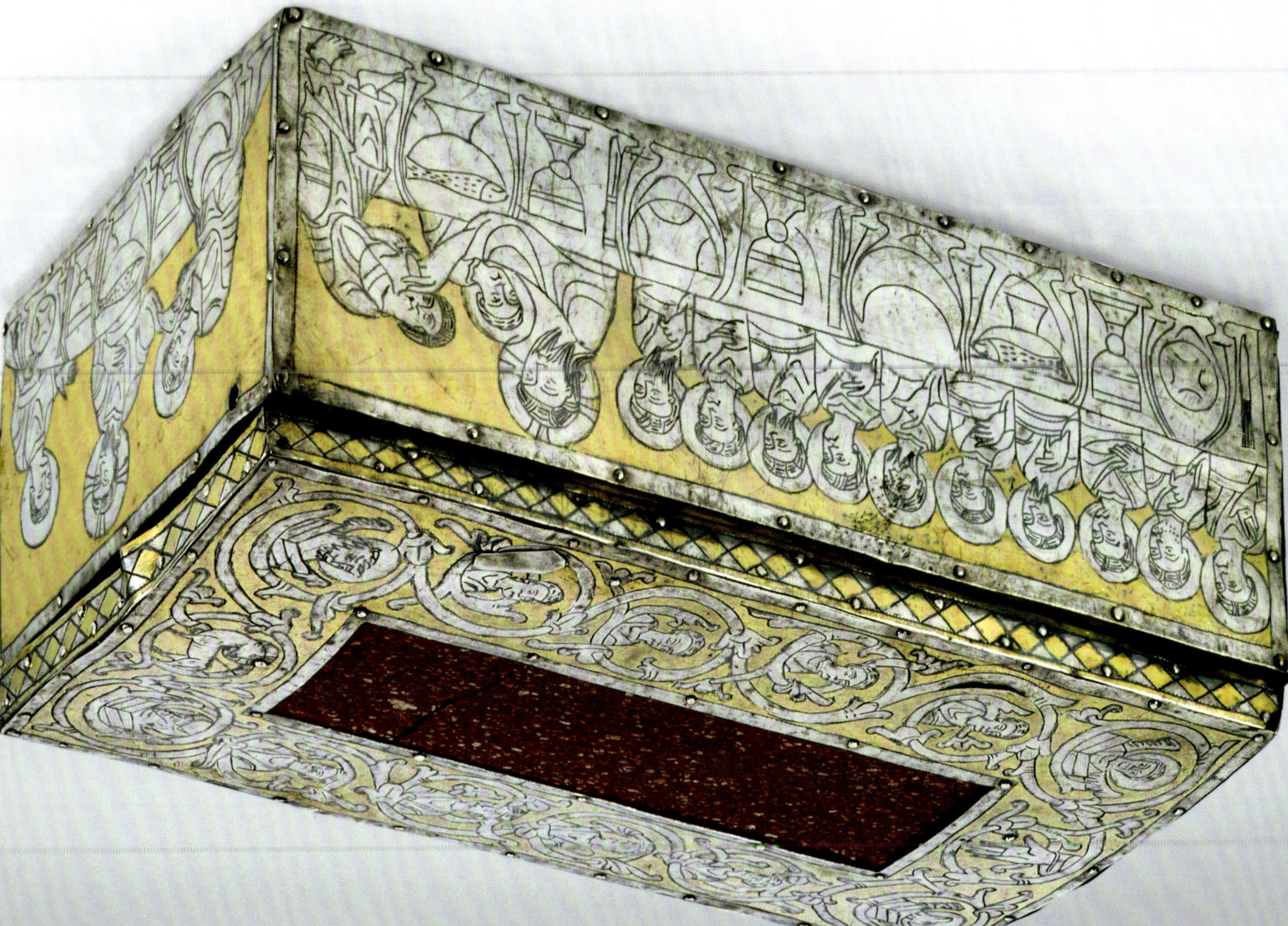

9 · Portable Altar

German (Hildesheim), ca. 1000
Silver with niello and gilding, porphyry, and unknown stone; wood core
$4\frac{1}{8} \times 10\frac{1}{4} \times 5\frac{7}{8}$ in. (10.5 × 26 × 15 cm)
Dom-Museum Hildesheim (DS 26)

Portable altars found utility in the field – in missionizing efforts, in battle, or on pilgrimage – providing a consecrated table for the celebration of the Eucharist beyond the walls of the church. Yet they also seem to have served in other ways. An image of Bishop Bernward of Hildesheim from the Precious Gospels (see Introduction, fig. 10) shows him within the confines of a magnificently appointed church with what may be a portable altar sitting prominently atop a fixed one. Far from being a mobile substitute, the portable altar would seem in that instance to be a supplement to the main altar – an attractive pedestal for paten and chalice, the vessels for the Eucharist's consecrated bread and wine.

This example, though clad in lustrous materials, is humbler than the several others that survive in whole or in part in the Hildesheim treasury. It eschews many of their showier elements – colorful enamels, carved ivories, decorative punchwork – in favor of engraved images on every side. However, the notably unsophisticated figural style sits comfortably within the range of artwork we associate with Bernward; the art he commissioned generally relied upon vivid colors, sumptuous decorative patterns, dramatic scale, or the inclusion of noteworthy components – not graphic virtuosity – to impress.

The front and back of the piece, showing the Last Supper and the Foot Washing, respectively, concern themselves with the Passion; the two ends, with the Meal at Emmaus and what is likely the Conversion of Paul on the road to Damascus, treat the impact of Christ upon his followers after his death. The Last Supper and Emmaus scenes seem chosen to emphasize the Eucharistic uses of an altar. (In the orderly lineup of the Twelve Apostles on the front and back, the artist seems to have particularly enjoyed the strong horizontal of the altar's long sides.) On the top appear the hand of God and the Paschal Lamb, symbols of the Four Evangelists, and the heads of four figures, presumably saints – appropriate motifs to frame the valuable porphyry slab at center, which, along with the relic inside, was the essential and therefore most important aspect of the altar.

The top is hinged to the rest of the altar, an unusual feature; it is not clear whether the hinge represents an alteration to the original design. This piece, along with several others, was recovered from the cathedral's main altar in the early nineteenth century, suggesting that, though it was no longer useful as a portable altar, it retained potency as a relic container.

M.H.

SELECTED REFERENCES: Brandt, "Tragaltäre im Hochaltar," 1989; *Bernward von Hildesheim und das Zeitalter der Ottonen*, 1993, vol. 2, pp. 478–79, no. VII-22 (Martina Pippal); *Schätze des Glaubens*, 2010, pp. 44–45, no. 9 (Michael Brandt).

10 · Bernward Cross

German (Hildesheim), after 1007/before 1022; base: 14th century
Silver with gilding
Overall (H. with base) 12 3/8 × 5 7/8 × 1 1/4 in. (31.2 × 14.9 × 3.2 cm); H. of cross 8 1/4 in. (20.9 cm)
Dom-Museum Hildesheim (DS 6)

One of the most precious objects of Ottonian art, this beautiful crucifix is cast in silver, selectively gilded, and engraved with inscriptions. Monumental in conception yet delicate in execution, it is not unlike the wooden Ringelheim Crucifix (cat. 8), translated into silver and gold. It also is reminiscent – for example, in the placement and form of the loincloth – of earlier ivory representations, such as that carved in relief about 1000 on a panel for Bishop Adalbero II of Metz (Metz Museums, 3550).

Despite being supported by a suppedaneum, the body of Christ hangs heavily, as is emphasized by his rounded stomach and the way the figure falls away from the cross. The work sensitively conveys his suffering and death with humanity and pathos. The placard above his head is inscribed: IE(SV)S NAZAREN(VS) / REX IVDEORV(M) (Jesus of Nazareth, king of the Jews).

Bishop Bernward, patron of this splendid object, included his name on the reverse of the placard (shown below), which is inscribed: BERNVVAR / DVS PRESVL / FECIT HOC. The inscription indicates that Bishop Bernward made or had this [crucifix] made – the Latin meaning is not clear – which is similar to the inscription on the back cover of the Precious Gospels (cat. 32). The *Vita Bernwardi*, a late twelfth-century biography, tells us the bishop was skilled in the arts, but we have no way to confirm that assertion.

Also on the reverse of the cross is an engraved list of relics encircling an image of the Lamb of God; the small relics were kept in a cavity in the body of Christ. The list reads: S(ANCTI) LAVRENTII M(ARTYRIS) // DE LIGNO S(ANCTE) CRVCIS S(ANCTI) [S]TEPHANI P(RO) T(O)M(ARTYRIS) // S(ANCTI) DIONISII M(ARTYRIS) (Saint Lawrence martyr, Wood of the Holy Cross, Saint Stephen proto martyr, Saint Denis martyr).

This object can be approximately dated, because Bernward obtained the relic of Saint Denis in 1006–7; he either acquired it at the saint's tomb outside Paris when accompanying Henry II, king of Germany, on a campaign or was given the relic by Robert II, king of the Franks, as his biographer Thangmar maintains. The crucifix was then made to house the precious relics, probably as a gift for the new Benedictine monastery of St. Michael in Hildesheim, before Bernward's death in 1022. It was possibly a processional cross and adapted to become an altar cross only in the fourteenth century, when a base was made for it.

Bernward's cross would have a lasting influence in the region. Very similar representations of Christ appear as much as two centuries after its creation, including on the Romanesque crucifix from the treasury of St. Godehard in Hildesheim (cat. 36).

C.T.L.

SELECTED REFERENCES: *Bernward von Hildesheim und das Zeitalter der Ottonen*, 1993, vol. 2, pp. 578–81, no. VIII-31 (Michael Brandt); Schulz-Mons, *Das Michaeliskloster in Hildesheim*, 2010, vol. 1, pp. 353–69.

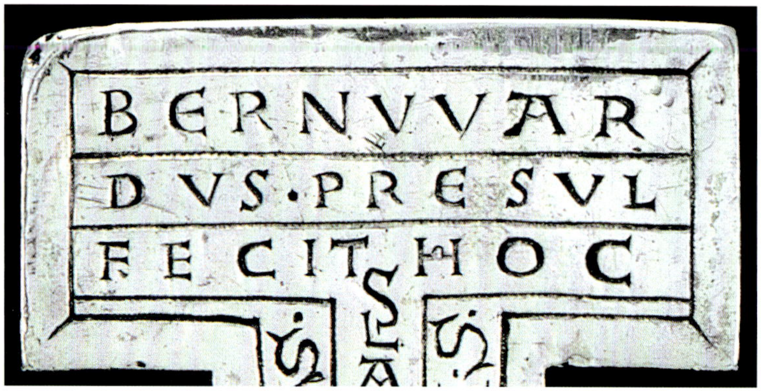

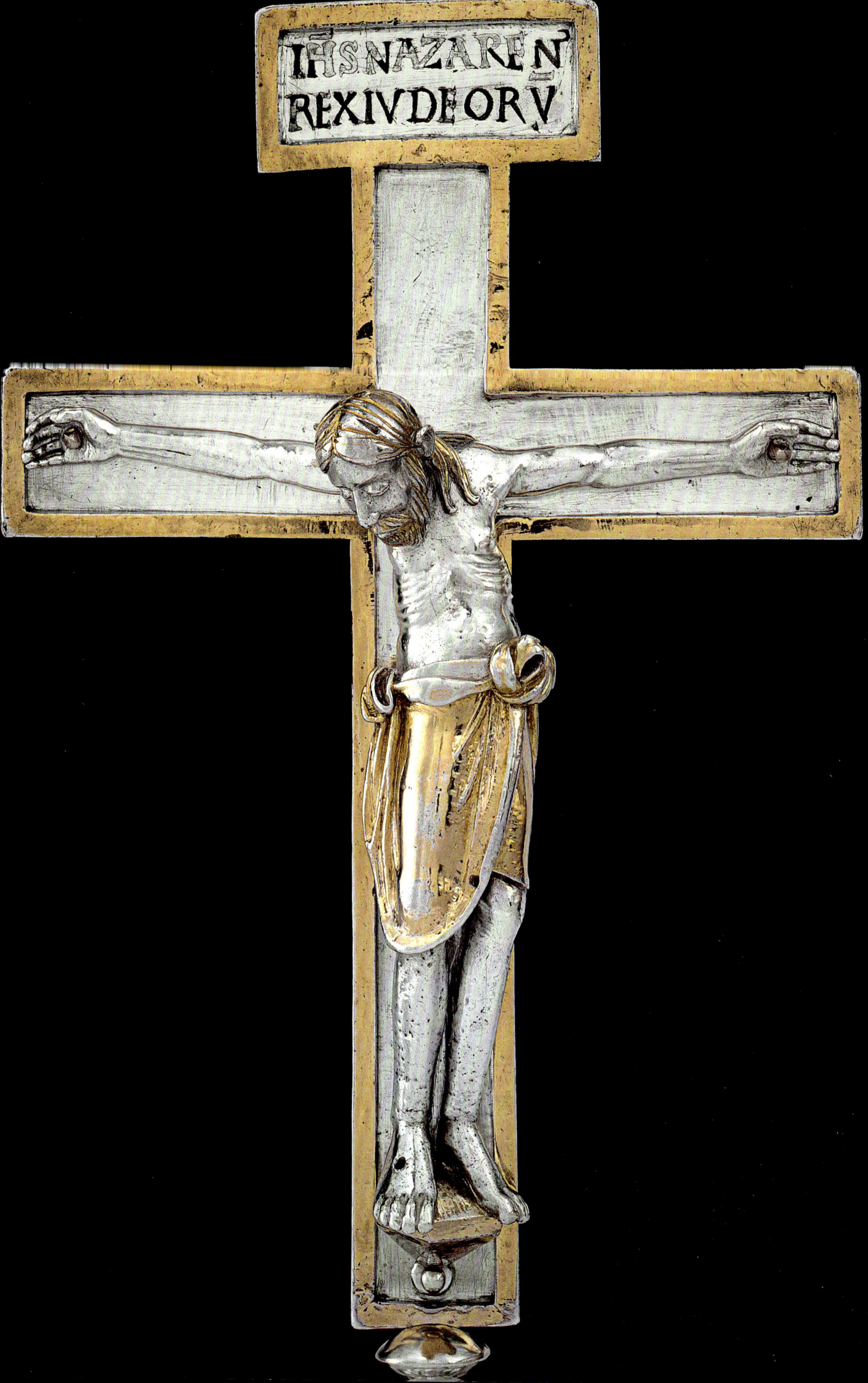
IHS NAZAREN
REX IUDEORU

11 · Bernward's Candlesticks (pair)

German (Hildesheim), before 1022
Silver with gilding and niello; iron core
H. 16 ⅛ in. (41 cm); 16 ⅝ in. (42 cm); Diam. 1 ¼ in. (3.2 cm) at knop
Dom-Museum Hildesheim (DS L 9)

Lavish candlesticks in precious metal are exceptionally rare in the Middle Ages, and this pair – a masterpiece of casting – is perhaps the most important to survive. The decoration teems with life amid a setting of abundant foliage: nude men riding dragons at the base; figures eating grapes, perhaps alluding to the Eucharist; and classicizing figures climbing the vine-covered shaft toward the light of the candles. Eagles flying near the top of the shaft may allude to the verse of the fifth-century poet Sedulius: "Flying high the eagle aspires to heaven, like the word of John" (Migne, *Patrologiæ cursus, series latina* 19.591). Even the knops (the stems' decorative rings) and drip pans are handsomely decorated. Set on an altar framing a cross or a gospel book, such candlesticks would symbolize the seeking of the true light of Christian doctrine.

Indeed, an illumination in the Precious Gospels, created about the same time, confirms that gilded silver candlesticks such as these ornamented Bishop Bernward's altar. Folio 16 verso (see Introduction, fig. 10) depicts a set of five tall candlesticks placed on a low plinth before the altar where Bernward offers his Precious Gospels to the Virgin.

According to the 1540 *Life of Saint Bernward*, this pair of candlesticks was found in Bernward's tomb when his remains were translated in 1194. The inscriptions on the base and on the top edge of the drip pan constitute a valuable document of artistic patronage. Both candlesticks bear Bernward's name and the same intriguing message: BERNVVARDUS PRESVL – CANDELABRVM HOC // + PVERUM SVVM PRIMO HVIVS ARTIS FLORE NON AVRO NON ARGENTO ET TAMEN VT CERNIS CONFLARE IVBEBAT (Bishop Bernward ordered his servant to cast these candlesticks in [or during] the first flowering of this art, not out of gold, not out of silver, and nevertheless as you discern [it here]).

The enigmatic reference to the material has been the subject of speculation; recent research suggests it could be electrum or Corinthian bronze, both alloys of silver, gold, and copper. The inscription may also allude to Christ's duality, as expressed by the Carolingian theologian Rabanus Maurus (died 856): "Jesus Christ is both God and man, just as electrum is mixed out of gold and silver" (Migne, *Patrologiæ cursus, series latina* 110.503D–504A). The "first flowering of this art" may refer to Hildesheim's mastery of the metallurgical arts in Bernward's time.

C.T.L.

SELECTED REFERENCES: *Bernward von Hildesheim und das Zeitalter der Ottonen*, 1993, vol. 2, pp. 581–84, no. VIII-32 (Michael Brandt); Brandt, "Bernward d'Hildesheim et ses trésors," 2010; Kingsley, "VT CERNIS and the Materiality of Bernwardian Art," 2012.

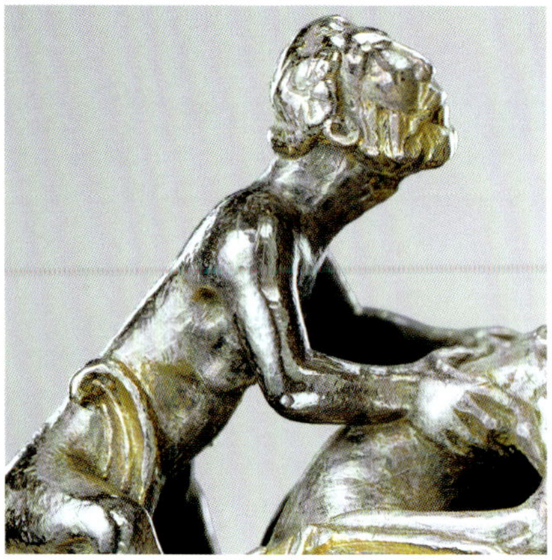

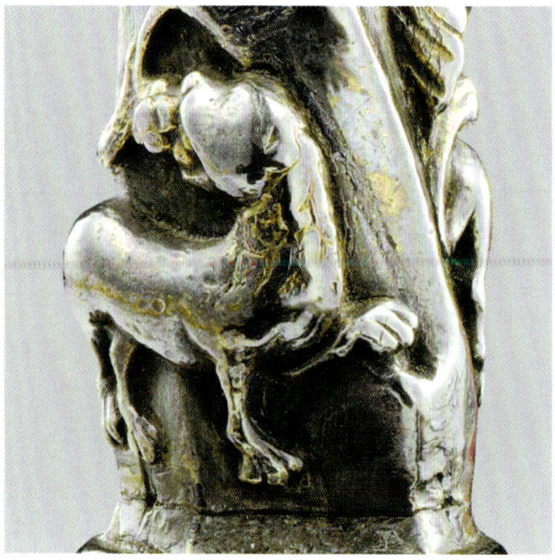

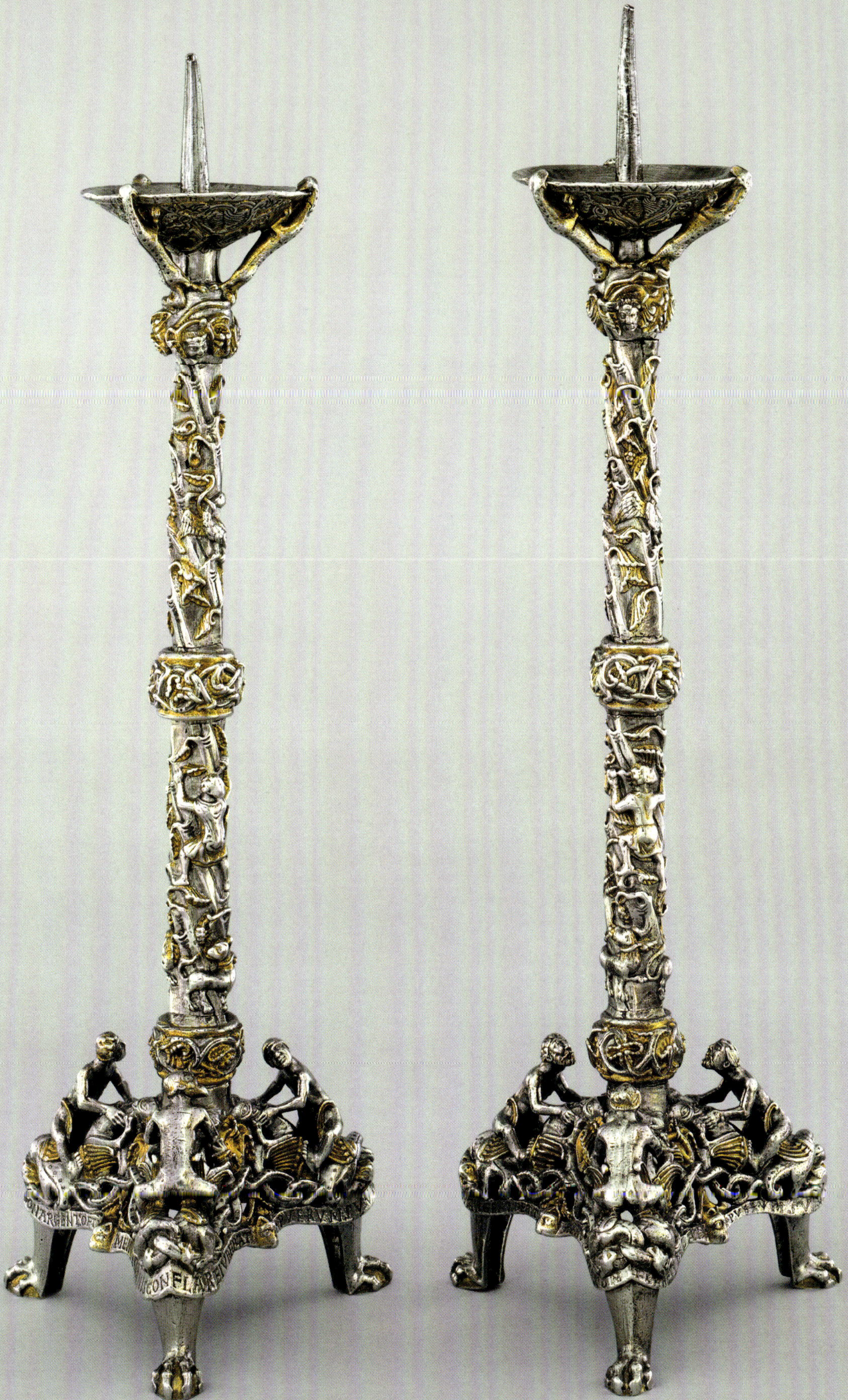

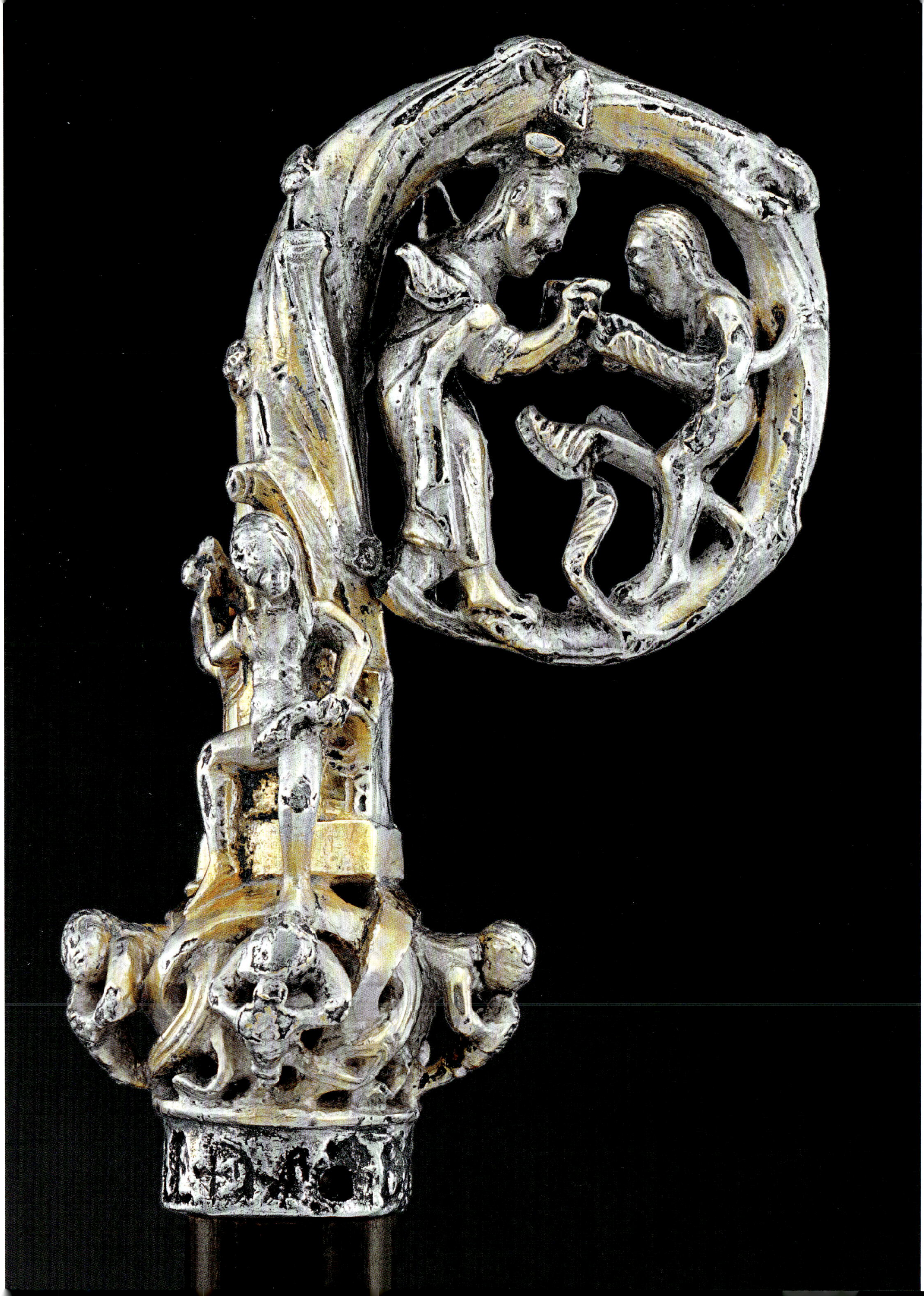

12 · Crosier of Abbot Erkanbald

German (Hildesheim), before 1011
Silver with gilding
Overall 4 ½ × 3 in. (11.3 × 7.5 cm) without stem
Dom-Museum Hildesheim (D3 7)

As a symbol of the office of the bishop and the principal insignia of his authority, lavish crosiers (staffs shaped like shepherds' crooks) were often special commissions; the upper part, the crook or curvature, is frequently decorative. This impressively ornate cast silver crosier was found in the tomb of Hildesheim's Bishop Henry III (reigned 1313–63) when it was opened in 1788, but it had nothing to do with him. The inscription at the base – ERKANBALD(VS) ABB(AS) – refers instead to Abbot Erkanbald, who presided over the monastery of Fulda from 997 to 1011. It is assumed that Erkanbald, a relative of Bishop Bernward, was given this crosier, almost certainly by Bernward himself, when he became abbot of Fulda or at least before becoming archbishop of Mainz, in 1011.

About that time there was a quarrel over the jurisdiction of the estates of Gandersheim Abbey, one of the most significant in Lower Saxony, with both Hildesheim and Mainz laying claim to it. Papal intervention finally favored Hildesheim over Mainz. The ecclesiastical dispute may somehow be connected to the gift of this crosier to Erkanbald, but the details have been lost to history.

Because the crosier is technically and stylistically linked to Bernward's Candlesticks (cat. 11), it almost certainly originated in the same workshop. It is a tour de force of narrative imagery. The knop (the central decorative ring) shows four small figures with water vessels, some damaged, personifying the Four Rivers of Paradise. On the stem and crook are a budding tree of twisted branches, Eve offering an apple, and Adam eating the forbidden fruit. The scene in the volute appears to show God condemning Adam after the Fall. God holds a book, indicating that only through the Scriptures can man be redeemed. The subject of the Expulsion from Paradise appears on no other crosier and seems at odds with the pastoral role a crosier signifies. Its specific meaning for Erkanbald is now lost, but it must have conveyed a particular spiritual, even political, message.

This crosier and Bernward's Candlesticks – both masterful works of casting by the lost-wax technique – testify to the high quality of metalsmithing and the revival of arts that Bernward's patronage fostered.

C.T.L.

SELECTED REFERENCES: *Bernward von Hildesheim und das Zeitalter der Ottonen*, 1993, vol. 2, pp. 570–78, no. VII-30 (Michael Brandt); *Für Königtum und Himmelreich*, 2009, pp. 436–37, no. 166 (Lothar Lambacher); *Schätze des Glaubens*, 2010, p. 37, no. 5 (Lothar Lambacher).

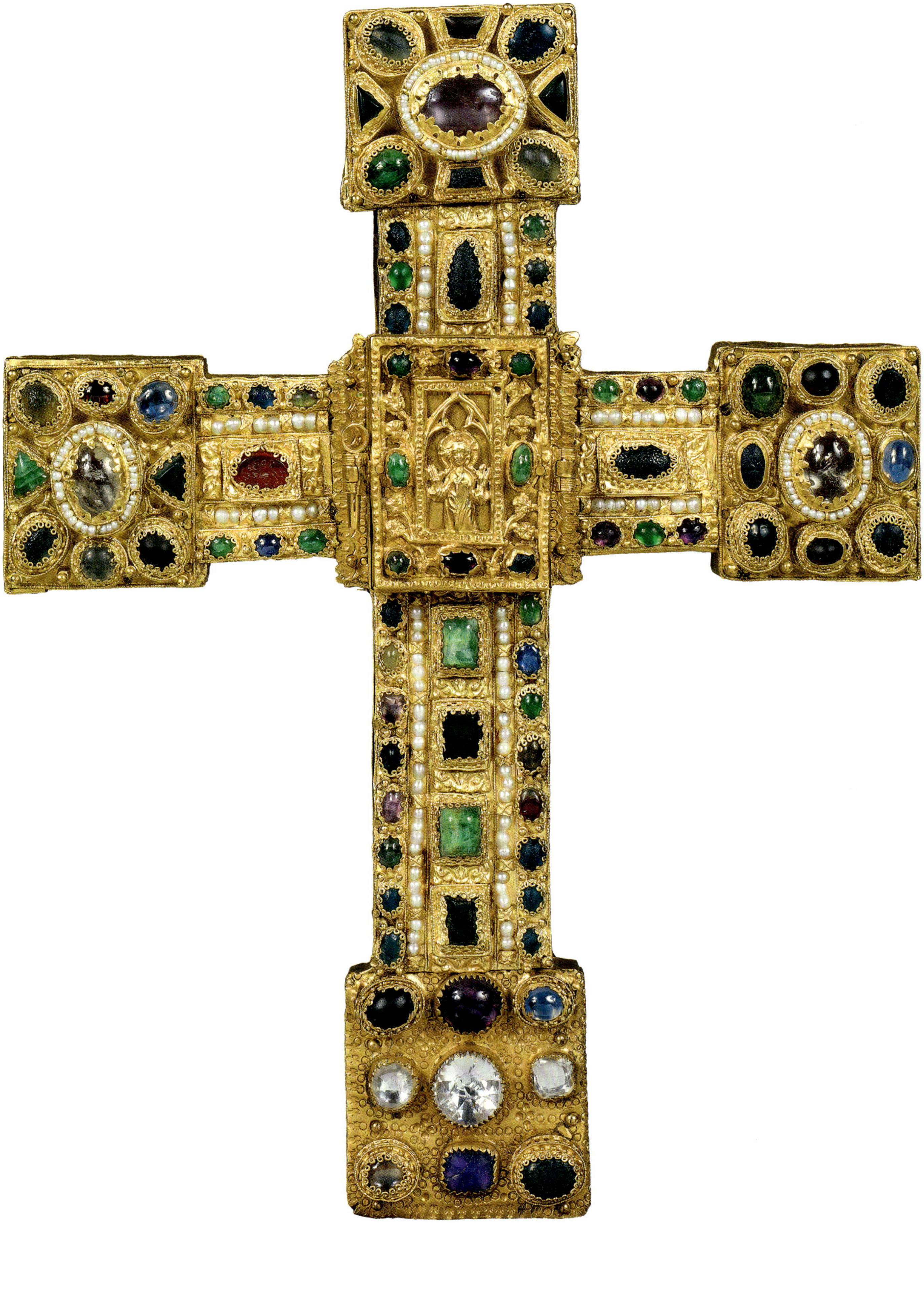

13 · Hezilo Cross

German (Hildesheim), before 1079
Gold, copper, pearls, and gems; wood core covered in silk
9⅝ × 7⅝ × 1¼ in. (24.3 × 19.2 × 3.2 cm)
Dom-Museum Hildesheim, on loan from the former collegiate church Zum Heiligen Kreuz in Hildesheim (DS L 113)

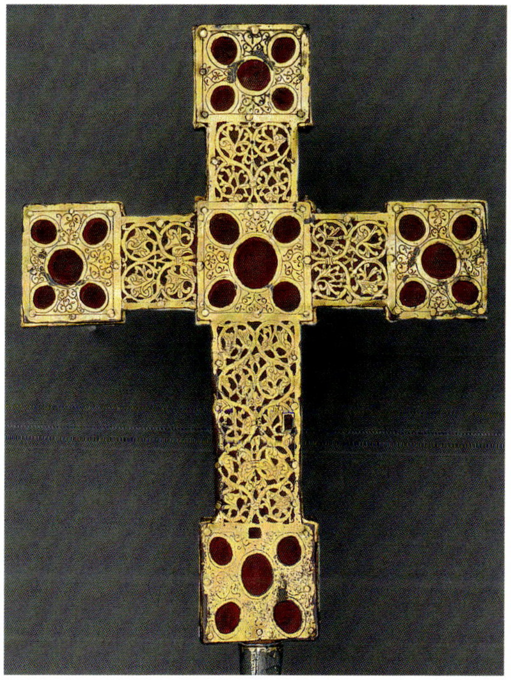

This cross, its front richly decorated with gemstones and pearls, is thought to have been donated by Bishop Hezilo (reigned 1054–79) to Zum Heiligen Kreuz, the collegiate church he founded in Hildesheim. Its luxuriousness reflects the value of the relic of Christ it preserves.

The relic was originally secured in the bottom part of the shaft, which could be opened. In the fourteenth century a small casket was built into the crossbeam, where the relic was housed from that point on. Its cover depicts Christ in the pose of an orant, standing with arms outstretched in prayer, beneath a trefoil arch. An inscription along the edge of the casket refers to Christ's act of salvation, relating it to the Old Testament's burnt offering: [C]RVX GENITV[M] TORRET SVAVE[M] PAT[ER] HAVRIT/[O]DORE[M] . . . CUIPA REPARAVIT GR[ATI]A VITA[M] (The cross burns the Son, and the Father accepts the sweet fragrance. Grace has restored life after it [had been destroyed] through guilt).

In a number of respects the cross echoes the famous Imperial Cross of about 1024 in Vienna's Weltliche Schatzkammer (Imperial Treasury), which contained the empire's most important relics – in particular, remnants of the True Cross and the Holy Lance. It shares its overall form, with a square panel at the center and at the ends of each beam. Within the squares, the arrangement of a central gem encircled by smaller precious stones also copies its well-known precedent. As on the Imperial Cross, the center stone in the top square is set horizontally. The tight, concentric arrangement of stones on the squares clearly contrasts with that of the shaft and crossbeams, whose vertical and horizontal orientations are emphasized by the rows of stones and pearls. In this too the Hezilo Cross resembles its Viennese precedent, though in contrast to the Imperial Cross the center axes are underscored by rows of larger stones. On the back, beneath the pierced metal cover, the wood core is visible, covered with red silk. A highly decorative symmetrical vine ornament takes up the motif of the Tree of Life and, like the inscription, suggests the life-giving importance of Christ's death on the cross.

The Hezilo Cross is one of the earliest examples of the Imperial Cross's influence – the cross with square terminals would become a common form in Hildesheim in the twelfth century (see cat. 30) – and its obvious borrowings may well reflect Bishop Hezilo's status as one of the most important politicians of his time. By referencing the Imperial Cross, Hezilo underscored his close relationship with the Holy Roman emperor, Henry III (reigned 1039–56), in whose court chapel he served. In 1051–52 he became provost of the collegiate church of St. Simon and St. Jude in Goslar, and in 1054 he was appointed chancellor for Italy.

C.H.

SELECTED REFERENCES: Jülich, "Gemmenkreuze," 1986–87, pp. 180–81; Wulf, *Die Inschriften der Stadt Hildesheim*, 2003, vol. 2, pp. 224–25; *Canossa 1077*, 2006, vol. 2, pp. 330–31, no. 437 (Michael Peter); *Schätze des Glaubens*, 2010, pp. 48–49, no. 11 (Michael Brandt).

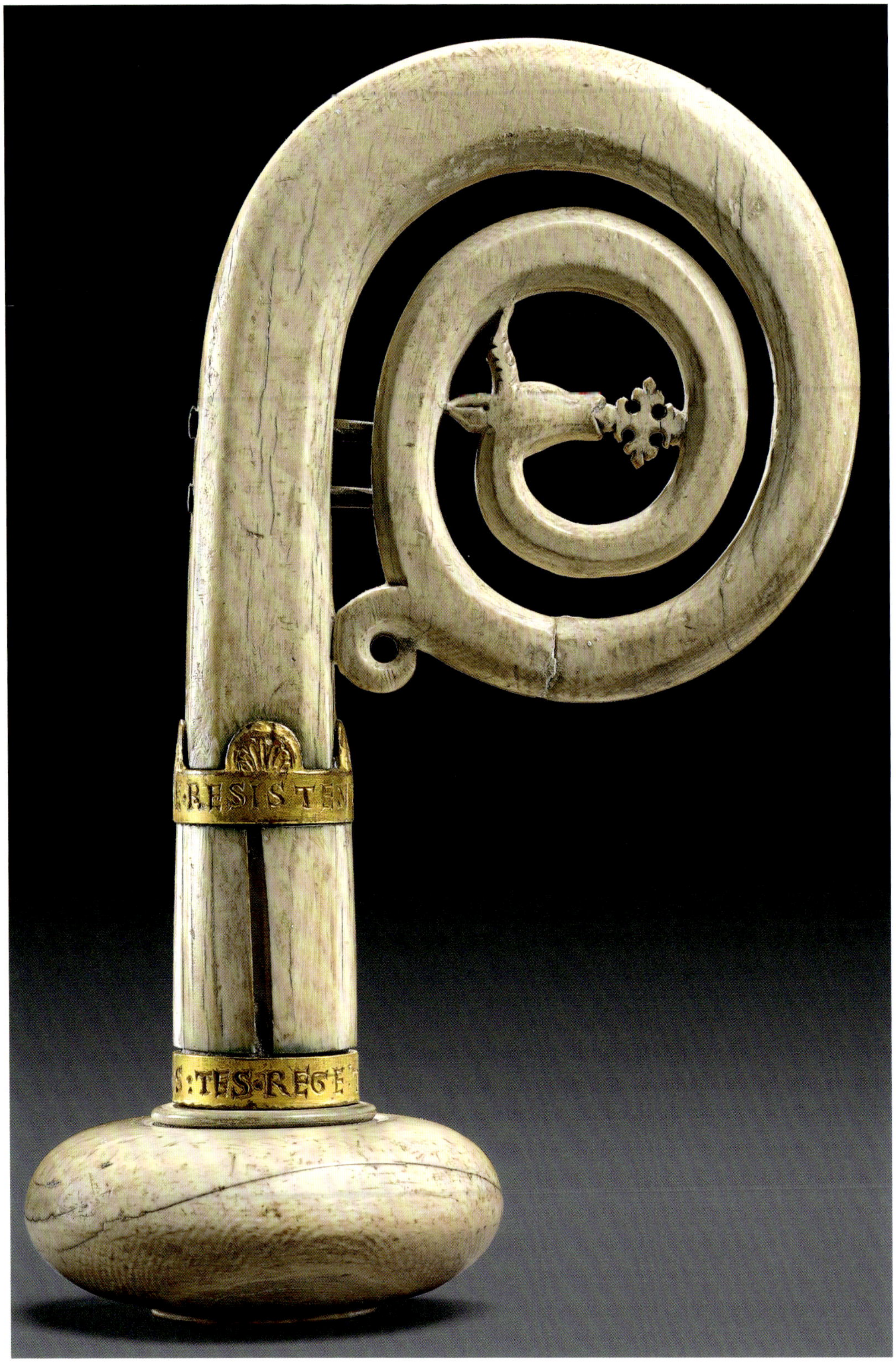
·RESISTEN
S:TES·REGE

14 · Saint Godehard's Crosier

Southern Italy, ca. 1133
Ivory, gilded and engraved copper, and wood
Overall 7⅞ × 5½ in. (20 × 13.8 cm); H. with stem 64¼ in. (163 cm)
Dom-Museum Hildesheim (DS 74)

This elegantly simple crosier is associated with Hildesheim's Bishop Godehard (reigned 1022–38), Bernward's immediate successor. However, it appears to have been made a century after Godehard's death, the work of an ivory carver in southern Italy; the metal bands at the base of the ivory may have been inscribed to honor Godehard following his canonization in 1131. The inscription reads: +STERNE RESISTENTES STAN // TES REGE TOLLE IACENTES (Throw down those who resist, help up those who have fallen). A fragment of another bishop's staff possessing a similar metal band was found in 1929 at St. Godehard's Basilica in the tomb of Abbot Theodoric, who died in 1204, suggesting that both may date to the same period.

In the center of the crosier's volute is the head of a gazelle, which terminates the spiraling form with a cross issuing from its mouth. Southern Italian ivory crosiers of similar conception exist in many European church treasuries; they often include creatures such as griffins, serpents, and exotic birds and frequently have a centralized cross as an integral part of the design. They were long believed to be the work of Muslim craftsmen during the Norman occupation of southern Italy and Sicily, but that is now an open question. Whether the gazelle – not in the pictorial repertoire of medieval bestiaries – is intended to be a variant of the serpent is impossible to determine.

The crosier belonged to the last monk of St. Michael's Church in Hildesheim before its secularization in 1803.

C.T.L.

SELECTED REFERENCES: Elbern and Reuther, *Der Hildesheimer Domschatz*, 1969, pp. 70–71, no. 74; *Der Schatz von St. Godehard*, 1988, pp. 86–88, no. 28 (Michael Brandt).

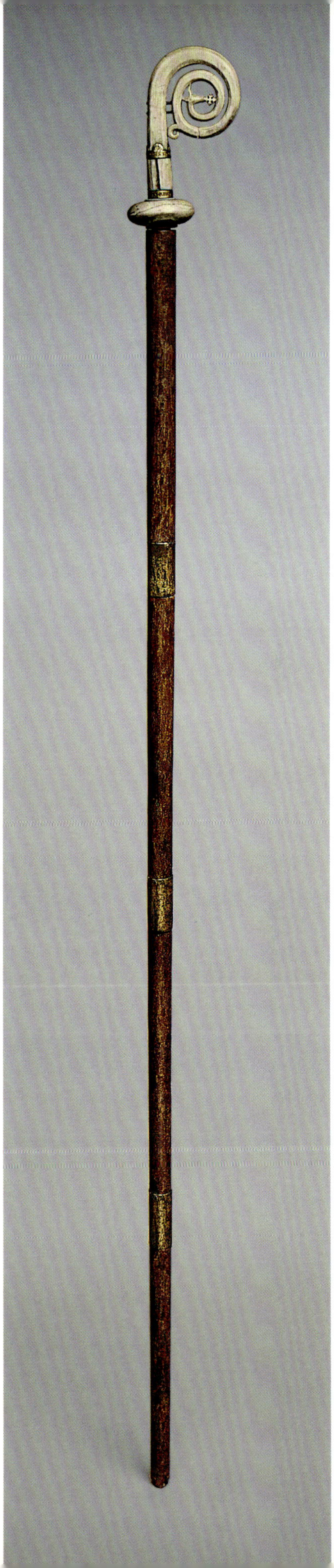

15 · Descent from the Cross

Italian, 12th century
Ivory
Overall 5 1/8 × 4 in. (12.9 × 10.2 cm)
Dom-Museum Hildesheim (DS 11)

This depiction in ivory of the Deposition displays Joseph of Arimathea awkwardly lowering the body of Christ from the cross toward the Virgin. Holding one hand to her chest, she stands on a stool to bring her head near that of her son. Opposite her, John the Evangelist is elevated on a rock as he holds his hand to his face in grief. Below, Nicodemus removes the nail from Christ's left foot with a pair of pliers. Above, busts of two angels flank the cross. The one on the left is presented calmly focusing on the action below, while the one to the right appears to be fleeing. The similarity of their poses to those often used for images of Ecclesia (Church) and Synagoga (Synagogue) may be a deliberate reference to the triumph of the Church through Christ's sacrifice for mankind.

This ivory traditionally was thought to be an eleventh-century Byzantine work. It resembles Byzantine depictions of the Deposition, like that on the elaborate cloisonné enamel Reliquary of the True Cross preserved in the cathedral treasury at Esztergom, Hungary (64.3.1). Its dating to the eleventh century was due to the inscription on the rim stating, "I, Bernward, bishop of Hildesheim, have executed this in the year 1006, in the twenty second year of my ordination, on the day of Saint Michael, archangel, in the name of the Lord." However, as Bernward's twenty-second year was 1014–15, the inscription is now thought probably to be a later addition. The poses of the angels, the unusual depiction of Mary and John the Evangelist raised from the ground, and the relatively crude detailing of the figures support an identification of the ivory as inspired by, rather than being, a Byzantine production.

Numerous copies of Byzantine works are known from northern Italy, especially Venice, where this work may have been carved. Records at Hildesheim from 1438 contain references to a plaque with a similar theme on a book cover. Byzantine ivory icons, or ivories imitating Byzantine themes, were often arranged as the central element of book covers in the West (see cats. 1, 32). The holes in the upper border of this plaque suggest it was put to a similar use.

H.C.E.

SELECTED REFERENCES: *Bernward von Hildesheim und das Zeitalter der Ottonen*, 1993, vol. 2, pp. 554–55, no. VIII-21 (Arne Eggebrecht and Hans Jakob Schuffels); *Glory of Byzantium*, 1997, pp. 493–94, no. 329 (Charles T. Little); *Byzanz*, 1998, pp. 102, 157, no. 42 (Gudrun Bühl).

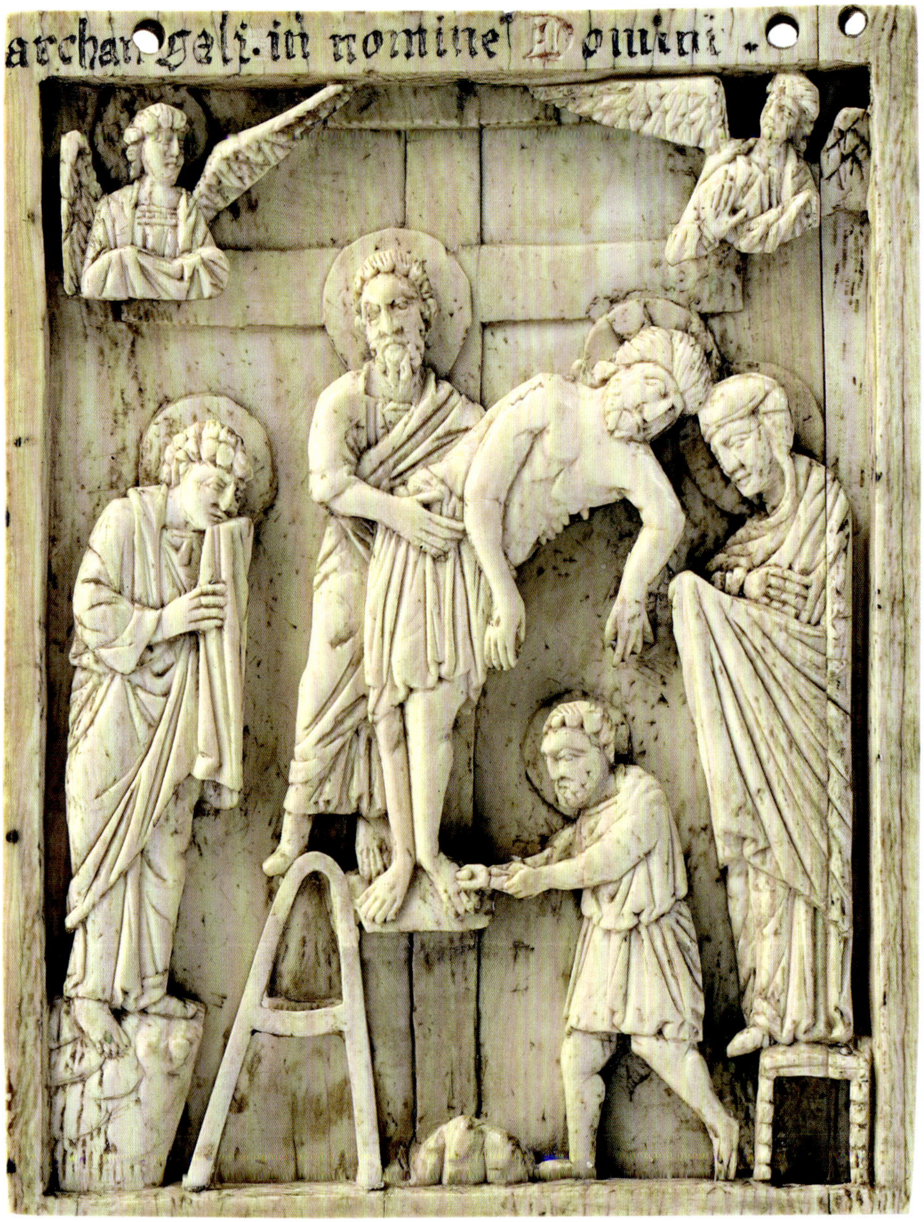
archangeli · in nomine Domini ·

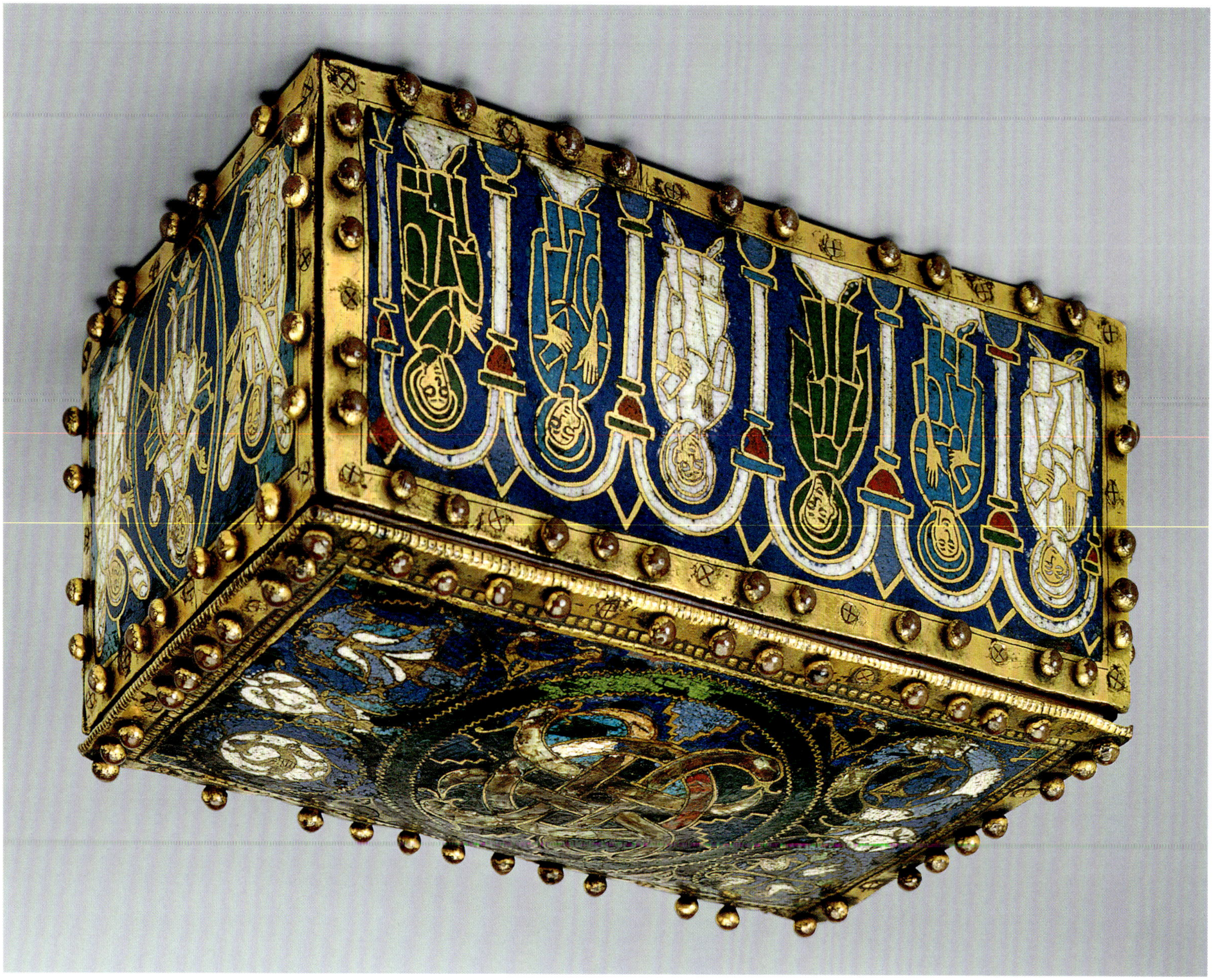

16 · Portable Altar

Northern German, early 12th century
Copper with gilding and champlevé enamels,
mounted on a modern copper casket
3 ¾ × 8 ½ × 3 ¾ in. (9.5 × 21.5 × 9.5 cm)
Dom-Museum Hildesheim (DS 21)

At the center of this casket's lid, a peg has been cut off; it was most likely part of a stud for a detachable cross. The casket thus served as a small portable altar.

It is made of hammered copper sheets and decorated on the top and sides with enamels in bright colors, predominantly shades of cobalt blue, turquoise, white, and deep green. The ends of the casket present christological scenes, with the crucified Christ between Longinus and Stephaton on one end and Christ enthroned in a mandorla, with two adoring angels, on the other. On the long sides are twelve figures with halos, probably the Twelve Apostles, beneath round-arch arcades. The lid is adorned with medallions with serrated edges encircling images of stylized plants, animals, and human figures. The piece is one of a group of ten bright-colored enamel caskets so similar in terms of pictorial program, style, and technique that they are assumed to have come from the same workshop. The assured provenance of four pieces from northern Germany would place that workshop in the area north of Hildesheim and south of the North and the Baltic Seas.

Whereas the christological scenes are similar among the group, the pictorial composition on the lid of the Hildesheim casket is unique. The design impressively combines geometric figures with floral motifs and animal ornaments that recall early medieval forms. The opening for the central cross is positioned at the middle of a large roundel filled with four symmetrically intertwined serpents. The motif of the serpent biting its own tail suggests the ancient cosmic symbol of a monster encircling the world, which in a Christian context was associated with the cross as a symbol of salvation.

C.H.

SELECTED REFERENCES: Nørlund, "Early Group of Enamelled Reliquaries," 1933; Lasko, *Ars Sacra 800–1200*, 1972, pp. 175–76; Springer, *Kreuzfüsse*, 1981, pp. 91–102; *Schatzkammer auf Zeit*, 1991, pp. 123–26, no. 33 (Neil Stratford).

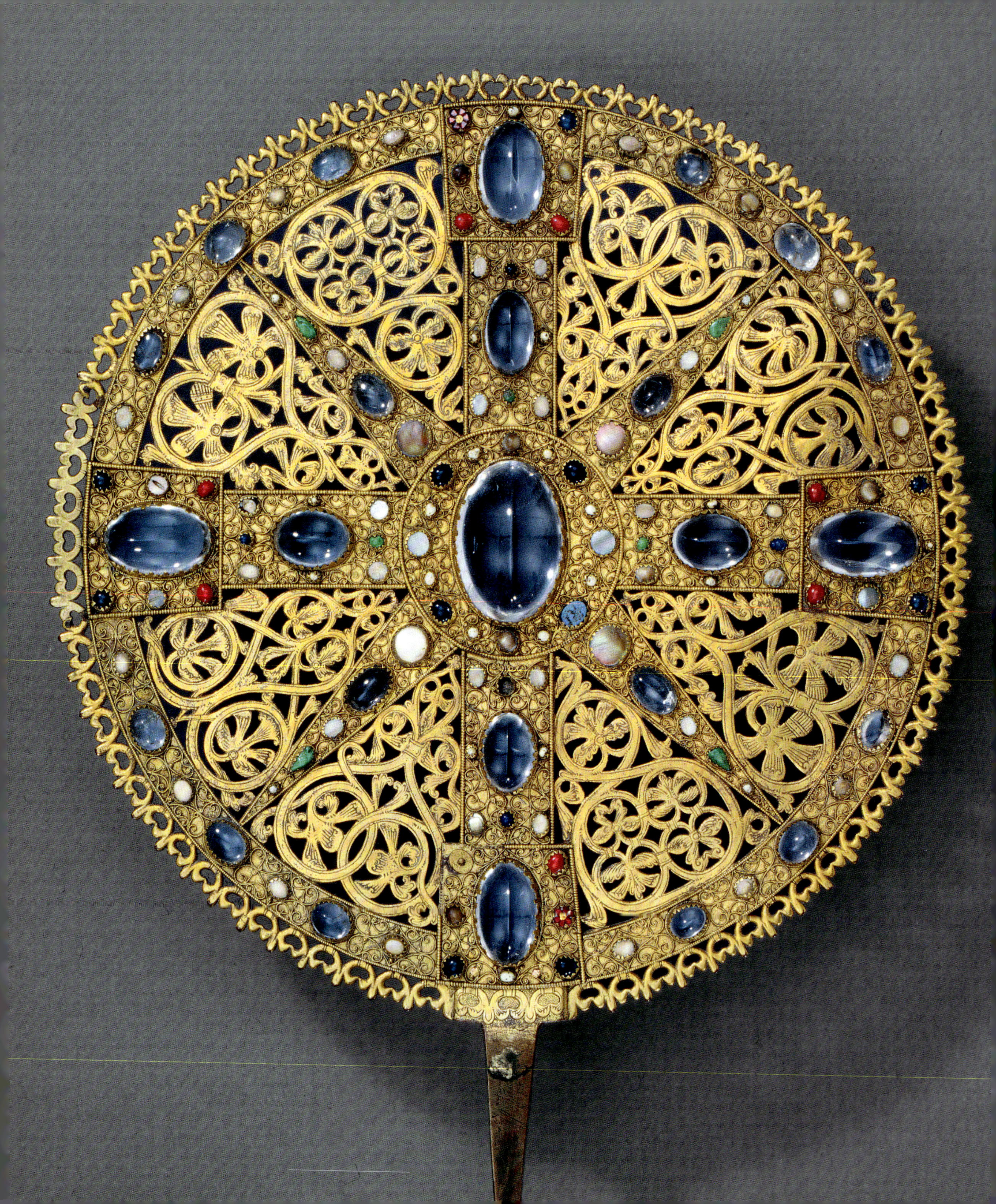

17, 18, 19 · Liturgical Fans

German (Hildesheim), ca. 1130–50
Gilded copper alloy, rock crystal, semiprecious stones, and ancient intaglios
Diam.: 17) 16 3/8 in. (41.5 cm); 18) 13 3/8 in. (34 cm); 19) 13 1/8 in. (33.3 cm)
Dom-Museum Hildesheim (DS 27a–c)

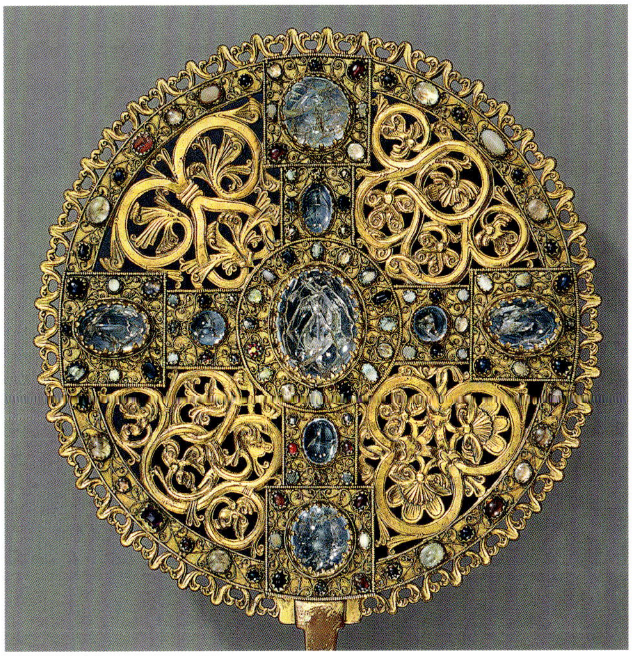

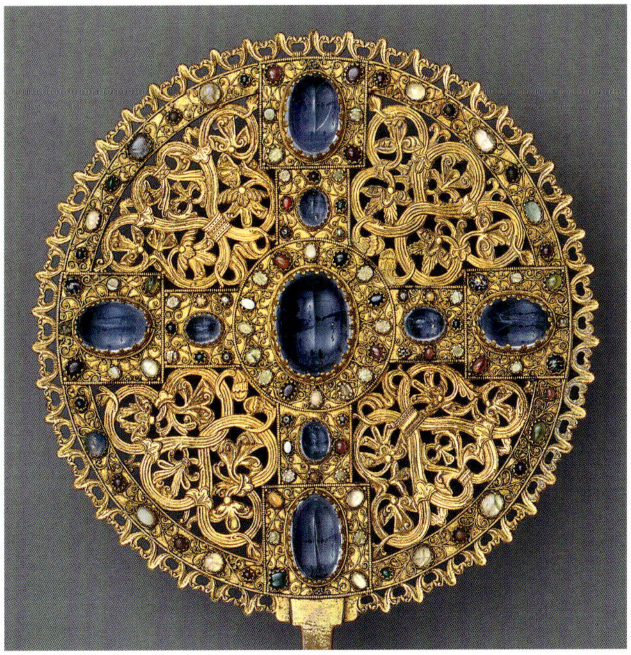

Flashing with translucent rock crystal and brilliant gilded copper, this astounding trio of openwork disks embellished with crosses constitutes a unique surviving ensemble. Though not mentioned in any inventory, they were enshrined in the seventeenth-century retable (the decorative altarpiece) set behind the high altar of Hildesheim Cathedral, where they were still to be seen in 1856, the largest at the center, flanked by the smaller pair. Homogeneous in overall impression, each is subtly differentiated from the other in the foliate patterns of the pierced openwork and the engraved designs. The larger disk is further distinguished by the introduction of a star-shaped pattern, the use of filigree and ancient intaglios on the front, and the use of *vernis brun* on the reverse. The close correspondence between the foliate openwork patterns of these pieces and the crest on the Godehard Shrine (see Introduction, fig. 19), created to house the saint's relics about 1130–40, suggests the approximate date for the creation of the fans.

The presence of such objects in the church apparently derives from the practice, known as early as the fifth century, of fanning the altar ceremonially. Here, however, the materials logically employed for that purpose – such as feathers or parchment – have been replaced by heavy, gem-studded copper. Because of its weight, a metal fan seems unwieldy at best, suggesting that these fans' presence in the church was more symbolic than practical. Still, equally large, disk-shaped metal fans are used today in the Orthodox liturgy. Fans made of metal or ivory are mentioned among the possessions of churches across Europe from as early as the ninth century and were used until the sixteenth century. In the Hildesheim examples, the piercing of the metal might be seen as an accommodation that both reduced the weight and allowed increased air flow. The triangle-shaped tongue at the bottom of each fan allowed it to be slotted into a long handle.

B.D.B.

SELECTED REFERENCES: Braun, *Das christliche Altargerät in seinem Sein und in seiner Entwicklung*, 1932, pp. 657, 660, table 141, no. 560; *Abglanz des Himmels*, 2001, pp. 221–22, nos. 5.1–5.3 (Ursula Mende), illus. pp. 210–11; *Bild und Bestie*, 2008, pp. 250–51, no. 6 (Michael Brandt); *Schätze des Glaubens*, 2010, pp. 64–65, no. 22 (Michael Brandt).

20 · Arm Reliquary

German (Hildesheim), 1130–40
Gilded copper
Overall (with base) 18⅞ × 14⅝ × 7⅞ in. (48 × 37 × 20 cm)
Dom-Museum Hildesheim, on loan from the church of St. Maurice, Hildesheim (L 1994-2)

Compared to the many rich treasures from Hildesheim, this reliquary of gilded copper is humble in its material and spare in its decoration. It is, nonetheless, an exceptional object.

The hand is gracefully posed, the fingers slightly curved and the thumb opposed in almost balletic counterpoint. The accomplished engraved decoration on the sleeve simulates rich fabric, an effect intensified by the gentle wrinkling seemingly caused by the flex of the wrist.

Reliquaries in the form of an arm were frequently created to house relics of bishops or patron saints of various vocations. This one is for a military saint, which is unusual but perfectly aligns with the dedication of the monastic church from which it comes: to Saint Maurice, commander in the third century of the Roman army's fabled Theban Legion. The church of St. Maurice, in the eponymous village of Moritzberg, near (and today part of) Hildesheim, later became a parish; its archives indicate that this was one of two arm reliquaries set on the high altar for important feasts.

Packets of relics inside this piece are identified by inscriptions as containing the arm bone of a member of the Theban Legion as well as bones of Saint Gereon, the legendary head of the Theban Legion in Cologne; his relics were unearthed there in 1121, more than eight hundred years after his death. It has been suggested that the cross emblazoned in *vernis brun* on the underside of the reliquary's shield-shaped base is the earliest to identify Saint Gereon by the golden cross that was found on his chest when his relics were disinterred.

The form of this arm reliquary is exceptional in two important regards. First, the position of the hand, with the fingers slightly cupped and the thumb opposed, is highly unusual. It would appear that the fingers once held an object, perhaps of precious metal. This pose is distinct from the sign of benediction more typically found on arm reliquaries (see cat. 33). The base of the reliquary, in the form of a shield, also is unique. In addition to its clear reference to the saint's military career, the base has the advantage of stabilizing the characteristically slim and top-heavy form of the reliquary, facilitating its safe placement on an altar.

B.D.B.

SELECTED REFERENCES: Ehlers and Kötzsche, *Der Welfenschatz und sein Umkreis*, 1998, pp. 358–59, pl. 5 (Michael Brandt); *Abglanz des Himmels*, 2001, p. 187, no. 4.15 (Michael Brandt); Hahn, *Strange Beauty*, 2012, p. 140.

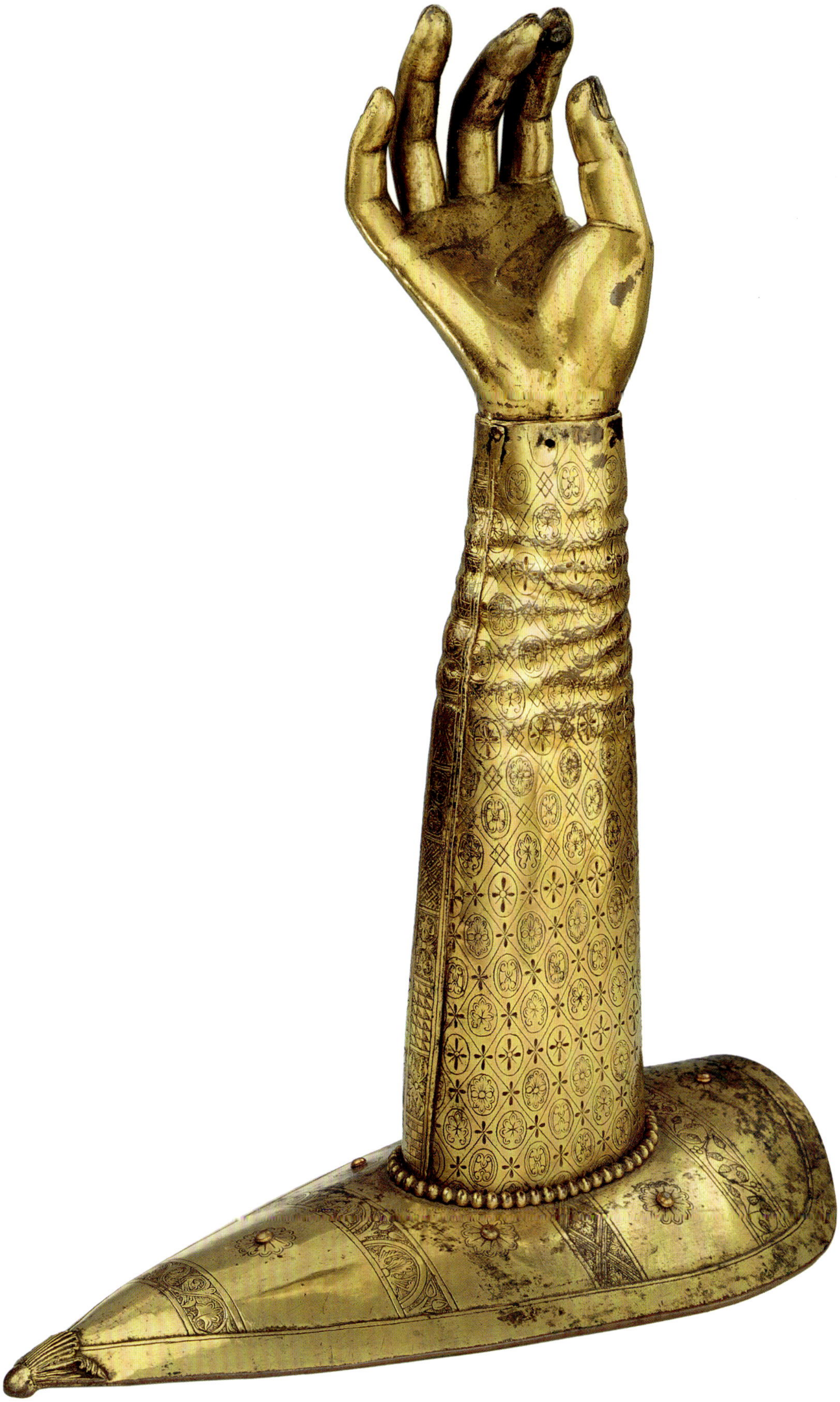

21 · Ratmann Sacramentary (front cover)

German (Hildesheim, St. Michael's), 1159; restored 1400
COVER: *copper, partly gilded, and rock crystal over leather*
MANUSCRIPT: *tempera, gold, and silver on parchment*
Cover 13 ¾ × 9 ⅝ in. (35 × 24.5 cm); 202 leaves
Only front cover is exhibited.
Dom-Museum Hildesheim (DS 37)

Christ trampling the head of a beast under each foot, a common subject in medieval art across Europe, is presented with particular power and efficacy on this book cover – complete with the graphic detail of the animals' tongues hanging from their mouths. The image vividly evokes God's role as protector, as expressed in Psalm 91:13: "Thou shalt walk upon the asp and the basilisk; and thou shalt trample underfoot the lion and the dragon."

In his left hand Christ holds an open book inscribed: EGO SUM DOMINUS, DOMINUS VESTER [QUI EDUXI VOS DE TERRA AEGYPTI], a text widely used in medieval liturgical chant that refers to God leading the Israelites out of Egypt, reinforcing the theme of God as protector of his people. In his right hand is a globe, inscribed: CAELUM ET TERRAM EGO INPLEO (do not I fill heaven and earth, saith the Lord; Jeremiah 23:24), a reference to God's omnipresence. To either side of Christ's halo are the Greek letters alpha and omega, emblematic of his being "the beginning and the end," as described in the Book of the Apocalypse.

Framing the whole is a long inscription that begins at the upper left and runs counterclockwise: + CVNCTA / REGENS × ADVERSA × PREMENS × INIMI/CA × COERCENS // + NOS / HVMILES × SALVA × MAIESTAS × QVESU/MUS × A[L]MA (Majesty, who reigns over all things, who crushes those who oppose you, and who casts away those who are not with you, save us lowly creatures, we beseech you, caring one).

Eight rock crystals are mounted in the frame of the book cover: four round ones at the corners, a square at either side, and an oval at top and bottom. The settings of the rock crystals vary, and the stones have clearly been reset over time. Under the corner rock crystals are small paintings on parchment representing the symbols of the Four Evangelists, holding scrolls with the opening words of their gospels. One of the square stones protects an inscription naming the donor, a monk called Ratmann, who presented the manuscript to St. Michael's in 1159 for the service of the high altar. Ratmann's image can be seen inside the manuscript, kneeling at the feet of Saint Michael and Saint Bernward, the monastery's patrons.

B.D.B.

SELECTED REFERENCES: *Bernward von Hildesheim und das Zeitalter der Ottonen*, 1993, vol. 2, pp. 605–7, no. IX-9 (Renate Kroos); *Heinrich der Löwe und seine Zeit*, 1995, vol. 1, p. 512, no. G31 (Michael Brandt); *Abglanz des Himmels*, 2001, pp. 133–34, no. 3.9 (Harald Wolter-von dem Knesebeck), illus. p. 122; Wulf, *Die Inschriften der Stadt Hildesheim*, 2003, pp. 240–41.

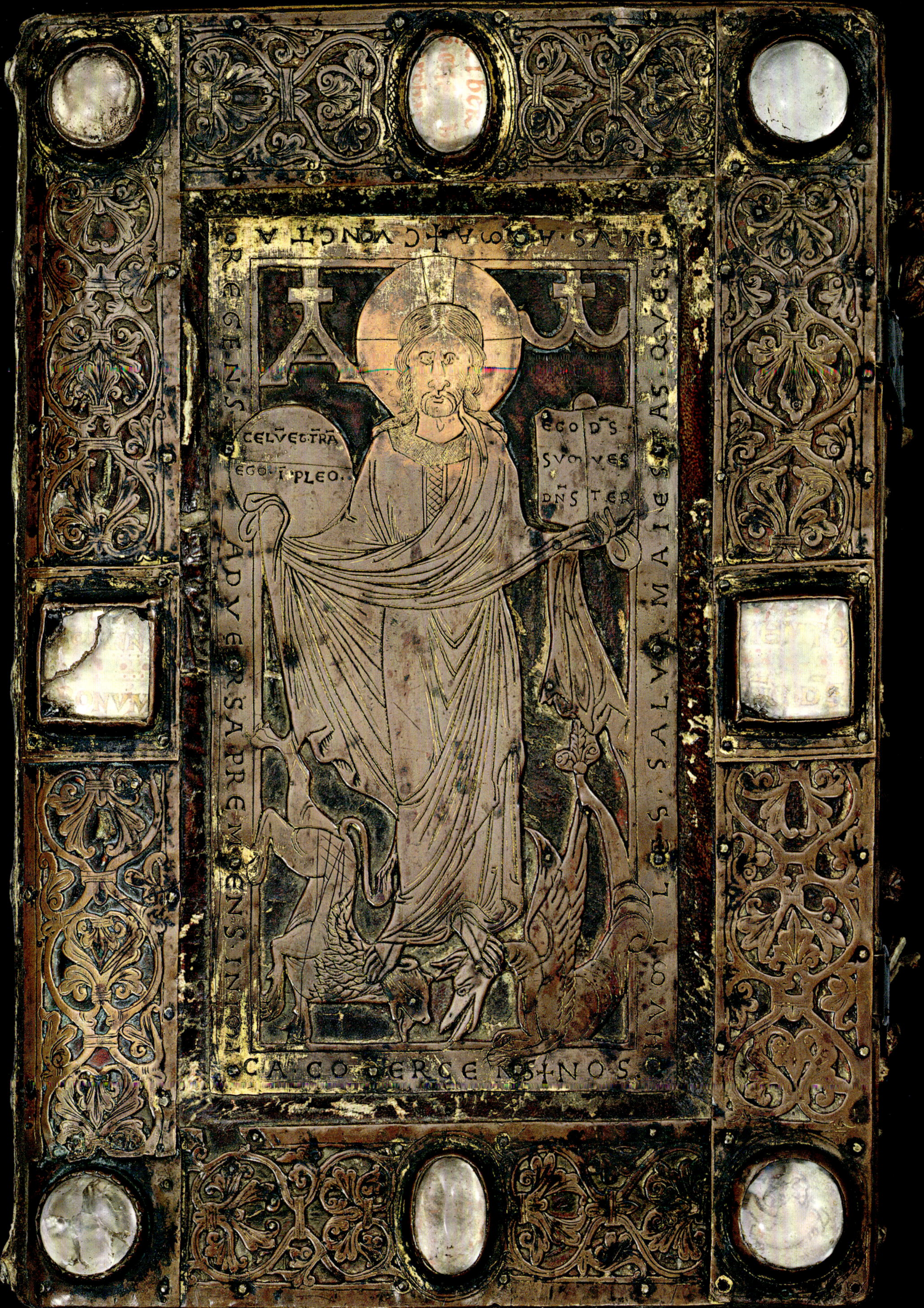
CELVET TRA
EGO I PLEO
EGO DS
SVM VES
DNS TER

22 · Pair of Altar Candlesticks

Mosan region, ca. 1160
Cast bronze, engraved, chiseled, and gilded, with niello(?) and traces of silver
H. 9 ½ in. (24 cm)
Dom-Museum Hildesheim (DS 22a–b)

The Mosan region (in present-day Belgium, the Netherlands, and Germany) was among the most innovative centers for metalwork in the Middle Ages, renowned especially for its outstanding objects of precious metal and enamel. Its use of allegory and didactic inscriptions strongly influenced Saxon workshops, although Mosan art drew more heavily upon classical style and used iconographic typology more systematically. A particularly rich decorative and iconographic program distinguishes this pair of Mosan candlesticks, which was given to the treasury of St. Mary's Cathedral in Hildesheim by its bishop Eduard J. Wedekin (reigned 1850–70).

The stems are adorned with a motif of leaves opening into a corolla. The bases rest on three feet in the form of winged dragons, and small lions clamber over the bases' edge. Three female allegories are seated on top of each candlestick's base. One (pictured to the left on the facing page) displays personifications of the continents, each holding a fragment of the disk representing the Earth and a second attribute: Europa is armed with a sword and shield, on which is written BELLUM (war); Asia bears a receptacle inscribed DIVITIE (wealth); Africa, her breast bared, holds the book of science (SCIENTIA). The other candlestick bears allegories of medicine (MEDICINA), conflict (CONFLICT[VS]), and theory and practice (THEORICA / PRACTICA), whose attributes are, respectively, a vase, two fighting snakes, and two busts of young men. While allegorical personifications are common in Mosan art, with recurring figures of Theological and Cardinal Virtues inspired by antiquity, the subjects here are highly unusual. The candlesticks' complex and rare iconographic program may well evoke the totality of the universe, illuminated by the light of the candles above.

The candlesticks' allegorical figures are similar in figurative style to a number of works by Mosan goldsmiths dating to the 1160s, such as the Evangelists on the portable altar of the Benedictine monastery of Stavelot (Musées Royaux d'Art et d'Histoire, Brussels, 1590), the archangels on the foot of the gilded copper cross at the Victoria and Albert Museum, London (7938-1862), and the statuette of Prudence in Paris (Musée du Louvre, OA 5908). Thus the candlesticks can be securely attributed to Mosan workshops of the 1160s, of which they are among the most original creations.

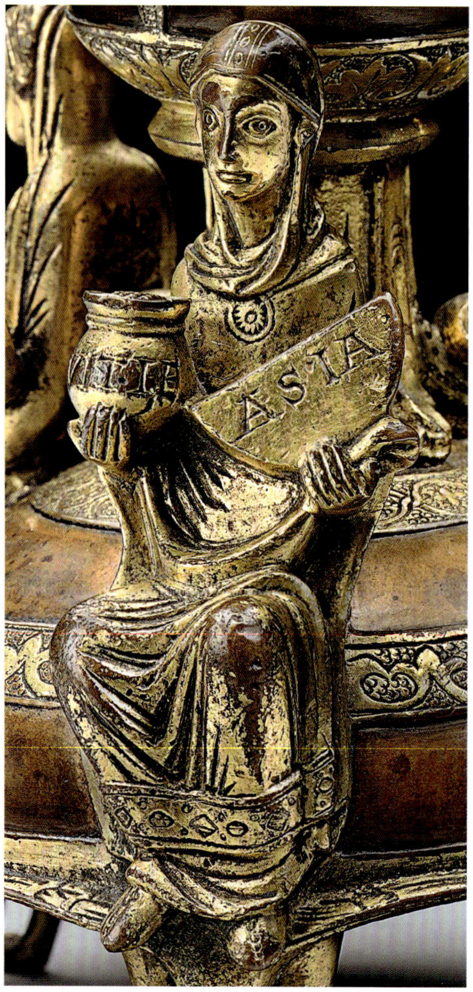

C.D.

SELECTED REFERENCES: Elbern and Reuther, *Der Hildesheimer Domschatz*, 1969, pp. 34ff., no. 22; *Schatzkammer auf Zeit*, 1991, pp. 126–29, no. 34 (Ursula Mende); *Schätze des Glaubens*, 2010, p. 78, no. 31 (Lothar Lambacher).

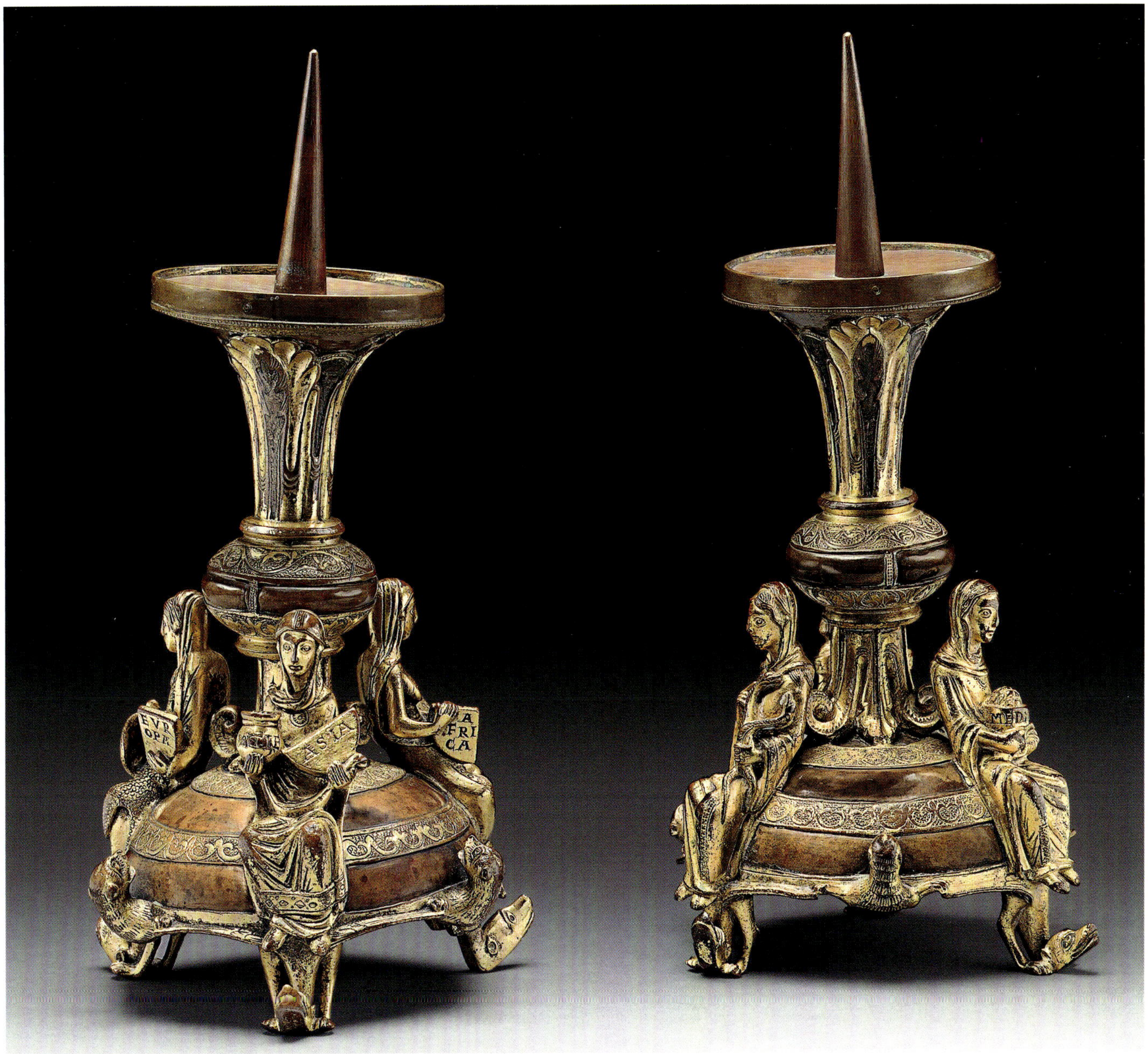
ASIA
A
FRI
CA

23 · Cross on a Pyx

German (Hildesheim), ca. 1160
Copper alloy with gilding
Overall 14 ½ × 6 ¼ × 6 in. (36.8 × 15.7 × 15 cm)
Dom-Museum Hildesheim (DS 17)

The unique form of this object, with a crucifix placed on a casket, makes discernment of its intended purpose difficult. The casket has been interpreted as a pyx (a receptacle for the host) to be used for the Holy Communion of the Sick; its interior has compartments where oil and hosts could have been stored. On the back is a separate opening, which could have housed relics. The cross on top adds to the vessel's multifunctional use, as it also could have served as an altar cross.

Standing on the four paws of a lion, the casket takes the form of a building with a central plan and engraved ornamentation on its roof. A canopy emerging from battlements bridges to a knob with openwork tendrils. Rising from the knob is the head of a lion, whose mouth holds the crucifix. Christ is depicted in a form typical of Romanesque bronze crucifixes, with an almost weightless, upright body attached to the cross; open eyes; and a slightly inclined head without a crown. The modest cross, accentuated by a raised edge, shows engraved tendrils on its back, with the Lamb of God in the center and the symbols of the Evangelists at the ends.

The cross is not part of the original cathedral treasure; it came from the collection of Bishop Eduard J. Wedekin (reigned 1850–70), who actively accumulated churches' treasures after ecclesiastical institutions were dissolved during the secularization at the beginning of the nineteenth century. According to his notes, Wedekin found the cross in Escherde, about six miles west of Hildesheim. However, as the Benedictine convent of Escherde was not founded until about 1200, the object certainly came from elsewhere. One possibility is St. Michael's Abbey in Hildesheim, which had close contacts with the nuns in Escherde and may have provided the cross as collateral for a loan in the fifteenth or early sixteenth century. Due to financial strains in the decades before the Reformation, many Benedictine institutions sought loans; some objects given as collateral were never redeemed, such as the so-called Bernhard Chalice (cat. 42) in St. Godehard's Basilica. That may well have been the case with this cross.

The similarity of a crucifix (cat. 24) from St. Michael's indicates that both came from the same workshop, which was active in Hildesheim during the third quarter of the twelfth century. Furthermore, the ornamentation seen on the casket, with its characteristic tendril leaves on the lid and the openwork knob, can be found on Hildesheim works since the 1130s – for example, on the Godehard Shrine (see Introduction, fig. 19) and the set of liturgical fans (cats. 17, 18, 19). Several corresponding motifs are on the bust of Emperor Frederick Barbarossa (*Barbarossakopf*) in Cappenberg Abbey, a former Premonstratensian monastery church near Dortmund, Westphalia; the bust's possible origin in a Hildesheim or Saxon workshop requires further study.

G.L.

SELECTED REFERENCES: Springer, *Kreuzfüsse*, 1981, pp. 148–52, no. 28; *Abglanz des Himmels*, 2001, p. 226, no. 5.13 (Ursula Mende); *Bild und Bestie*, 2008, pp. 252–53, no. 7 (Michael Brandt).

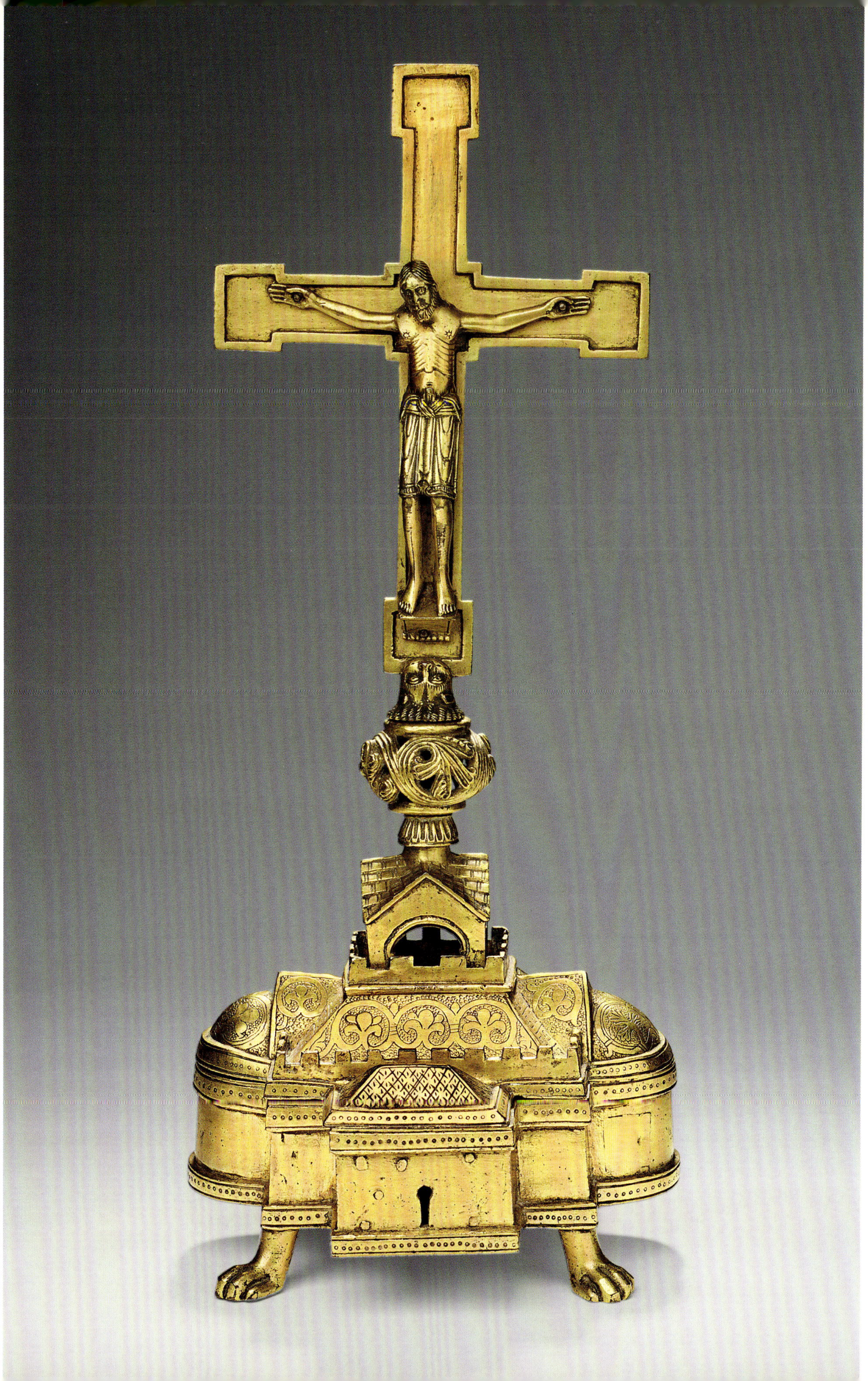

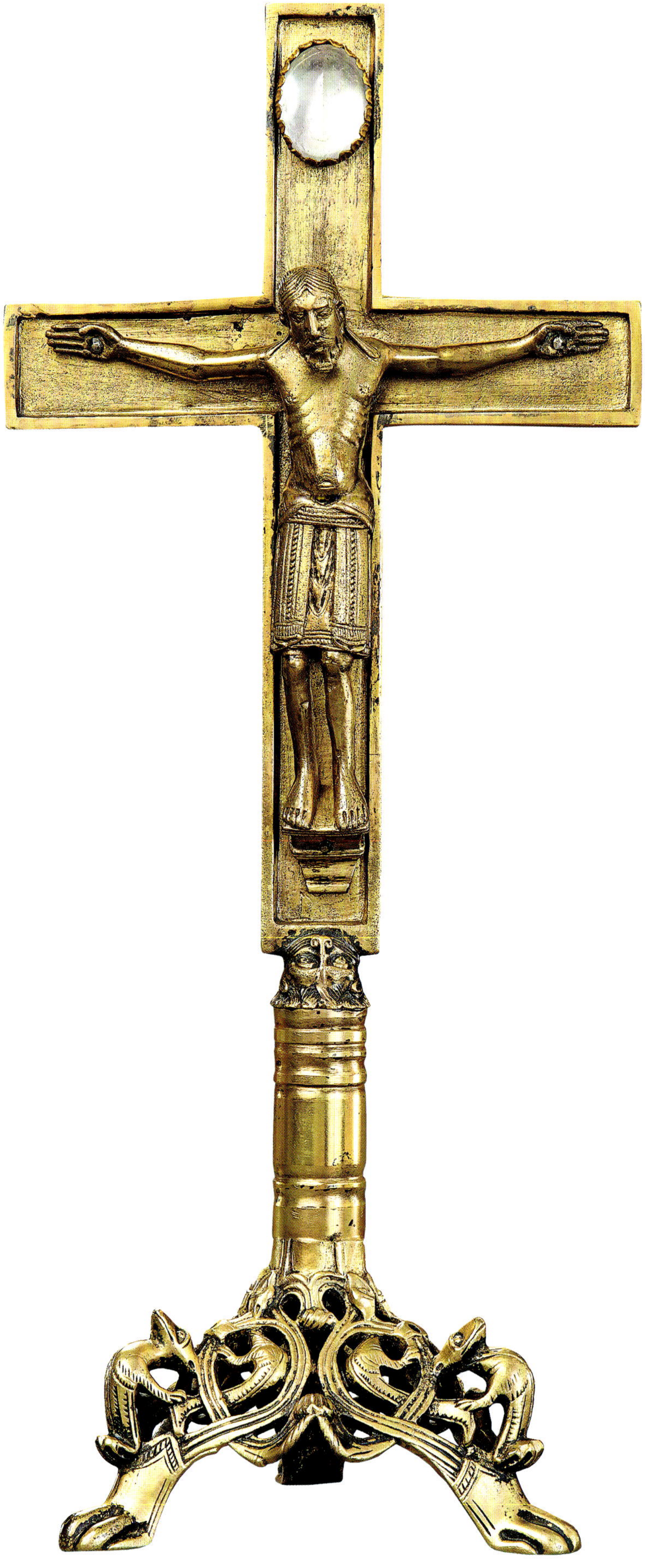

24 · Altar Cross

German (Hildesheim), third quarter of 12th century
Bronze, cast and engraved, with modern gilding and rock crystal
Overall 11 5/8 × 5 × 3 7/8 in. (29.5 × 12.7 × 9.8 cm); *H. of corpus* 4 1/4 in. (10.6 cm)
Dom-Museum Hildesheim (DS 12)

The cross and its base are characteristic works of twelfth-century Hildesheim workshops in their form and ornamentation. However, they are connected by a much later cylindrical interface. Thus it is not clear whether the current arrangement of components, which can be traced to at least 1840, reflects the original concept or is a later combination; it is worth noting that the form of the base resembles that of a candlestick, which may have been reused here. The cross was in the possession of St. Michael's Abbey in 1640, but it remains open whether the base was part of the cross then.

The cross is positioned on the throat of a lion, as is another cross in the cathedral treasury (cat. 23). The depiction of Christ – fairly erect, without any suggestion of dangling – is typical of the twelfth century: His knees are only slightly bent, his body subtly swings to the right, and his eyes are wide open. In those respects as well the two crosses closely relate, pointing to the same workshop active in Hildesheim in the third quarter of the twelfth century.

The back side of the cross is embossed with the Lamb of God and the symbols of the Evangelists in medallions at each end. A fifteenth-century inscription mentions a number of relics – from the True Cross and from Saints Bernhard, Bernward, Margaret, Jacob, Gregory, Fabian, and Sebastian – that were probably kept in the hollow back of Christ.

The base stands on three paws of a lion (like those seen in cat. 23), entwined with tendrils and dragons. Additional dragons with birdlike snouts arch backward over each paw. The foliate ornaments of the base find a parallel in the slightly older or perhaps contemporary base of a cross now in the Kunstgewerbemuseum Berlin (K 4165). Examples of bases with a simpler design possibly from the same workshop as the Hildesheim cross can be found at the church of St. Jacob in Stendal (Saxony-Anhalt, Germany) and the Diözesanmuseum in Freising (Bavaria), testifying to a flourishing production and wide distribution.

Like the Ratmann Sacramentary (cat. 21) and the Small Bernward Cross (cat. 25), this cross was produced for the abbey after permission was granted to venerate Bernward in 1150; together the three pieces are evidence of the abbey's extensive refurbishment in Bernward's honor.

G.L.

SELECTED REFERENCES: *Bernward von Hildesheim und das Zeitalter der Ottonen*, 1993, vol. 2, p. 613, no. IX-13 (Beate Braun-Niehr); *Abglanz des Himmels*, 2001, p. 225, no. 5.11 (Ursula Mende); Mende, "Romanische Bronzen," 2001, pp. 204–5.

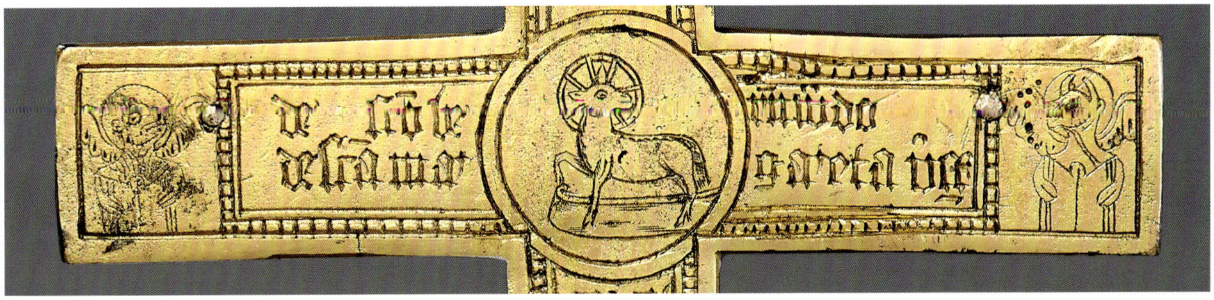

25 · Processional Cross (so-called Small Bernward Cross)

German (Hildesheim), ca. 1170–80
Copper alloy, gilding, filigree, rock crystal, and semiprecious stones
19 ½ × 12 ⅝ × 1 ⅝ in. (49.5 × 32 × 4 cm) *with tang*
Dom-Museum Hildesheim, on loan from the church of St. Magdalen (L 1989-6)

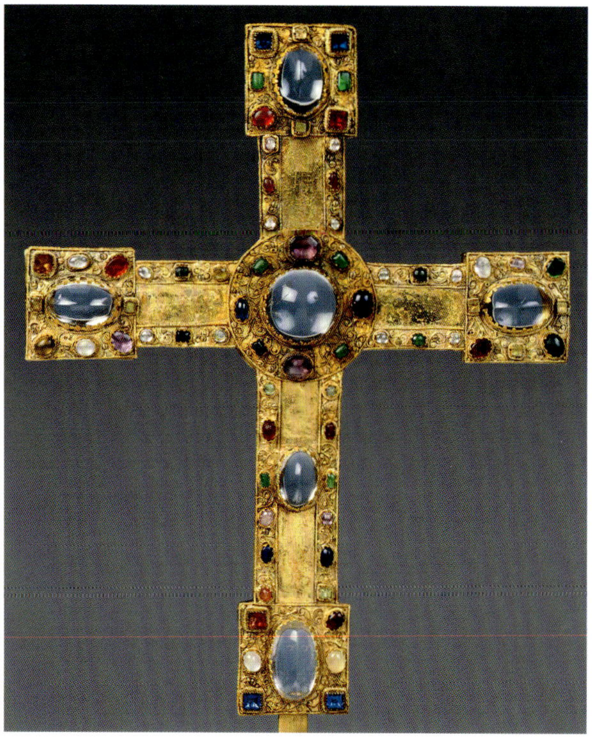

The form of this cross, with a circular field in its intersection and square terminals, follows a classical Romanesque model depicting the cross as a sign of victory. It is complemented by semiprecious stones that are traditional medieval symbols of the resurrected Christ and the Heavenly Jerusalem. The back side shows engraved tendrils with leaves, alluding to the cross as the Tree of Life.

The only reference shedding light on the cross's possible provenance is a note in which Johann Michael Kratz, the nineteenth-century Hildesheim archivist and historian, mentions it as an object owned by the church of St. Magdalen. Since that church received all the major treasures from St. Michael's Abbey after its secularization in 1803, this cross was likely previously part of St. Michael's treasure. The cross's general form testifies to that provenance, as it partly imitates the famous Bernward Cross of about 1150 (see Introduction, fig. 20), which was made for a cross relic that Emperor Otto III presented to Bernward, who donated it to the church. Furthermore, both crosses were restored about 1787 using the same kind of screws.

A number of objects in various media that were produced during the extensive refurbishing of St. Michael's after it obtained the concession in 1150 to venerate Bishop Bernward were patterned after works from Bernward's time. As the bishop was venerated not only as founder and major donor of the monastery but also as an artist himself, his donations and commissions were regarded as near relics worthy of copy. In addition to this cross, an example of such imitation is the crucifix from St. Godehard's Basilica (cat. 36), which recalls the silver Bernward Cross (cat. 10) from the early eleventh century.

The Small Bernward Cross was probably made in a Hildesheim workshop that was active in the third quarter of the twelfth century. Two contemporary Hildesheim book covers from St. Godehard's, today both in the treasury of St. Peter's Cathedral in Trier, Germany (Hohe Domkirche, Domschatz, nos. 69, 70), correspond in their details to the Small Bernward Cross. However, the form of the latter's tendrils and filigree had been popular since about 1130, when technical and artistic innovations gave rise to a great number of goldsmith and metalwork commissions, such as the three flabella (ceremonial fans) from the cathedral (cats. 17, 18, 19).

G.L.

SELECTED REFERENCES: *Schatzkammer auf Zeit*, 1991, pp. 136–38, no. 38 (Michael Brandt); *Abglanz des Himmels*, 2001, p. 191, no. 4.25 (Michael Brandt).

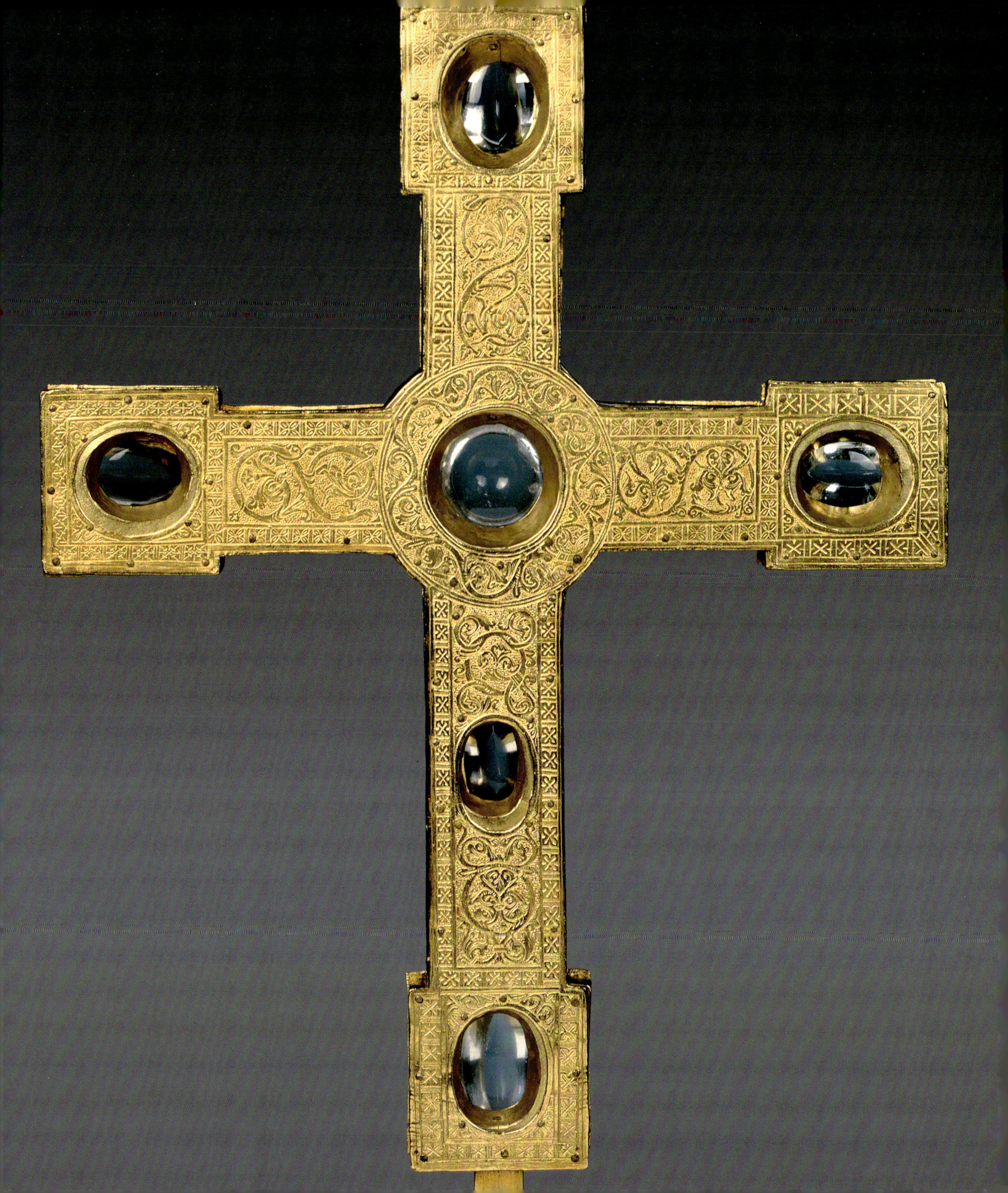

26 · Domed Reliquary

German (Hildesheim), ca. 1170–80
Gilded copper, champlevé enamel, and rock crystal; wood core
9 × 6 3/8 × 4 5/8 in. (22.8 × 16.2 × 11.5 cm)
Dom-Museum Hildesheim (DS 20)

Domed with a great rock crystal and raised on short feet that mimic animal paws, this reliquary's shape is fairly rare. The large spherical crystal ennobles the otherwise modest container, and it dramatically draws attention to and magnifies the precious relics that are stored within it, in a space carved out of the stone.

Bust-length images of saints and angels appear on the enameled and gilded copper plaques that sheathe the sides and the slanted roof. Defined only by summary engraving against an enamel ground limited to blues of varying intensities, the saints' and angels' heads are framed in white halos; they represent virtually indistinguishable generic types. A partial inscription on the base names the Twelve Apostles.

This reliquary was a bequest to Hildesheim Cathedral by its bishop Eduard J. Wedekin (reigned 1850–70), who amassed a collection of church treasures after the secularization of ecclesiastical institutions in 1803.

B.D.B.

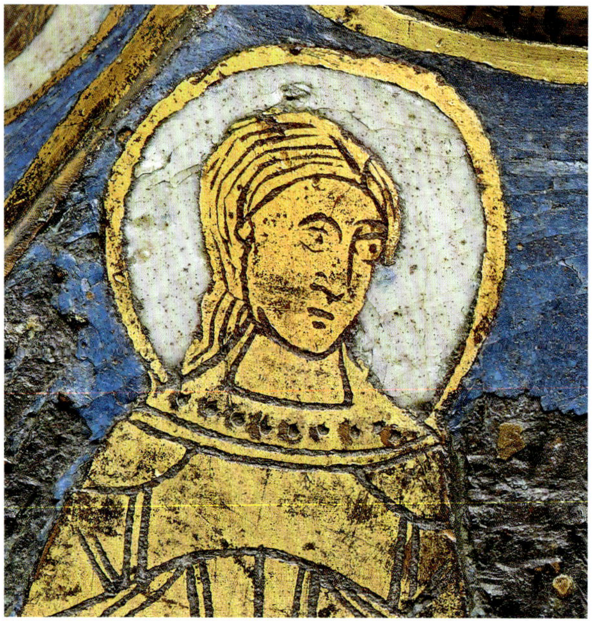

SELECTED REFERENCES: *Schatzkammer auf Zeit*, 1991, pp. 134–36, no. 37 (Michael Brandt); *Abglanz des Himmels*, 2001, pp. 188–89, no. 4.19 (Michael Brandt), illus. p. 164.

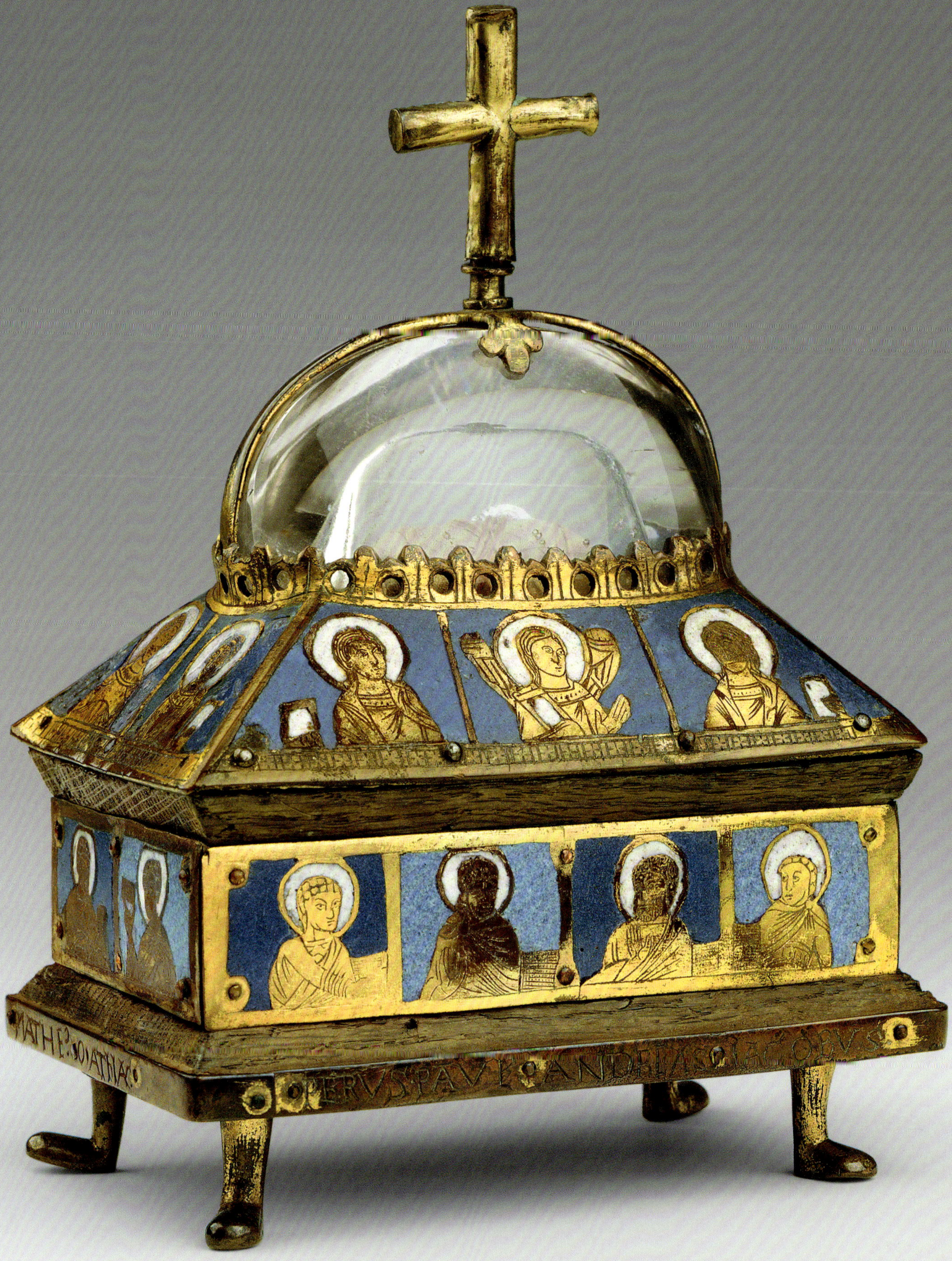

27 · Six Enamel Plaques

German (Hildesheim), late 12th century
Champlevé enamel, copper alloy, and gilding
TWO VERTICAL PLAQUES: *each 13 × 4 3/8 in (33 × 11 cm);*
FOUR HORIZONTAL PLAQUES: *each 4 3/8 × 15 3/8 in. (11 × 39 cm)*
Dom-Museum Hildesheim (DS 30)

Since their creation in the second half of the twelfth century, these plaques, with small scenes from the life of Christ, have served as decorative elements on at least two objects in Hildesheim. From the seventeenth century until the end of the nineteenth, they adorned the predella, or decorative base, of an altarpiece that stood in a side chapel of Hildesheim Cathedral. A wood panel discovered in the cathedral's crypt in 1898 gives a clue to an earlier context for the plaques. (The illustration below shows the plaques superimposed on the panel in their presumed original positions.) Rectangular recessed compartments at the panel's outer edges correspond to the size and shape of the plaques, which may once have served as a border for a now missing central element. Still visible in the center is the imprint of the sort of geometric design often used to organize representations of Christ in Majesty, which suggests one possibility for the centerpiece's theme.

Five of the plaques treat the Passion and post-Resurrection events in Christ's life; the sixth represents the Nativity. The wood matrix suggests that at one time two more plaques would have filled out the border, perhaps extending the Nativity sequence or offering scenes from Christ's ministry. One plaque may well have elaborated upon the Resurrection events by including scenes of the Women at the Tomb and the Noli Me Tangere (Christ appearing to Mary Magdalen) – notable absences in an otherwise extremely thorough post-Resurrection cycle. No matter the iconography, the size and shape of the wood panel argue against the plaques having served as decoration for a portable altar, as was long assumed. Recent scholarship has offered up the possibility of the wood panel having served as the antependium (the decorative front cover) of a standing altar.

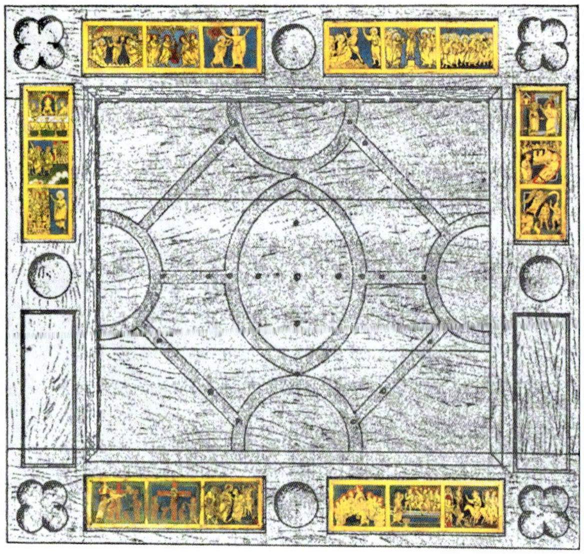

In technique and style, the plaques conform to the work of metalsmiths from the area around Hildesheim and in the Rhineland. Those artists and their patrons favored narrative sequences, rather than the typological scenes often found in Mosan enamelwork (from the Meuse River valley, in present-day Belgium, the Netherlands, and Germany). Also in contrast to their Mosan counterparts, the Saxon and Rhenish artists tended to leave the figures in reserve, setting them against patches of colored enamel. The silhouetted figures gain remarkable clarity and thus become ideal vehicles for engraved linear effects, akin to the draftsman's art. A trial "sketch" on the back of one of the plaques (see p. 132) reinforces this point. This haunting image of a bearded man is notably of a much higher quality than the finished figures on the front, raising the possibility that the master of the workshop may have used the back of the plaque as a guide for the lesser metalsmiths who were left to complete peripheral pieces such as these.

M.H.

SELECTED REFERENCES: *Ornamenta ecclesiæ*, 1985, vol. 1, pp. 294–95, no. B 78 (Ingrid Westerhoff-Sebald); *Abglanz des Himmels*, 2001, p. 185, no. 4.11 (Michael Brandt); *Schätze des Glaubens*, 2010, pp. 88–89, no. 38 (Michael Brandt).

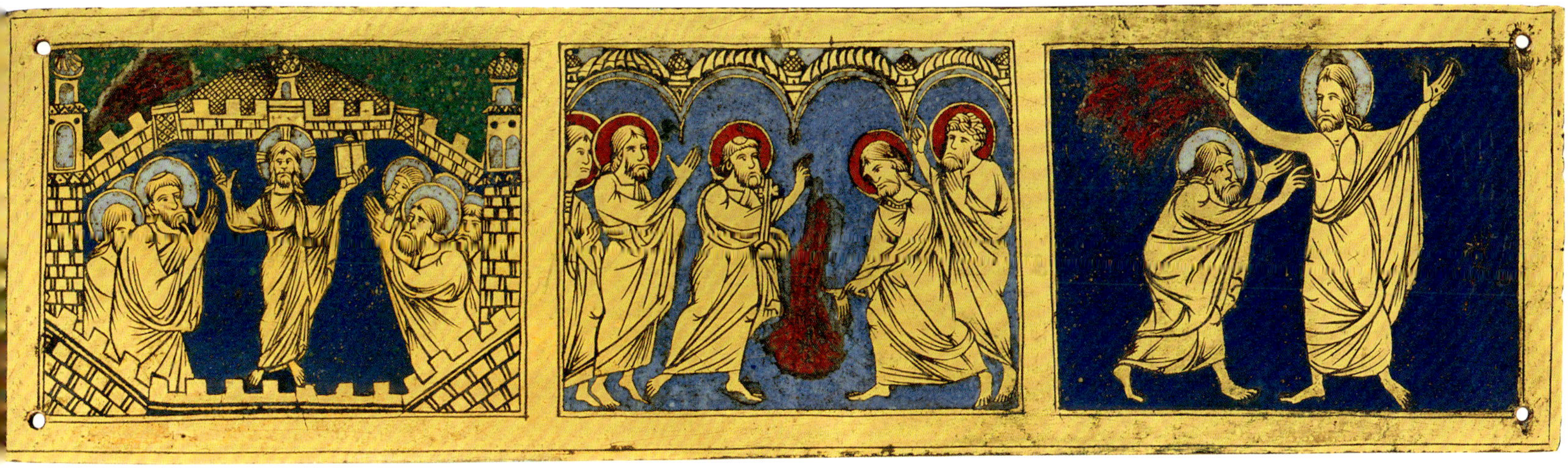

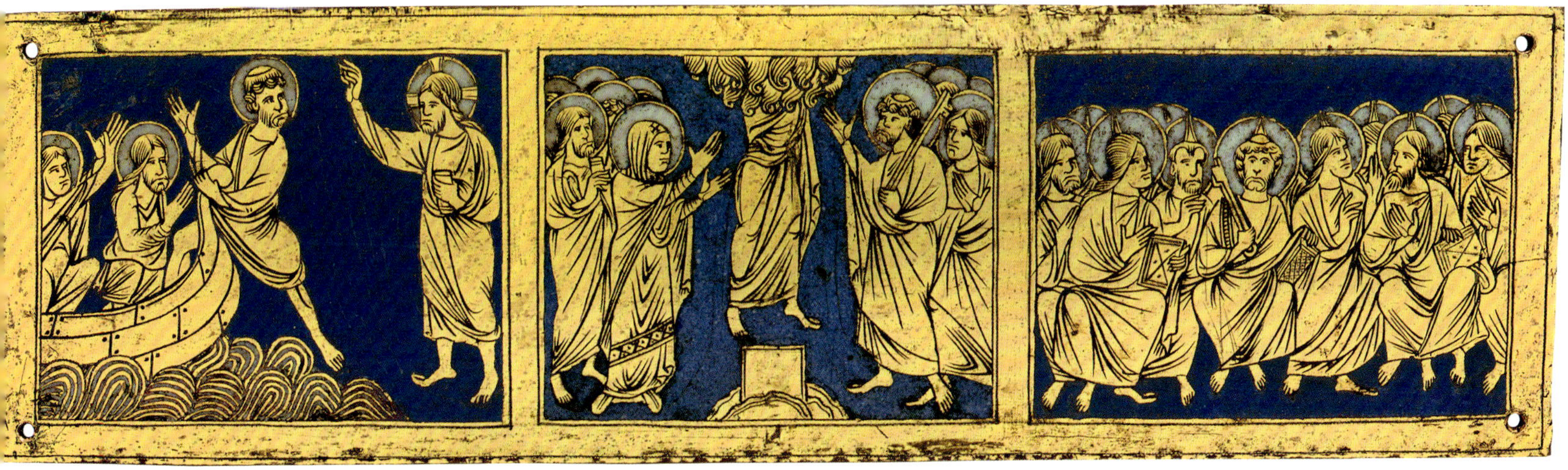

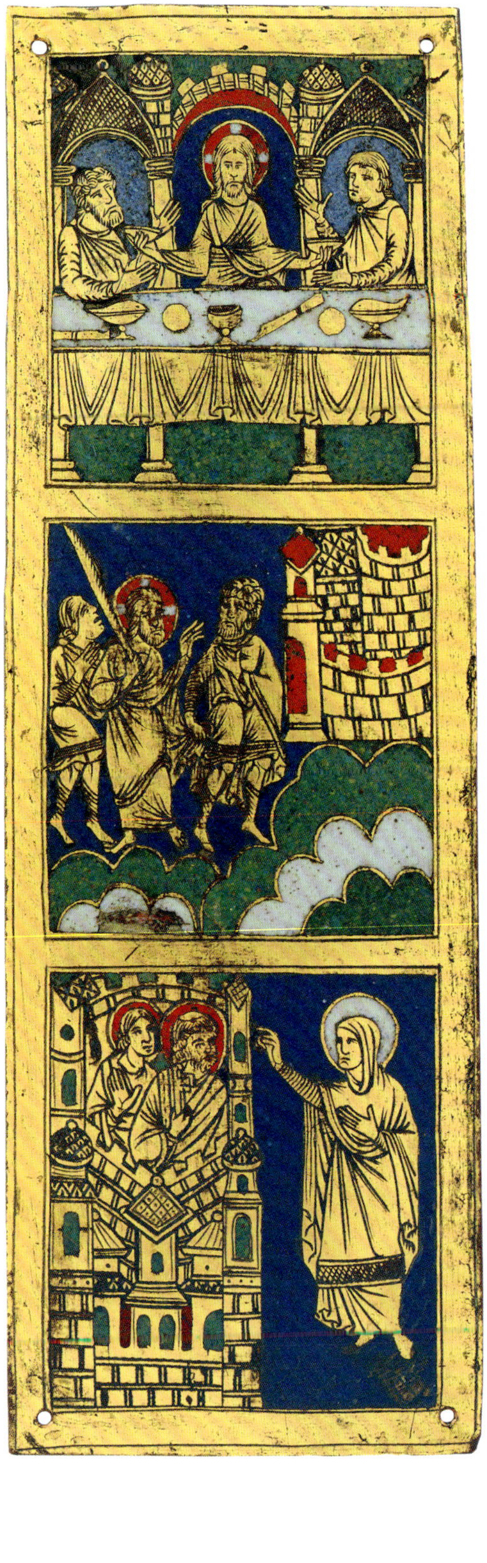

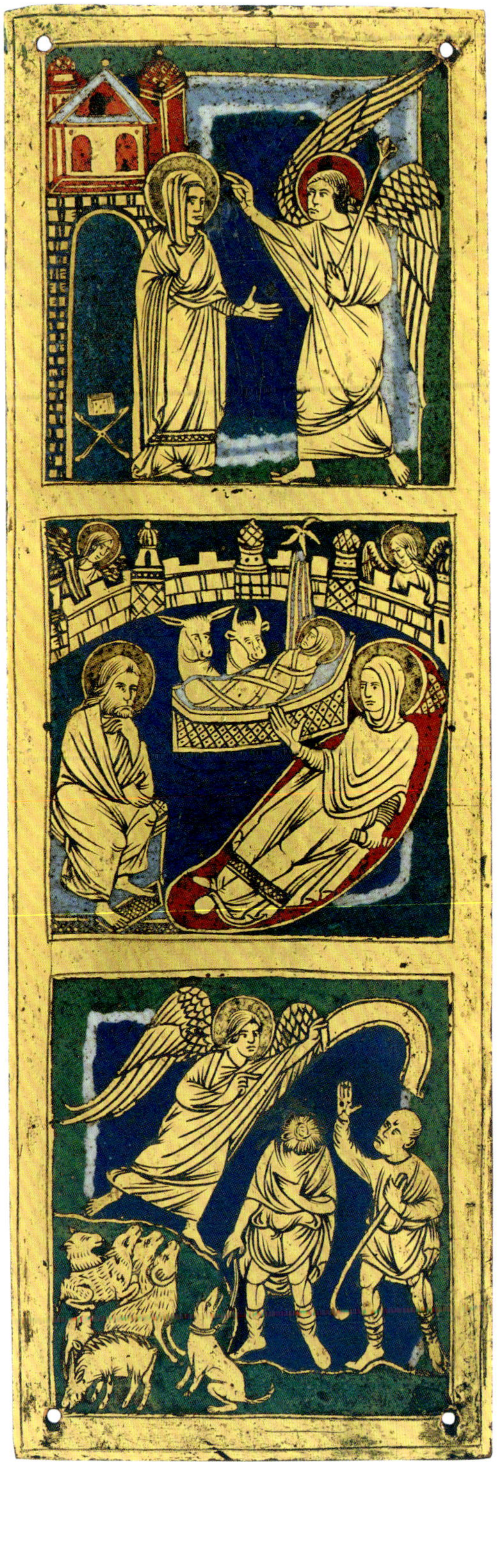

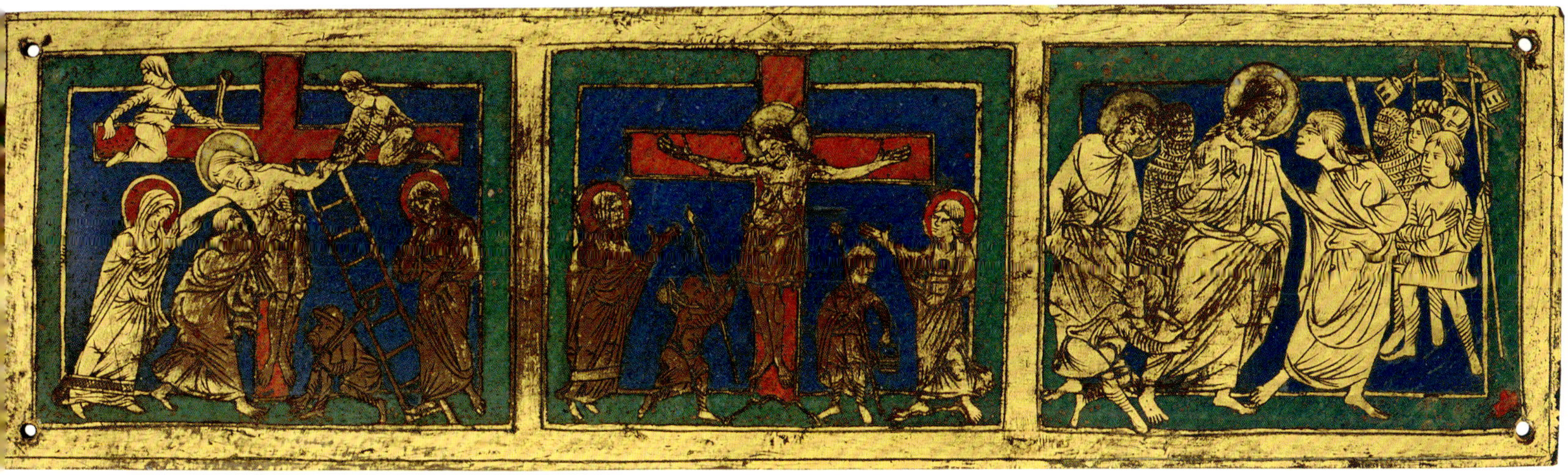

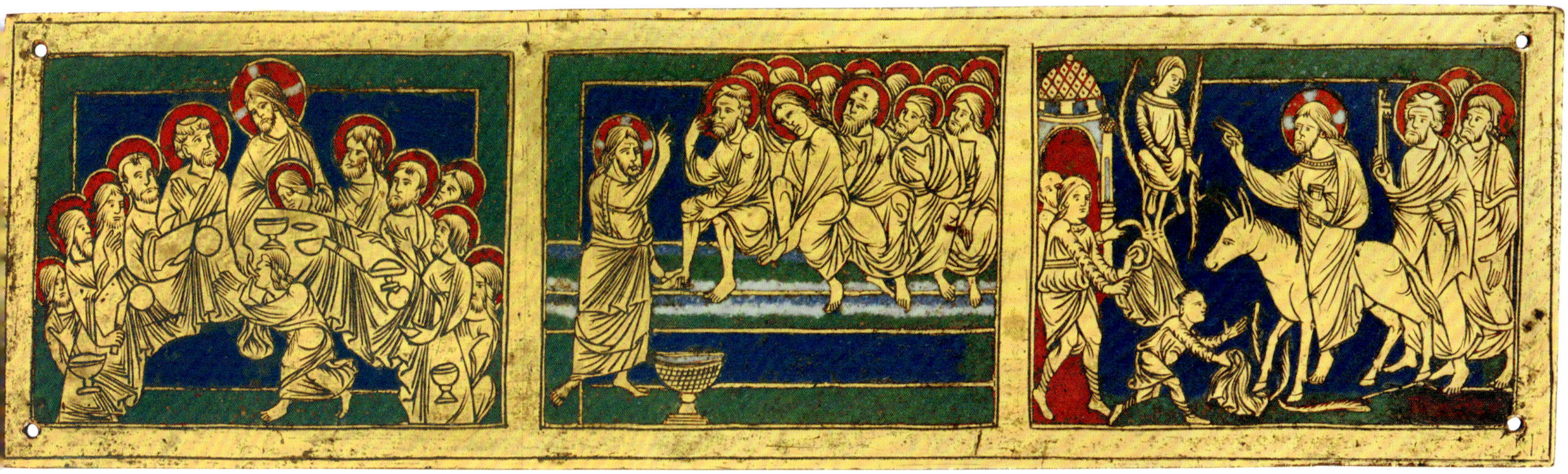

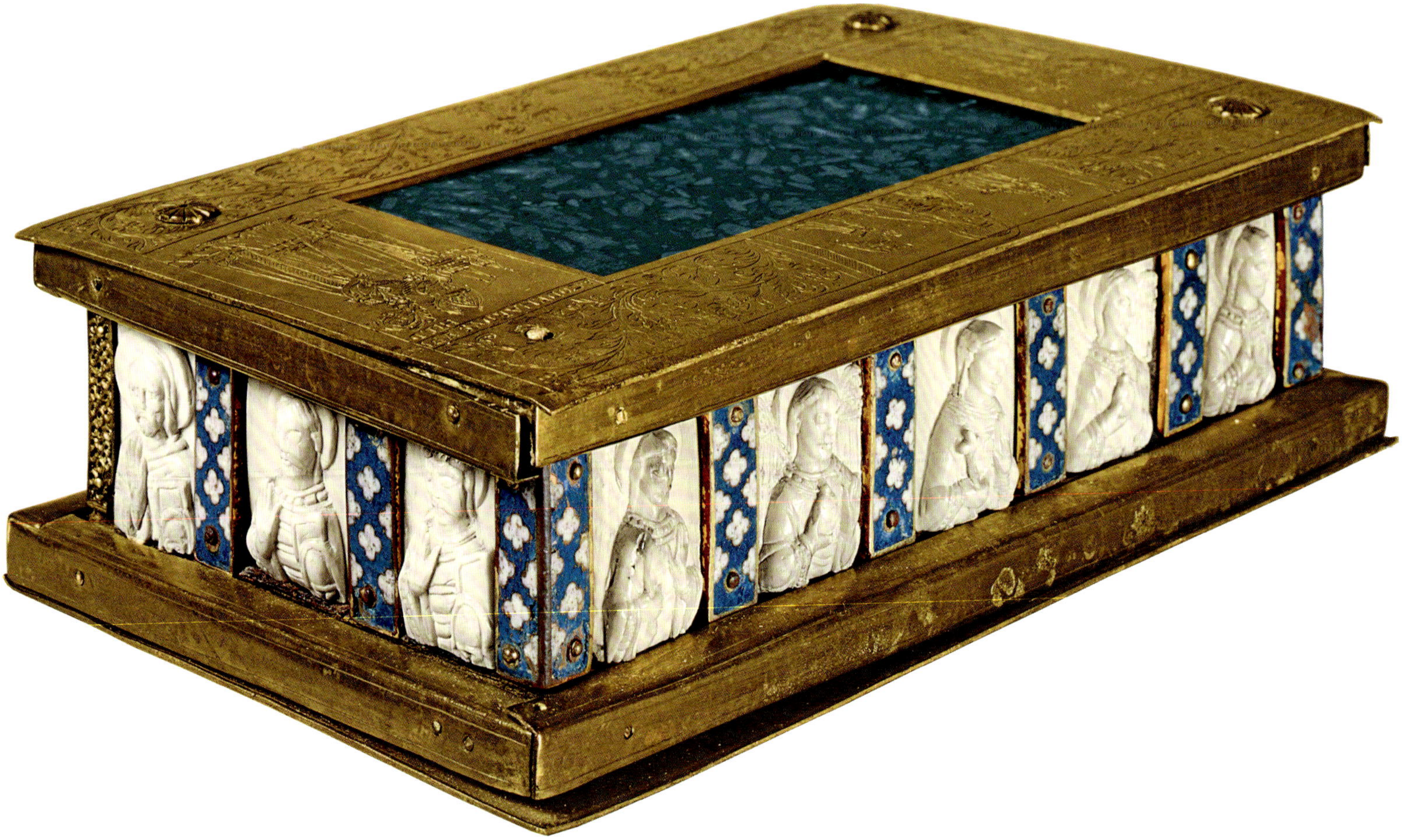

28 · Portable Altar

German (Hildesheim), second half of 12th century, with later repairs
Serpentine, walrus ivory, champlevé enamel, and gilded copper; wood core
2 7/8 × 9 7/8 × 5 3/4 in. (7.3 × 25 × 14.5 cm)
Dom-Museum Hildesheim (DS 25)

The diminutive size of this altar suited the needs of priests when traveling or taking the sacrament to the sick. The serpentine plaque centered on the top provides the flat surface for the placement of a chalice and paten, while the images of saints apparently serve as a "cloud of witnesses" (Hebrews 12:1) to the solemn celebration of Mass.

Bust-length images of saints carved in walrus ivory appear on the sides, framed by enameled bands. On one long side Christ is flanked by Saints Peter and Paul, each with an apostle at his side. On either short end are three apostles. Mary is at the center of the other long side, accompanied by two angels and two holy virgins. Prominently set on top, framing the central serpentine plaque, are engraved images of saints directly linked to Hildesheim: Bernward and Godehard, successive eleventh-century bishops of Hildesheim; Epiphanius, a fifth-century bishop of Pavia, whose relics were translated to Hildesheim in the mid-tenth century; and the Virgin, patron of the cathedral. While not medieval, those images probably reprise the altar's original program.

To judge from the repairs, this portable altar was still in use in the sixteenth century; subsequently it was stored with two others (cats. 9, 29) in the high altar of Hildesheim Cathedral. When it was discovered in 1833, pieces of parchment and paper were under the serpentine plaque; the texts written on them were not recorded, and they have since disappeared.

B.D.B.

SELECTED REFERENCES: Brandt, "Tragaltäre im Hochaltar," 1989; *Abglanz des Himmels*, 2001, p. 193, no. 4.32 (Michael Brandt), illus. p. 179.

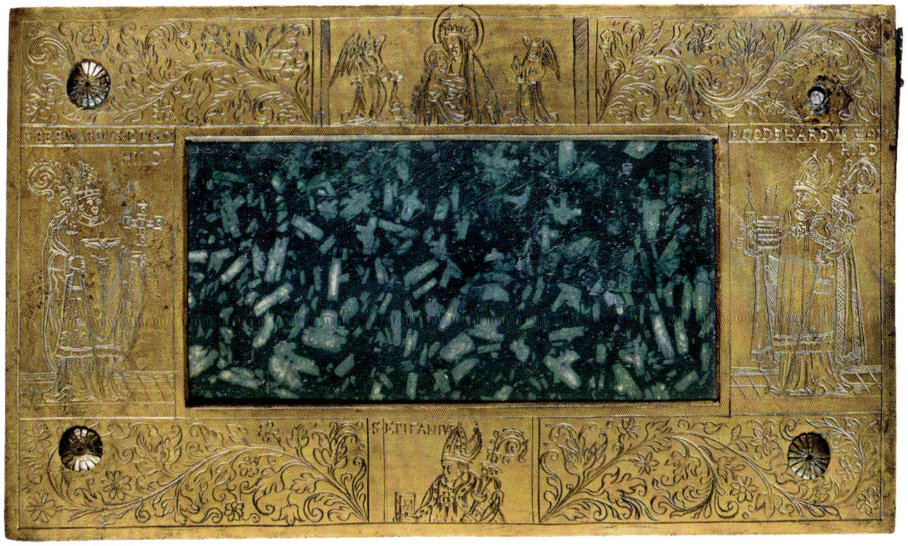

29 · Portable Altar

German (Hildesheim), last quarter of 12th century
Marble, gilded silver, gilded bronze, gilded copper, émail brun, *and walrus ivory; wood core*
5 ½ × 11 ⅞ × 7 ⅜ in. (14 × 30 × 18.5 cm)
Dom-Museum Hildesheim (DS 24)

The buttery tones of the ivory carvings along the sides and of the marble plaque on top are handsomely complemented by the gilded copper sheets that originally completely sheathed the wood core of this handsomely proportioned portable altar.

It was found in the high altar of Hildesheim Cathedral in 1833, along with two other portable altars (cats. 9, 28). One long side of this example represents Christ with four apostles; on the other long side are the Virgin Mary and an entourage of apostles and other saints. Mary is flanked by Saint Christopher (patron of nearby Braunschweig, in an early representation) holding the Christ Child and Saint John the Baptist with a lamb. (It has been suggested that the presence of Christopher and John the Baptist might have reflected the altar's relic contents, as those saints are not customarily linked to Hildesheim.) All twelve apostles are depicted in the ivories around the piece, including Peter (with keys), Thomas (with a carpenter's square), Philip (with a crosier), and Bartholomew (with a knife) – an early example of the use of attributes to single out certain apostles. (The apostle shown to the right is not thus identified.)

A gilded copper plaque affixed to the underside bears the image of a priest, the donor, with the portable altar in his hands.

B.D.B.

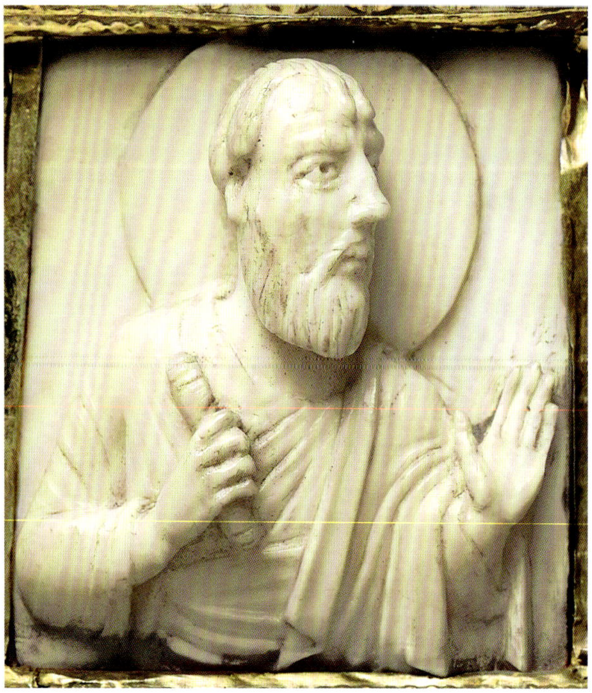

SELECTED REFERENCES: Goldschmidt, *Die Elfenbeinskulpturen*, 1914–26, vol. 2 (1918), no. 86; *Die Zeit der Staufer*, 1977, vol. 1, no. 626; Brandt, "Tragaltäre im Hochaltar," 1989; *Abglanz des Himmels*, 2001, pp. 193–94, no. 4.33 (Michael Brandt), illus. p. 179.

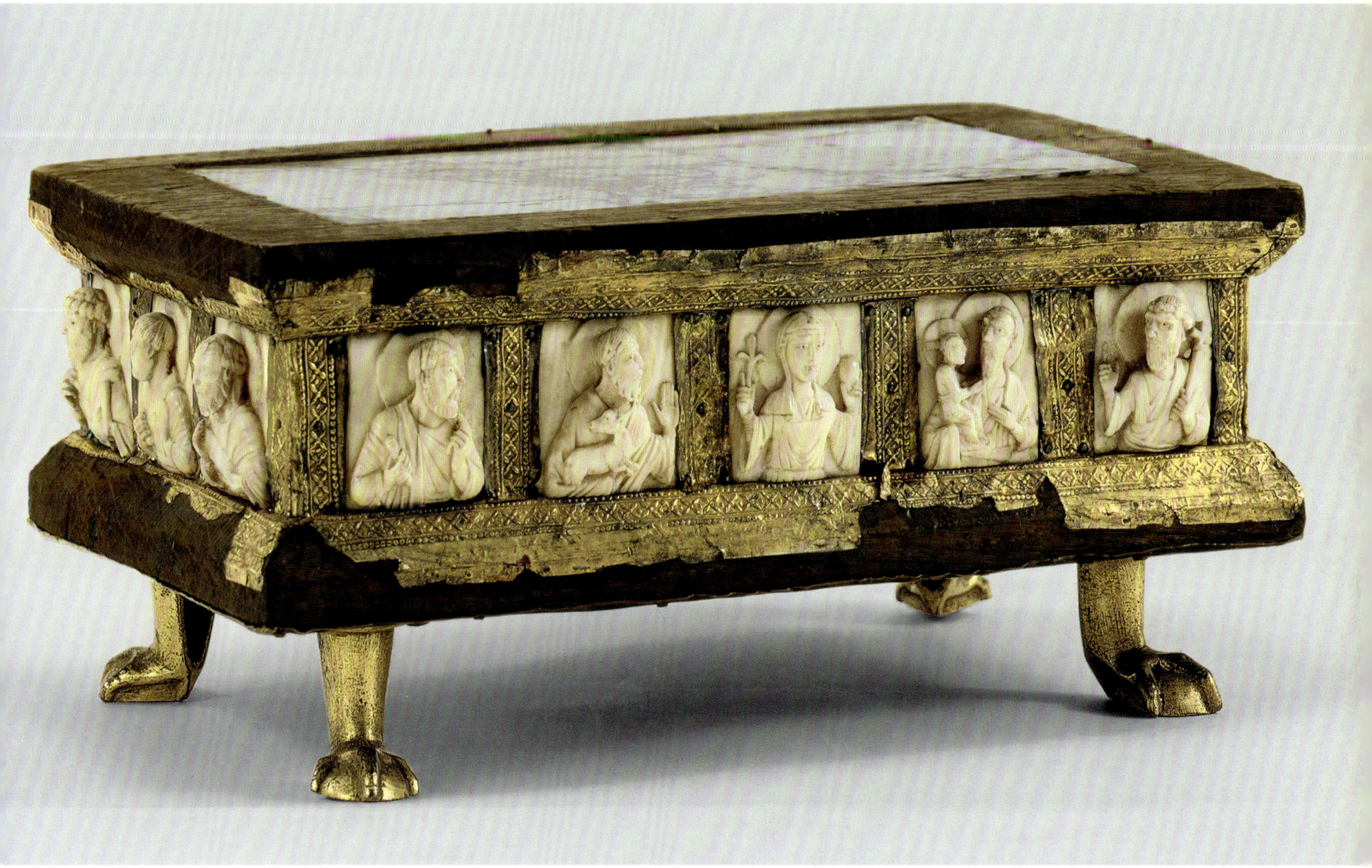

30 · Reliquary Cross

German (Hildesheim), ca. 1180–90
Gilded silver, rock crystal, semiprecious stones, and ancient intaglios; wood core
27 × 12 7/8 × 1 3/8 in. (68.5 × 32.5 × 3.5 cm) with tang
Dom-Museum Hildesheim (DS L 112)

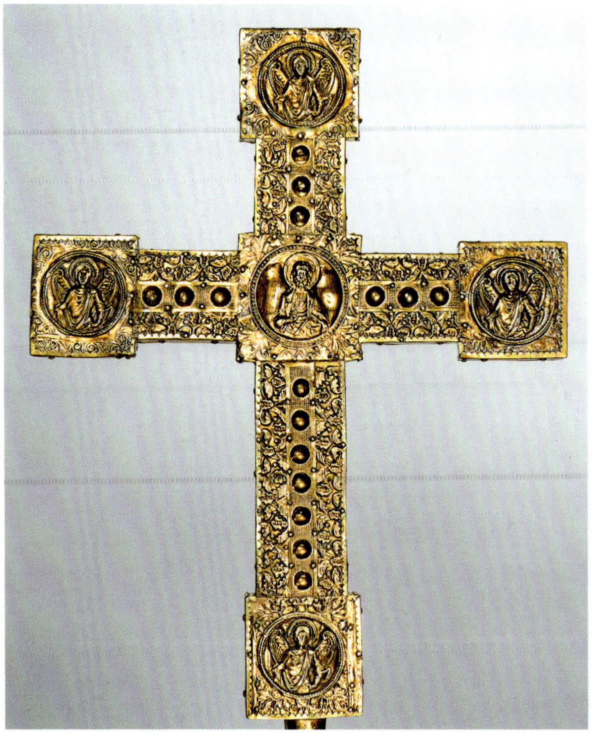

After the Crusaders captured Jerusalem in 1099, the fervor among European Christians for relics of the True Cross redoubled. The secular and religious leaders of Europe eagerly sought to obtain fragments of the cross when they traveled to Jerusalem to visit the Church of the Holy Sepulcher. As the powerful duke of Saxony and Bavaria, Henry the Lion (ca. 1130–1195) was one of those privileged to procure such a relic, whether during his pilgrimage to Jerusalem (1172–73) or during his two meetings in Constantinople with the Byzantine emperor, who lavished him with gifts.

According to an undated document, now lost, Henry was traditionally believed to have presented the relic to the Church of the Holy Cross in Hildesheim after his safe return in 1173, and to have had it framed at the center of this cross. Alas, there is no evidence supporting the legend. The cross does not appear in an inventory of the cathedral's valuables undertaken by city officials in 1546, after the Reformation; no link to Henry the Lion is asserted in an eighteenth-century reference to the reliquary cross.

If doubt surrounds an association of this cross with Henry, there is none about the importance of the relic it enshrines; it is proclaimed by the dazzling array of jewels and goldsmiths' techniques. Gems of rock crystal, prized for its translucence, are prominently set at each of the terminals, while the entire front of the cross is framed by smaller rock crystals and colored gems. Late Roman intaglios appear on both the right and bottom terminals; some gems, notably one set in the left terminal, are pierced, as they would be for stringing, a clear indication of reuse. Others appear to be replacements of originals, substituted over the course of centuries. The ordered profusion of gems and their placement conform to the tradition of reliquary crosses since the flourishing of Ottonian art, beginning in the mid-tenth century.

Every inch of the precious gilded surface is decorated. In addition to the abundant gems, delicately hammered leaf patterns, characteristic of twelfth-century work, cover the surface, above all on the arms of the cross, both front and back; filigree wires overlay the terminals and center. The exacting techniques – including the filigree, more typically associated with Carolingian and Ottonian metalwork and uncommon by this point – are detailed in the early twelfth-century treatise *On Divers Arts* (or *Schedula diversarum artium*), an encyclopedic guide to the methods of medieval art that focused particularly on goldsmithing.

A medallion with the half-length figure of Christ blessing is set at the center of the reverse. Angels set in roundels appear at each terminal, where one would expect to find images of the four authors of the Gospels; the angels are similar to those on the cover of the Precious Gospels (cat. 32). The small image of the crucified Jesus on the front of the cross was added later, likely in the sixteenth century, and, as is typical of medieval goldsmiths' work, there appear to be other, minor modifications as well, including the addition of red fabric behind the relic.

B.D.B.

SELECTED REFERENCES: *Abglanz des Himmels*, 2001, p. 191, no. 4.26 (Michael Brandt), illus. p. 172; Peter, "Das sogenannte Kreuz Heinrichs des Löwen," 2007–8; *Schätze des Glaubens*, 2010, pp. 94–95, no. 41 (Lothar Lambacher).

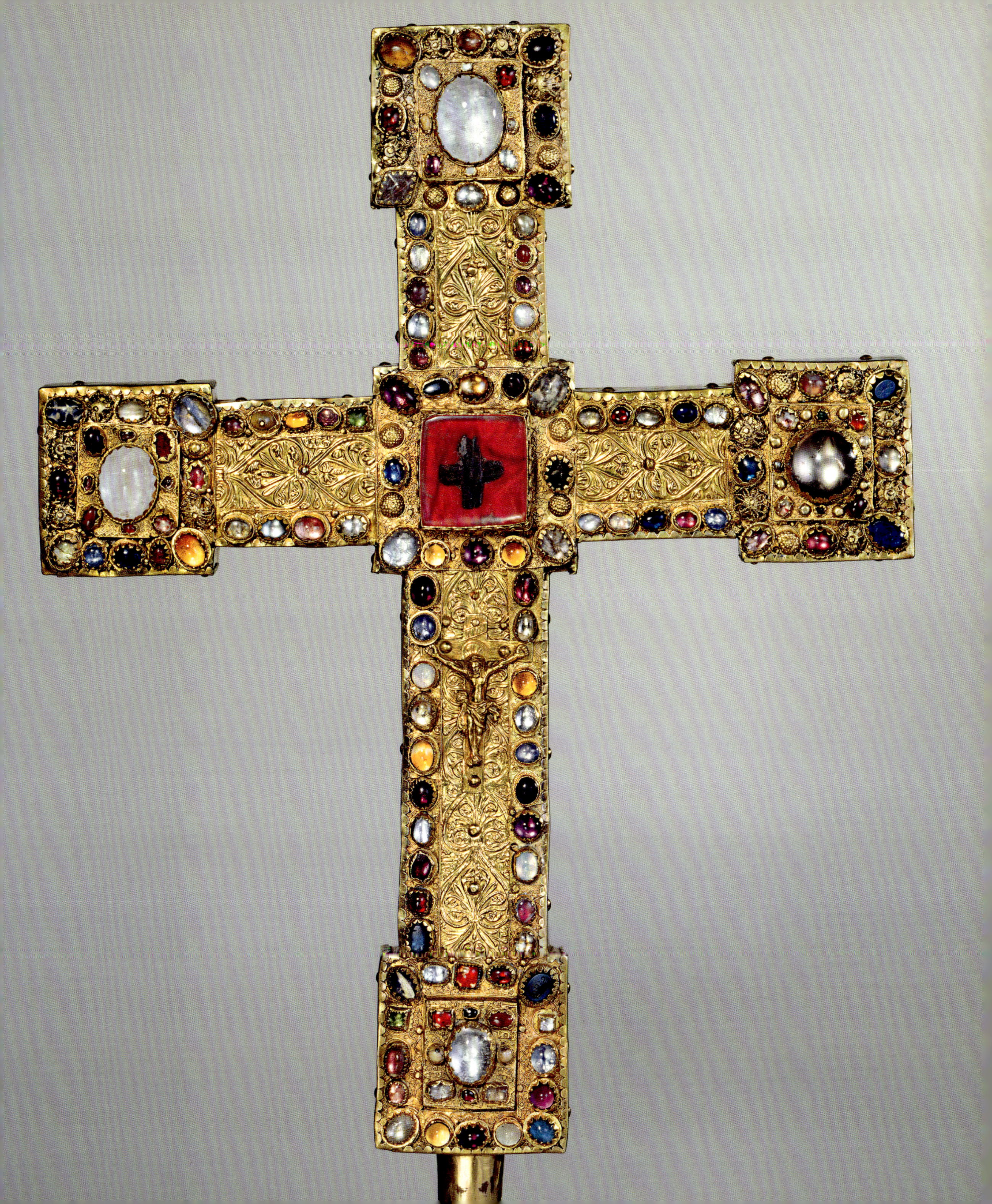

31 · Reliquary of Saint Oswald

German (Hildesheim) or possibly English, ca. 1185–89; partly restored 1779
Gold, silver, gilded silver, niello, cloisonné enamel (a few replaced), gems, pearls, and antique cameos and intaglios; wood core
H. with crown 18 ¾ in. (47.5 cm); Diam. of base 10 ⅝ in. (27 cm)
Dom-Museum Hildesheim (DS 23)

Imposing in size, rich in materials, and impeccably crafted, this bust is one of the great surviving masterpieces of medieval goldsmiths' work. It was created to house the skull of Saint Oswald, king of Northumbria, in northern England; the skull, wrapped in silk, has been preserved in the reliquary to this day.

The saint's curling hair peeks out from beneath his crown, and he has an equally full beard. The pupils of the eyes are niello (a black alloy of sulfur and metal that is fused by heat to engraved metal surfaces), giving Oswald a piercing gaze that is typical of medieval bust reliquaries. The saint's prayerful, charitable life and noble death in 642 at the hands of Penda, the pagan king of Mercia, are alluded to in the niello inscription that encircles the middle of the reliquary.

The inscription engraved around the octagonal base refers to God's role as the crowner of kings, and the base is ringed by images of eight monarchs – all but one of whom ruled over part of England, and most of whom were venerated as saints. Oswald himself has pride of place at the center. The others, identified by an inscription added in the fourteenth century, are Adalbert (prince of Northumbria, died 740); Edmund (king of East Anglia, died 870); Alfred (king of Wessex, died 899); Canute the Great (died 1035); Edward the Confessor (king of England, died 1066); and two not named here as saints: Ethelwold (king of East Anglia, died 664) and Sigismund (presumably the sainted king of Burgundy, died 524). The royal portraits alternate between golden images against niello grounds and niello images against gold grounds; the lunettes just above, representing symbols of the Evangelists and the Four Rivers of Paradise, similarly alternate.

The inherently high cost of the reliquary's materials, especially the profusely bejeweled crown, and the remarkable ensemble of sainted English kings suggest English royal patronage. Henry the Lion, duke of Saxony, and his second wife, Matilda, daughter of Henry II, the Plantagenet king of England, are recorded as the donors of two reliquaries to the cathedral; that this is one of them seems almost irrefutable.

The niello work is remarkably accomplished, with sure draftsmanship in the drapery, hair, and scrolling backgrounds. The technique is seen throughout the twelfth century, often in Plantagenet domains, including on the diminutive reliquary of Saint Thomas Becket in the Metropolitan Museum's collection (17.190.520).

The crown is curiously ill-fitting and utterly distinct in workmanship from the bust. Rulers sometimes gave their own crowns to church treasuries to be set on bust reliquaries of saints, as was done with later examples at Prague Cathedral and Saint-Denis in Paris; whether that is the case here is unknown. The crown comprises a number of earlier elements, including the large Roman cameo at the center front. Two gold plaques with cloisonné enamels are decorated with filigree on the crown's outer and inner sides, but the mounts for the gems pierce the original decoration on the inside, clear indications of reuse.

B.D.B.

SELECTED REFERENCES: *Kirchenkunst des Mittelalters*, 1989, pp. 135–60, no. 9; *Abglanz des Himmels*, 2001, p. 190, no. 4.23 (Michael Brandt), illus. pp. 168–70; *Schätze des Glaubens*, 2010, pp. 90–91, no. 39 (Lothar Lambacher).

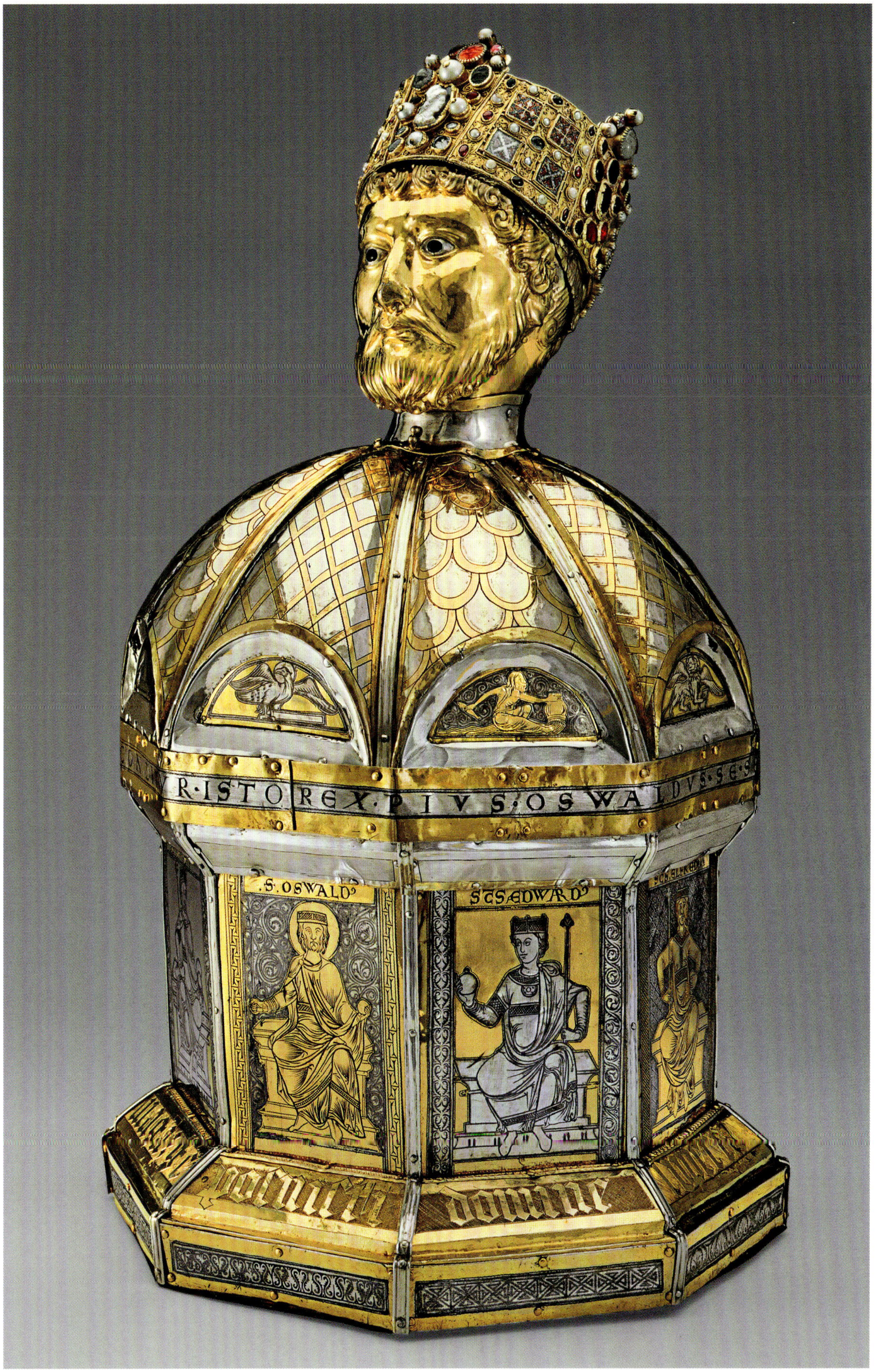
REX·PIVS·OSWALDVS
S·OSWALD
domine

32 · Precious Gospels of Bernward (front and back covers)

German (Hildesheim), ca. 1015; refurbished ca. 1194
COVERS: *silver and gilded silver with niello, filigree, semiprecious stones, and late 10th-century Byzantine (Constantinople) ivory on wood foundation*
MANUSCRIPT: *tempera, gold, and silver on parchment*
Overall 11 × 7⅞ in. (28 × 20 cm); 232 leaves
Only front cover is exhibited.
Dom-Museum Hildesheim (DS 18)

Bishop Bernward's Precious Gospels, lavishly illuminated with scenes from the life of Christ, is decorated with a bejeweled cover whose centerpiece is the sole remaining ivory panel of a Byzantine triptych depicting the Deesis: Christ standing between the supplicating Virgin and Saint John the Baptist, who act as intercessors for humankind. (That arrangement is characteristic of Byzantine art; Western depictions of Christ in Majesty more commonly place him in the company of the Four Evangelists.) The two other panels of the original icon likely showed saints.

Many important Constantinopolitan ivories survive only because they were sent to the West, where they no longer served as devotional objects but frequently were incorporated into deluxe bindings of precious manuscripts, a practice unknown in Byzantium. This ivory certainly arrived in the West as a gift of diplomatic exchange; Bernward may have acquired it while still a member of the court of Otto III, before his elevation to bishop. Its use as centerpiece both honors the Byzantine icon and enriches the prestige of Bernward's gospel. The ivory is inscribed: SIS RIA QVESO TVO BERN / VVARDO TRINA POTESTAS (I pray that the threefold power is merciful to Bernward).

The front cover was renewed in the late twelfth century to enhance Bernward's reputation, either to help secure his canonization, which took place in December 1193, or, following his canonization, to stimulate veneration of the new saint. The refurbishment incorporated elements from Bernward's time, including the small gilded silver crucifix below the Byzantine ivory, some of the antique intaglios, and precious and semiprecious stones. The decorative gilded silver filigree that frames the Byzantine ivory and the repoussé gilded silver symbols of the Evangelists were also added.

The back cover (see p. 93) contains an Ottonian silver and partly gilded engraved image of the Virgin Hodegetria (She Who Shows the Way – Mary gesturing toward the Child she holds, indicating that he offers the way to salvation). The Christ Child holds the host, and MP OY (Mother of God) is inscribed near the image. The Virgin Hodegetria was a characteristic Byzantine subject, and this figure was clearly inspired by a Byzantine icon, probably in ivory. The Virgin is surrounded by an inscription celebrating Bernward's art and patronage, indicating that he wanted the great works he donated to memorialize him: HOC OPV[S] EXIMIV[M] / BERNVVARDI P[RE]SVLIS ARTE FACTV[M] CERNE D[EV]S MATER ET ALMA TVA (Behold, God and thy gracious Mother, this prominent work, created through the art of Bishop Bernward).

His donation of this gospel book to the Benedictine abbey of St. Michael in Hildesheim is commemorated again inside, on folio 16 verso (see Introduction, fig. 10): "This small book of the Gospels, with a devoted mind / the admirer of Virginity hands over to you, Holy Mary, / Bishop Bernward, only scarcely worthy of this name, / and of the adornment of such great episcopal investment." A portrait of Bernward adorns this page, and above the arch over his head is inscribed: "He presents [it], Christ, to you and to your holy mother."

C.T.L.

SELECTED REFERENCES: *Bernward von Hildesheim und das Zeitalter der Ottonen*, 1993, vol. 2, pp. 570–78, no. VIII-30 (Michael Brandt and Ulrich Kuder); *Das Kostbare Evangeliar des Heiligen Bernward*, 1993; *Glory of Byzantium*, 1997, pp. 466–68, no. 305 (Charles T. Little); Brandt, "Bernward und Byzanz," 2008; Brandt, "Bernward d'Hildesheim et ses trésors," 2010.

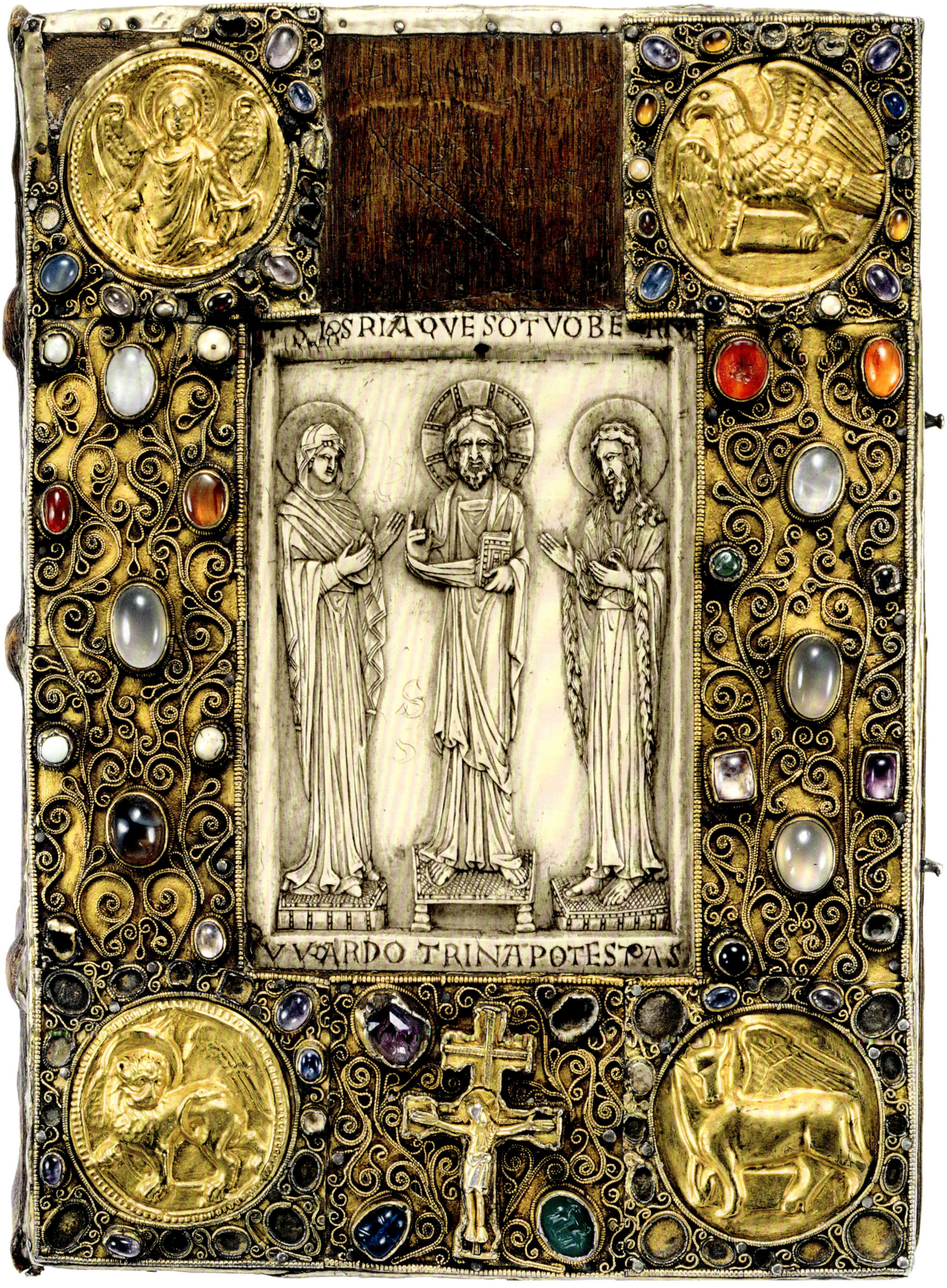
VVARDO TRINAPOTESTAS

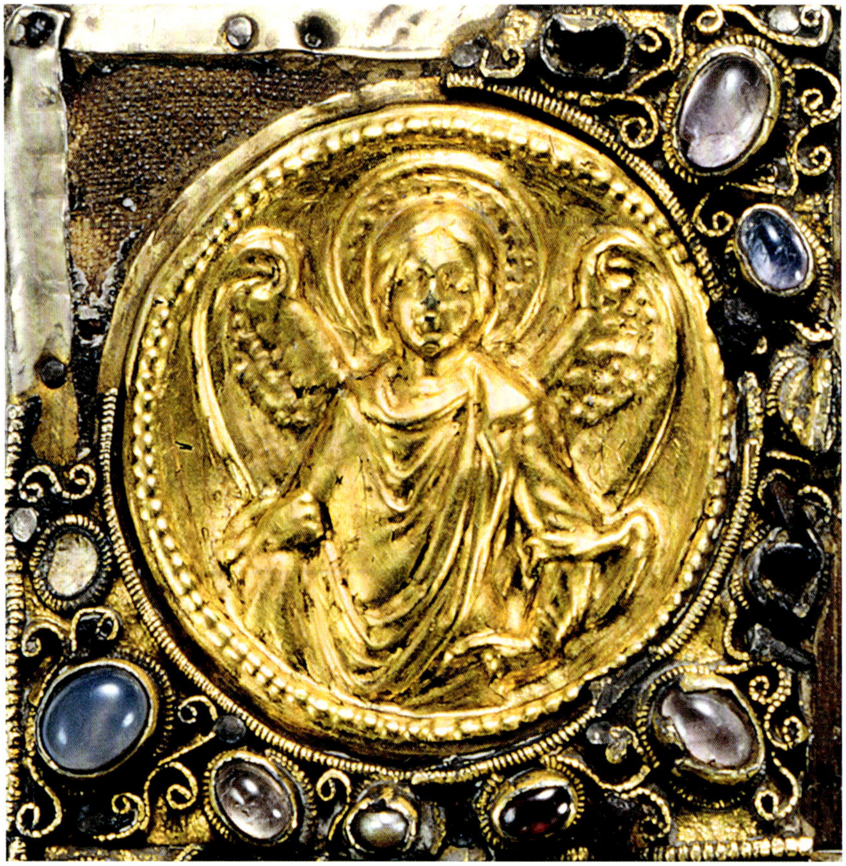

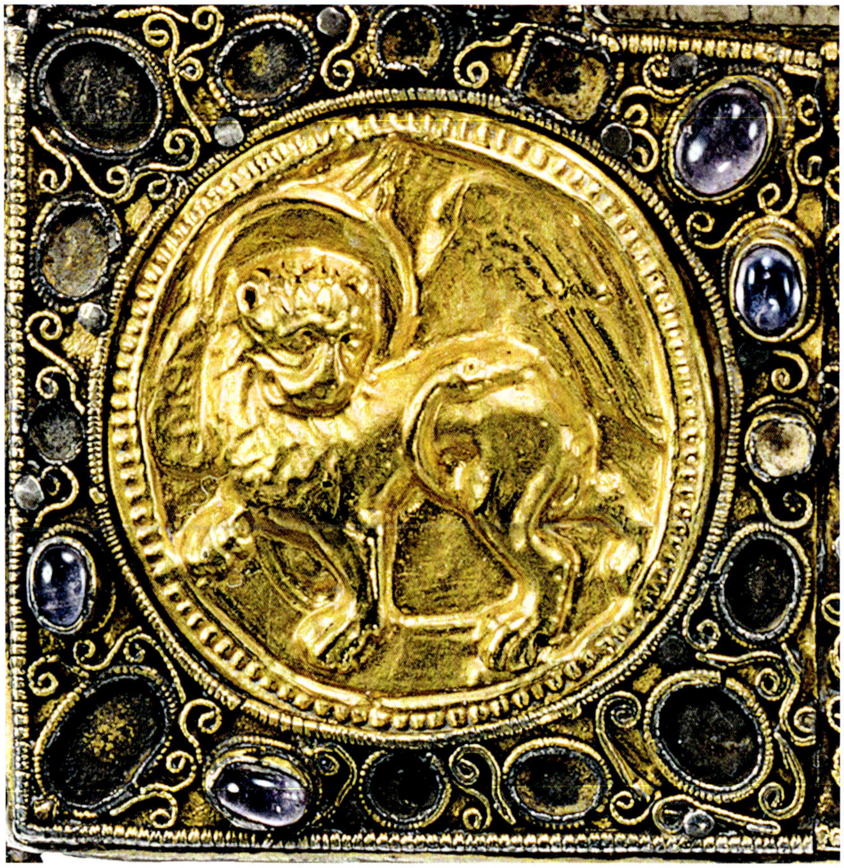

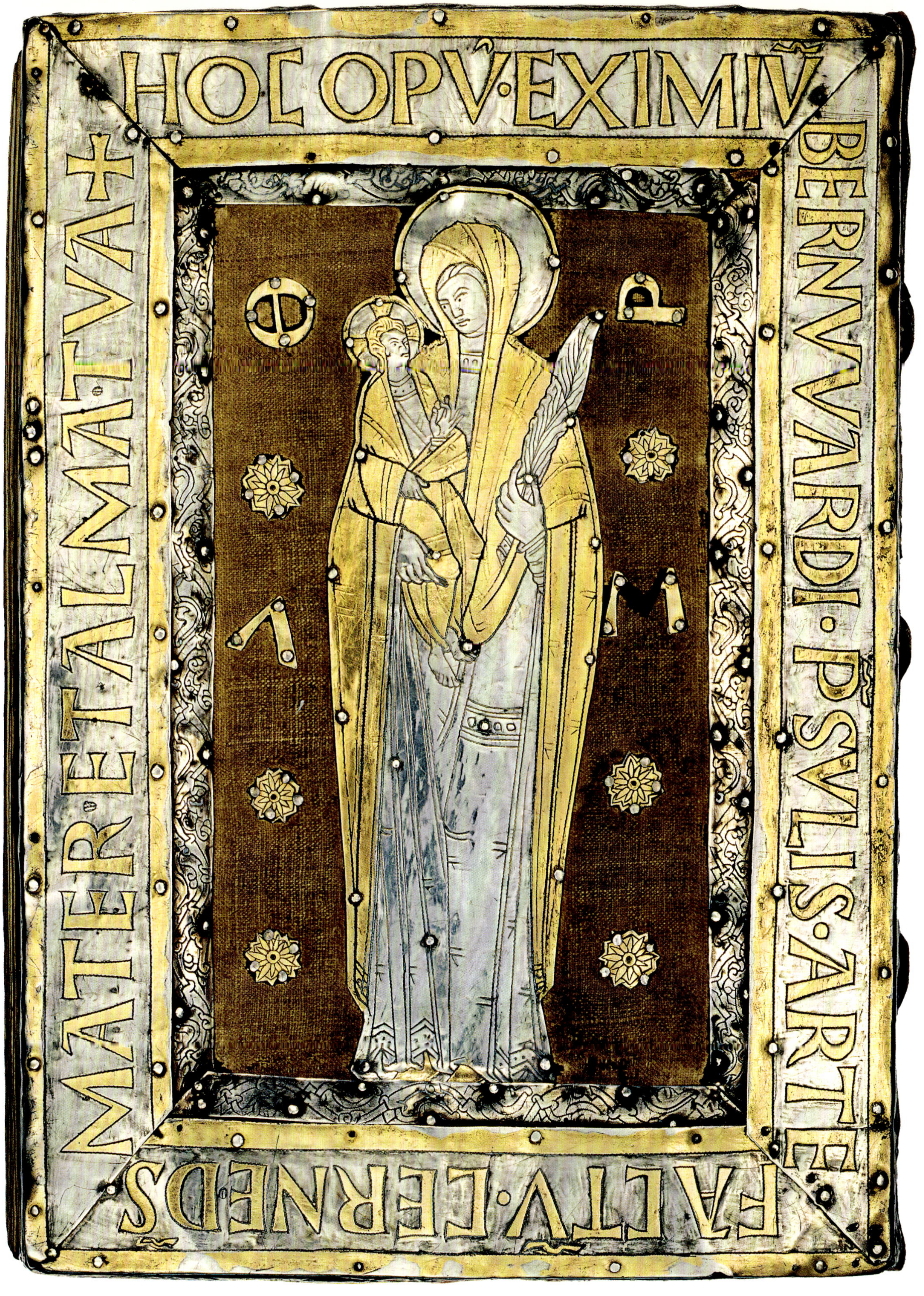
HOC OPV·EXIMIV
BERNVVARDI·PSVLIS·ARTE
FACTV·CERNEDS
MATER·ET·ALMA·TVA+

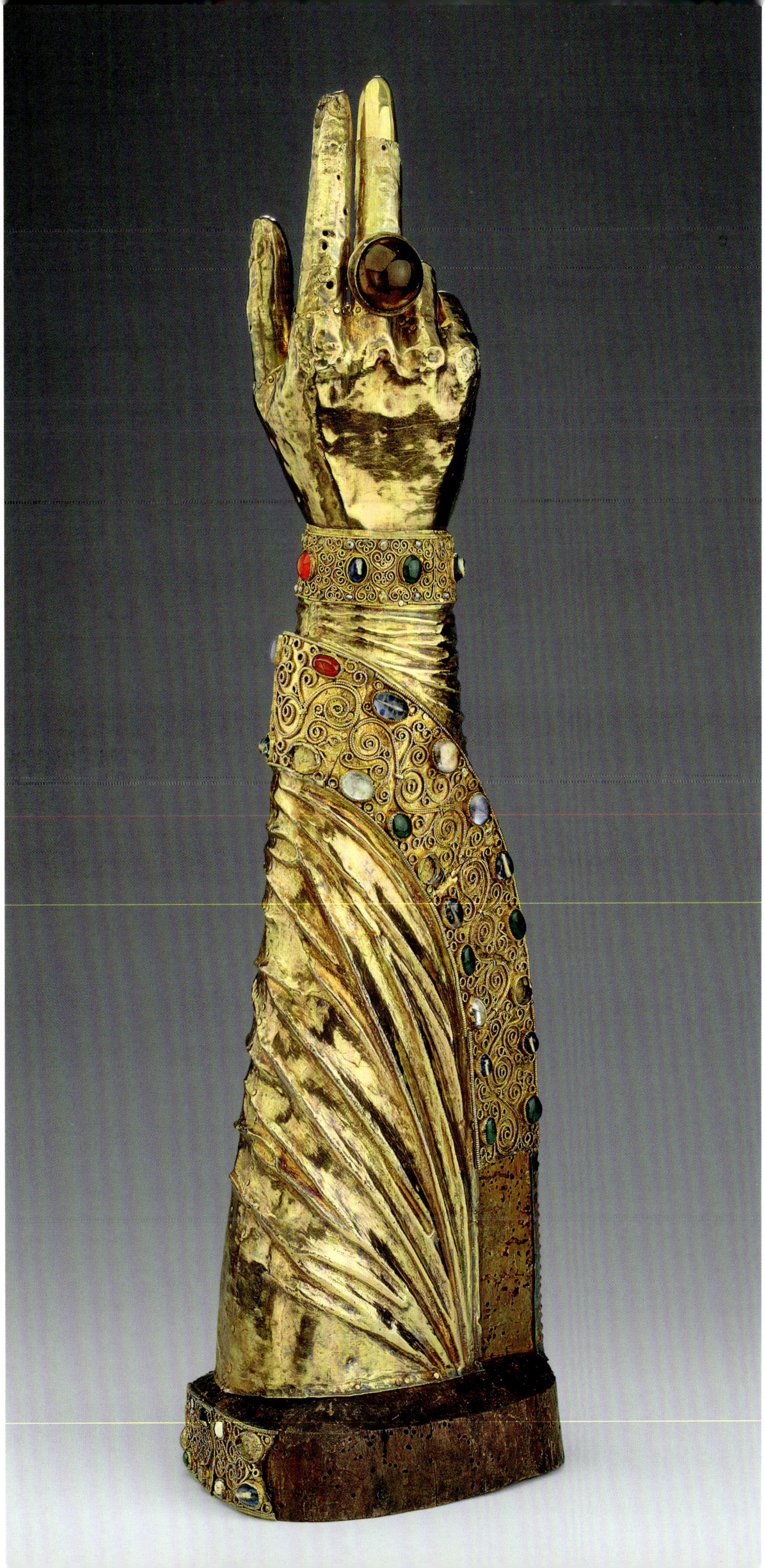

33 · Arm Reliquary of Saint Bernward

German (Hildesheim), ca. 1194
Silver, gilded silver, rock crystal, and semiprecious stones; wood core
Overall 21 ½ × 6 ⅛ × 4 ⅝ in. (54.5 × 15.5 × 11.6 cm)
Dom-Museum Hildesheim, on loan from the church of St. Magdalen, Hildesheim (L 1978-2)

This arm reliquary came from the treasury of the church of St. Michael and, though it no longer contains any relics, can be presumed to be one of the five arm reliquaries from the church described in an inventory prepared by city officials in 1542, after the Reformation. It can further be inferred to represent the arm of Saint Bernward. As an evocation of the canonized bishop of Hildesheim, this reliquary aptly represents the saint with his right hand raised in blessing; fittingly, the hand bears a ring, an episcopal attribute. The ring is one of three that once graced the finger; all may have been gifts added later.

Technically the workmanship – above all the distinctive scrolling pattern of the filigree that decorates the edge of the sleeve and the cuff – is very close to that of a head reliquary of Saint Bernward (Dom-Museum Hildesheim, DS 10). Both pieces are thought to have been created after the translation of Saint Bernward's relics in 1194; across Europe, unearthing a local saint's relics was frequently associated with commissioning a suite of reliquaries to honor the community's patron.

The construction of this arm reliquary is typical of examples across Europe up to the thirteenth century, with precious metal sheets laid over a wood core, partly visible today due to losses. Of particular elegance are the gemstones, carefully paired for color and size and set at regular intervals along the sleeve band and cuff. Burn marks visible in photos of the wood core of the saint's index finger and the metal patch on the third finger are among the sure indications that repairs have been made to the hand's metal sheathing.

B.D.B.

SELECTED REFERENCES: *Schatzkammer auf Zeit*, 1991, pp. 138–40, no. 39 (Michael Brandt); *Bernward von Hildesheim und das Zeitalter der Ottonen*, 1993, vol. 2, p. 624, no. IX-22 (Michael Brandt); *Abglanz des Himmels*, 2001, p. 187, no. 4.16 (Michael Brandt).

34 · Reliquary in the Form of a Ball

German (Hildesheim), ca. 1160–80
Painted maple
H. 6 ½ in. (16.3 cm); Diam. 6 in. (15.1 cm)
Dom-Museum Hildesheim (136)

This unusual object may be the only existing reliquary in the form of a ball. The lid construction is also highly uncommon and perhaps unprecedented: Tabs in the lid slot into the base, as on a modern-day teapot, so that the lid will not fall out once the tab is rotated into place.

Christ appears on the lid in the company of seven saints. With the exception of the Virgin Mary, who appears to be the figure at Christ's right, the bust-length images are largely unidentifiable now. Among them are men, women with veiled heads, and a charming knight with helmet and mail; it may be that they all represent saints whose relics were stored inside.

The lower half of the reliquary shows a repeating pattern of red rosettes inscribed in circles against a black ground, with highlights of blue green. The design, which the scholarly literature links to decoration in contemporary manuscripts, also calls to mind the fields of quatrefoils inscribed in circles often found on twelfth-century Limoges enamels. On both this reliquary and the enamels, the design is likely meant to mimic the patterns of luxury silks. By contrast, the spare bust-length images, rendered in black, approximate the understated effect of niello.

This reliquary may be the one that was found in the high altar of Hildesheim Cathedral in 1833, which had a similar shape, notwithstanding the summary description of the latter as depicting twelve apostles rather than Christ with seven varied saints. In the nineteenth century the reliquary was in the possession of Hildesheim's bishop Eduard J. Wedekin (reigned 1850–70), who bequeathed his valuable art collection to the cathedral chapter.

B.D.B.

SELECTED REFERENCES: *Kirchenkunst des Mittelalters*, 1989, pp. 107–18, no. 6b; *Schatzkammer auf Zeit*, 1991, pp. 132–34, no. 36 (Michael Brandt); *Abglanz des Himmels*, 2001, p. 185, no. 4.10 (Michael Brandt), illus. p. 158.

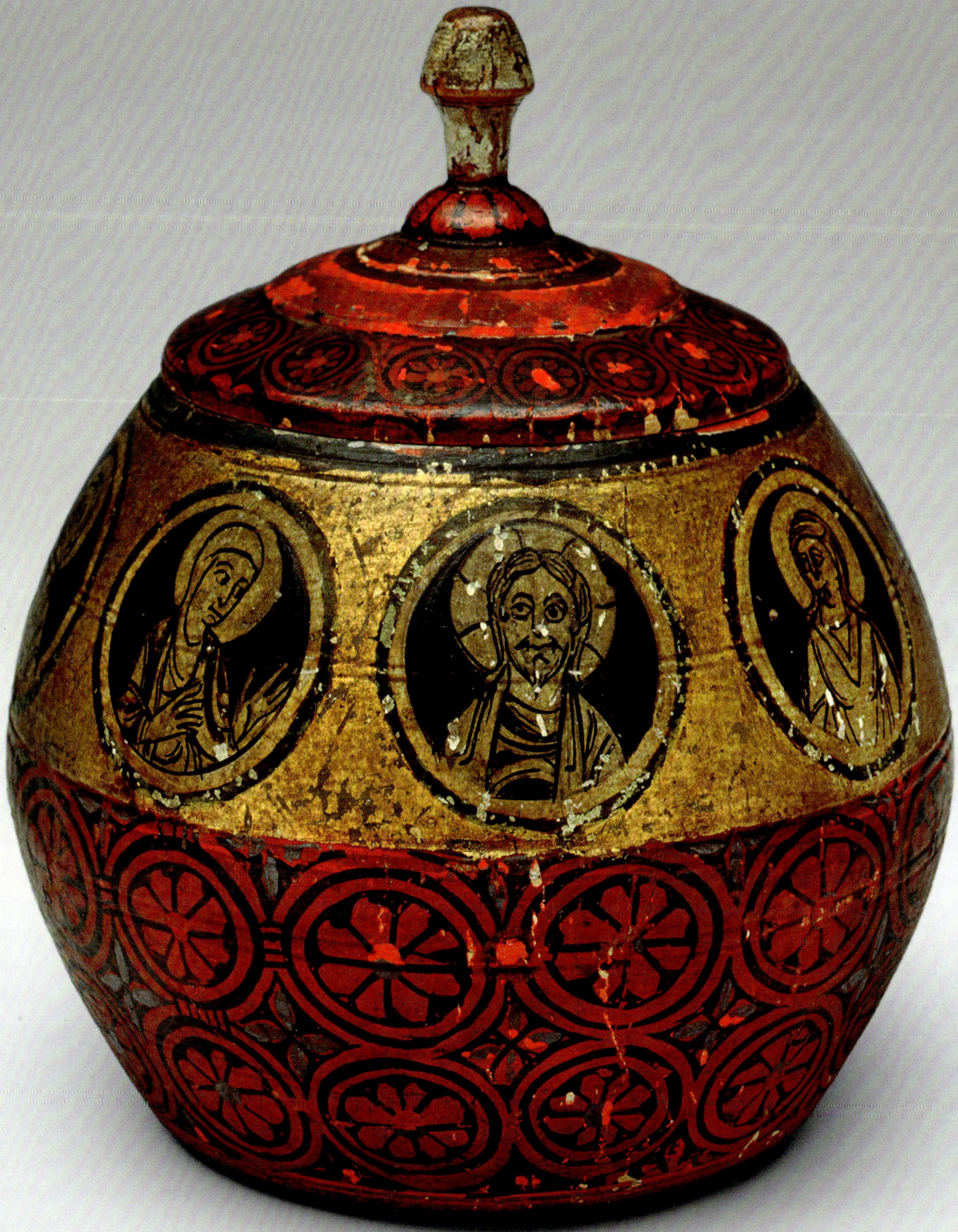

35 · Beaker (so-called Beaker of Saint Godehard)

German (Hildesheim), late 12th century
Root wood; cast silver, wrought, engraved, and stamped
H. 5 ⅜ in. (13.5 cm); Diam. 4 ¾ in. (12 cm)
Basilika St. Godehard, Hildesheim

This beaker was made for ablution; it was used to rinse out the mouth with wine after receiving communion. The inner lid depicts the blessing hand of God at the center, and the gilded image of Christ is juxtaposed opposite, on the bottom of the bowl. The outer lid carries another bust in its central circular field (opposite, below) – a figure with a book in his left hand but no further attributes for a clear identification. The beaker is covered with silver strips with foliate and tendril ornamentation, four on the lid and eight on the more richly decorated bowl. The lid and bowl are separated by a silver band with geometric ornament that is overlaid by engraved blossoms; those features were later additions.

There are no medieval texts mentioning the beaker, which is one of the few surviving medieval objects from the treasury of St. Godehard's Abbey. It was probably made during the tenure of Abbot Thidericus (1181–89), who also commissioned a portable altar today in the British Museum, London (1902, 6-25,1). The beaker was venerated as a relic of Saint Godehard (960–1038) since at least the early sixteenth century; the object is mentioned in a register of revenues and expenses for the year 1506 in the context of a restoration. The engraved silver band and blossoms date to that restoration campaign. About 1750 a new base and inner bowl of silver were added by the Hildesheim goldsmith Ernst Heinrich Meyer (ca. 1700–1774), retaining the original central image of Christ.

The attribution to Saint Godehard exemplifies a broad late medieval movement erroneously associating younger objects with the church's principal saints, as were the so-called Bernhard Chalice and Paten (cat. 42) and the paten of Bishop Gerhard vom Berge (cat. 47). In Saint Godehard's case, that was because his body was placed in a new shrine at Hildesheim Cathedral rather than moved to the monastery that Bishop Bernhard founded in Godehard's honor after his canonization in 1131. Thus the monks had to rely on objects ostensibly related to Godehard to attract attention to him from pilgrims and donors and to intensify his veneration. The legendary attribution of this beaker to Saint Godehard possibly explains why the Jesuit monk Johannes Dirking reported in 1674 that the beaker was used for ablution after communion was served to worshippers during the Feast of Saint Godehard and to pregnant women during complicated childbirths. (Godehard was traditionally invoked against birth pains and other ills.)

Stylistic comparisons suggest an origin in a Hildesheim workshop. The form of the twined leaves is characteristic of late twelfth-century Hildesheim works such as the choir screen at St. Michael's Church from about 1193 (see Introduction, fig. 7) and the arm reliquary of Saint Lawrence from the Guelph Treasure of Braunschweig Cathedral (Kunstgewerbemuseum, Berlin, W23).

G.L.

SELECTED REFERENCES: *Der Schatz von St. Godehard*, 1988, pp. 94–97, no. 31 (Michael Brandt); *Abglanz des Himmels*, 2001, p. 193, no. 4.31 (Michael Brandt).

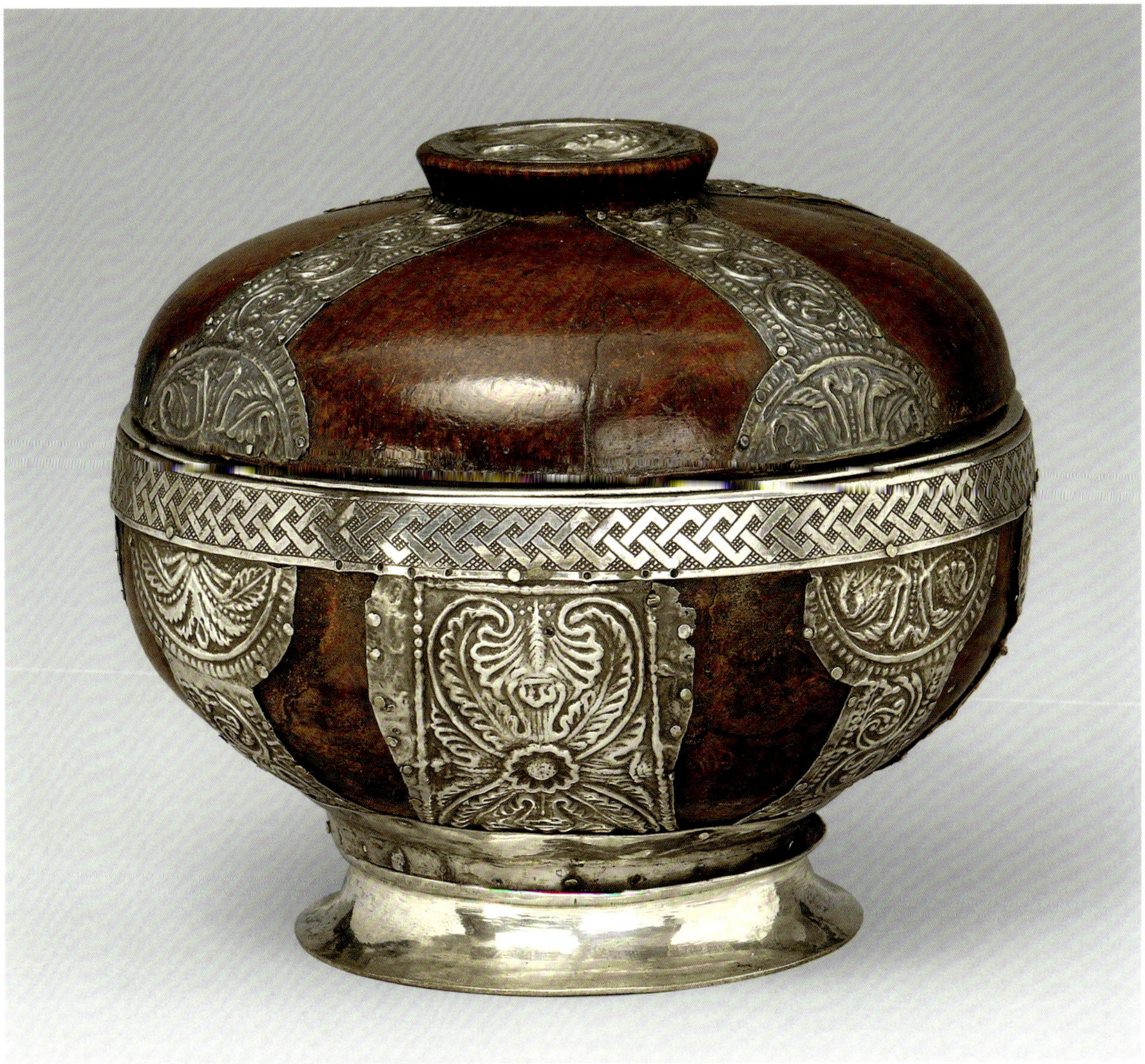

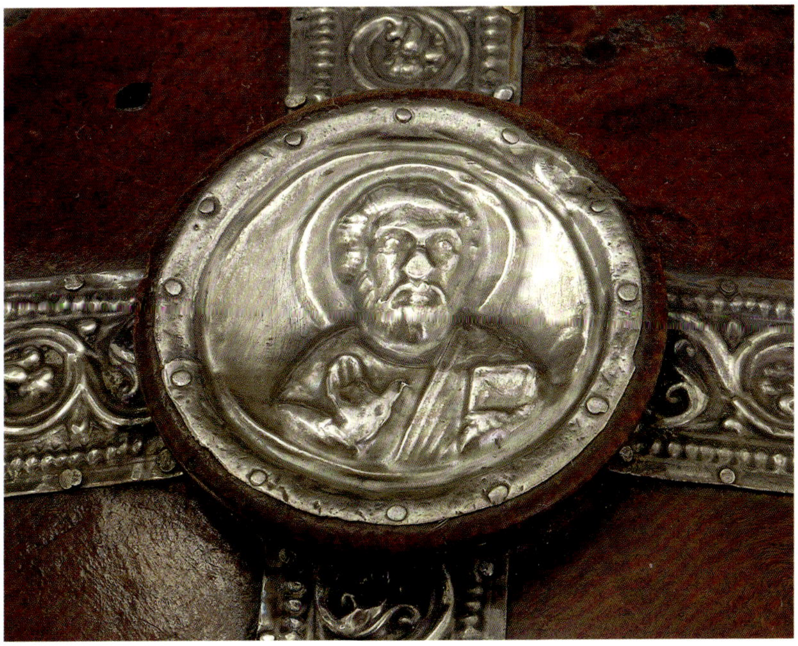

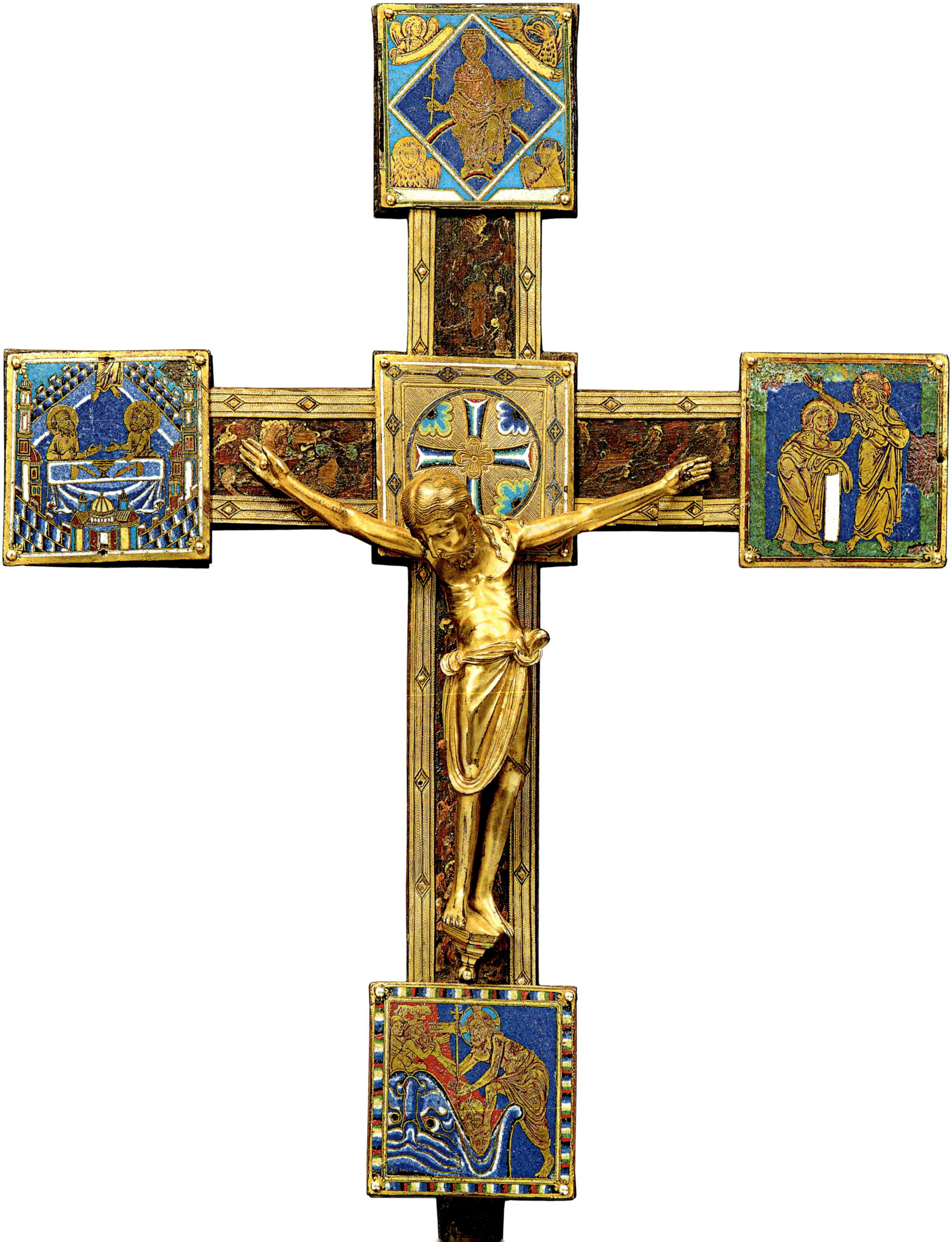

36 · Cross

German (Lower Saxony, Hildesheim[?]), ca. 1190–1200
Copper alloy, gilding, champlevé enamel, and marble; wood core
22 ¼ × 14 ¾ × 1 ⅛ in. (56.4 × 37.5 × 2.7 cm) with tang
Basilika St. Godehard, Hildesheim

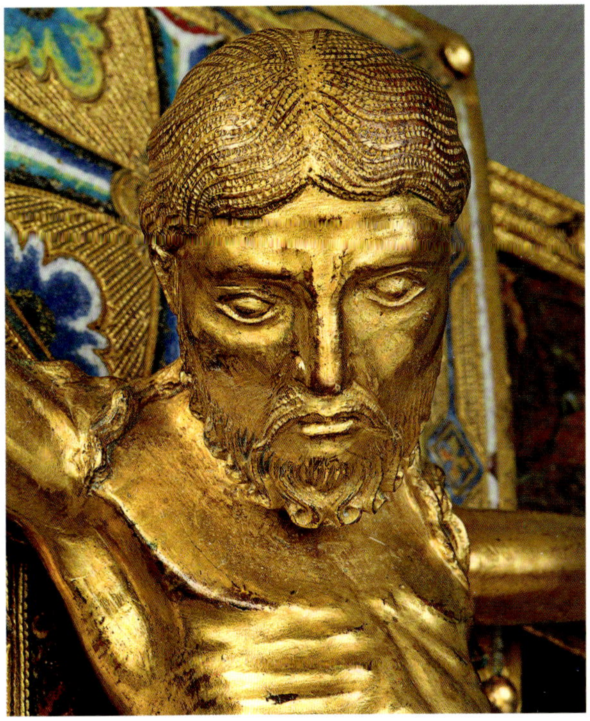

As this processional cross appears today, a gilded copper figure of Christ hangs limply from a cross that is colorfully adorned with marble facing and champlevé enamels. The enamel plaque at center serves as his cruciform nimbus. The enamels at the sides and bottom of the cross display scenes from after his death: his descent into Hell; his appearance to a doubtful Thomas after his resurrection; and the moment in which his companions at the table in Emmaus recognize him as their risen leader. At the top of the cross appears an unusual image of Ecclesia, the personified Church, on the Throne of Heaven, surrounded by symbols of the Four Evangelists. Plates of gilded copper worked in *vernis brun* adorn the cross's reverse side.

A thorough technical examination conducted in the early 1990s revealed that the cross at some unknown point had been cut down, reworked, and rearranged. The sculpted figure of Christ was covered with gilding, and multihued enamels were added to the central plaque that frames his head. It would seem that, in the original configuration, a simple bronze corpus, without gilding, and the halo plaque, ornamented exclusively with *vernis brun* technique, were affixed to what is now the back of the cross. The four other enamel plaques were always featured on the side they now occupy, but in a different arrangement, with the Ecclesia plaque at center, the Emmaus meal at top, and a now-lost plaque situated at left. The Hell and Thomas scenes were at the bottom and right, respectively, as today.

The original object created at the end of the twelfth century was thus a double-sided demonstration of the varied aesthetic effects at which metalworkers of Lower Saxony excelled. The original front of the cross emphasized copper's tonal qualities. The *vernis brun* plaques deal in patterns of dark and light, and matte and reflective, surfaces. The corpus would have achieved similar tonal effects through the volumes of the figure, the recessed folds of his garment, and the striations of his hair. The other side, by contrast, emphasized bright color, forceful line, and vivid storytelling. In the cross's earlier appearance, the scenes and compositions of the enamel plaques were cleverly attuned to their placement. The bilateral symmetry of the Ecclesia plaque made it well suited for its central position. Likewise, the figure ascending in the Emmaus plaque and the deep cavity on the Descent into Hell played off the upward and downward thrusts of the cross's shaft.

Even in its new incarnation, the entire cross retains a programmatic emphasis on Christ's death and resurrection, suggesting that both before and after its dramatic alterations it held special resonance during the Easter season. It has long belonged to the treasury of the former Benedictine monastery of St. Godehard in Hildesheim.

M.H.

SELECTED REFERENCES: Brandt, "Ein Hildesheimer Vortragekreuz," 1994; *Abglanz des Himmels*, 2001, pp. 191–92, no. 4.27 (Michael Brandt).

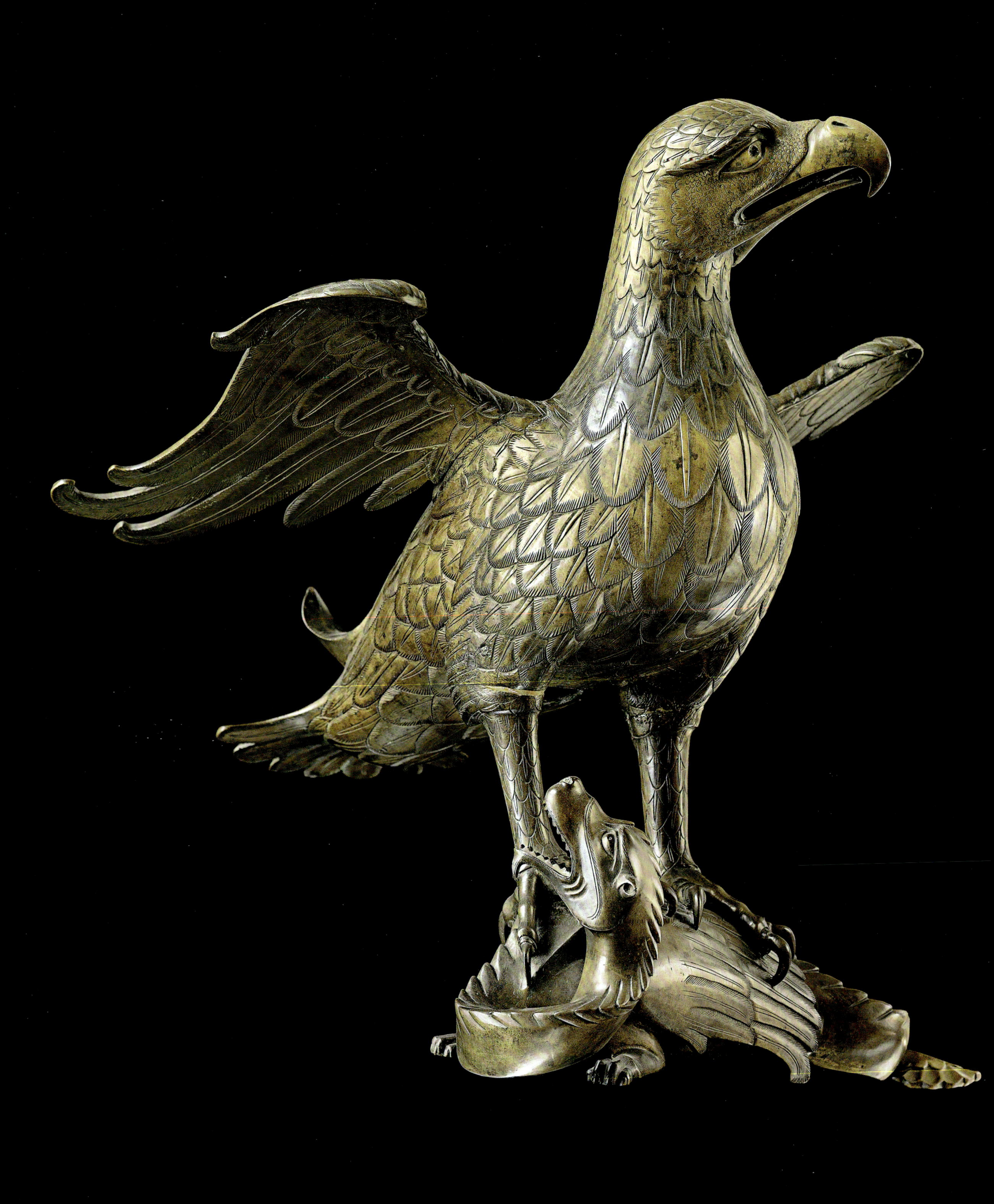

37 · Eagle Lectern

German (Hildesheim), ca. 1220
Copper alloy
Overall 22 5/8 × 19 1/8 × 26 7/8 in. (57.5 × 48.5 × 68 cm)
Dom-Museum Hildesheim (D 1984-2)

This finely cast lectern in the form of an eagle with outstretched wings grasping a dragon in its talons is a rare survivor among such medieval church furnishings. It was designed to support an open gospel book for readings during church services and likely would have risen on a support high above the floor. Prior to 1943 the eagle was incorporated into a Renaissance lectern of 1546 in Hildesheim Cathedral. Two large pins protrude from the flat underside of the dragon, but the medieval form of the support for the lectern is unknown. The only evidence of what such a monument might have looked like at the time is the famous thirteenth-century drawing of a lectern by Villard de Honnecourt (Bibliothèque Nationale de France, Paris, MS Fr 19093, fol. 7r).

Villard inscribed his drawing with the following statement: "He who wishes to make a lectern from which to read the Gospel, behold the best manner of making it. First there are three serpents which rest on the ground and over them a three-lobed slab, and above that three serpents of a different kind and columns of the same height as the serpents, and over that a triangular slab. After this, you can see for yourself in what manner the lectern is made. Here is its image. In the midst of the three columns there must be a rod to carry the knob on which the eagle sits." Villard's lectern shows seated figures, presumably Evangelists, writing below the eagle, and standing figures censing midway between the dragon feet and the eagle. As the sole examples of this form, the lost lectern Villard describes (presumably cast in metal, although Villard does not specify) and the Hildesheim lectern can be seen as precursors of numerous surviving Netherlandish lecterns from the late Middle Ages.

Villard's lectern was most likely northern French or Mosan, but the details of the Hildesheim piece compare closely with details of other works cast in Lower Saxony. For example, the engraved pattern of the eagle's feathers is similar to that on the outstretched wings of the Evangelist symbols on the baptismal font (cat. 38) from Hildesheim.

P.B.

SELECTED REFERENCES: *Bild und Bestie*, 2008, pp. 384–87, no. 54 (Michael Brandt); *Schätze des Glaubens*, 2010, pp. 98–99, no. 43 (Michael Brandt).

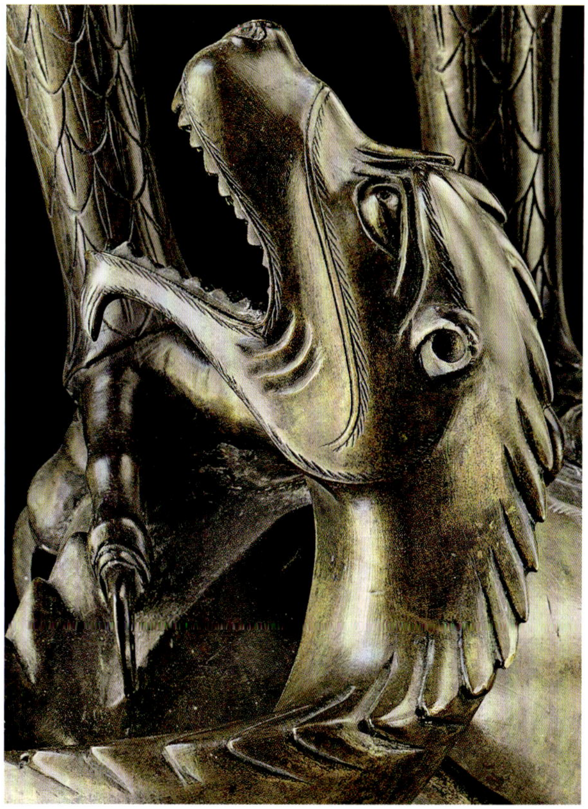

38 · Baptismal Font

German (Hildesheim), ca. 1226
Copper alloy, cast in eight pieces
Overall H. ca. 72⅞ in. (185 cm); BASIN: *H. 26⅜ in. (67 cm); Diam. 37¾ in. (95.9 cm) excluding hinges;*
LID: *H. 16⅛ in. (41 cm);* FINIAL: *H. 12⅝ in. (32 cm);* SUPPORTING FIGURES: *H. 18½ in. to 19¾ in. (47 cm to 50 cm)*
Hohe Domkirche Hildesheim

Hildesheim Cathedral's baptismal font is among the most accomplished and iconographically complex works cast in copper alloy to survive from the High Middle Ages, along with such monuments as the early twelfth-century font by Rainer of Huy in the church of St. Bartholomew, Liège, and the seven-branched candelabrum of about 1200 in Milan Cathedral (the so-called Trivulzio Candlestick). Northern Germany was known from an early date for its sophisticated metalwork, with production reaching a high point about the year 1000, under the patronage of Hildesheim's Bishop Bernward. Shortly after 1200 the city reemerged as a center for the casting of monumental works in copper alloy, exemplified by this richly decorated font.

The font is supported on the backs of four freestanding kneeling male figures representing the Rivers of Paradise, each with a downturned jug issuing a stream of water (see p. 106). The outside of the font is decorated with four scenes cast in relief, each set beneath a trefoil arch. The kneeling rivers below mark the divisions between these scenes: The Baptism of Christ (opposite) is flanked by the Parting of the Red Sea and the Ark Crossing the Jordan River, episodes from the Old Testament that were understood as prefigurations of the Baptism of Christ. Opposite the Baptism of Christ, the Virgin and Child are enthroned between the standing figures of Saints Epiphanius and Godehard, patrons of the cathedral. The kneeling donor on the Virgin's right is identified in an inscription as Wilbernus. Directly above each of the rivers, dividing the major scenes, is a half-length bust of one of the Cardinal Virtues, which in turn supports a twisted colonnette. Above each of the colonnettes is a Hebrew prophet within a roundel. Each of the prophets is surmounted by one of the four Evangelist symbols.

The conical lid of the font has four more major scenes in relief: Mary Magdalen, the repentant sinner, washing the feet of Christ; the personification of Charity (Misericordia) dispensing food and drink (see p. 107); Aaron and Moses flanking the flowering rod; and the Massacre of the Innocents. Those scenes, too, are separated by twisted colonnettes, and four figures from the Old Testament surmount the colonnettes – two more prophets and two kings. The font and its lid bear numerous Latin inscriptions. The prophets hold scrolls bearing quotations heralding the scenes, and the Evangelist symbols bear quotations underscoring the centrality of the sacrament of baptism. Lengthy inscriptions circumscribe the top and bottom rims of the basin and the rim of the lid. The lid is surmounted by a large foliate finial, which was cast separately.

The donor, Wilbernus – possibly the designer of the font's sophisticated program – is Wilbrandus of Oldenburg-Wildeshausen, who was dean at Hildesheim Cathedral in 1219–25. He is depicted kneeling at the feet of the Virgin wearing an alb and dalmatic; his liturgical vestments suggest that the font was created after he became bishop of Paderborn in 1226. An inscription on a simpler baptismal font in Osnabrück (where he was archdeacon in 1226–27), which was likely cast in the same workshop as the Hildesheim example, reveals that Wilbernus was its donor, too.

P.B.

SELECTED REFERENCES: *Bild und Bestie*, 2008, pp. 284–89, no. 21 (Michael Brandt); Höhl, *Das Taufbecken des Wilbernus*, 2009; *Schätze des Glaubens*, 2010, pp. 100–101, no. 44 (Lothar Lambacher).

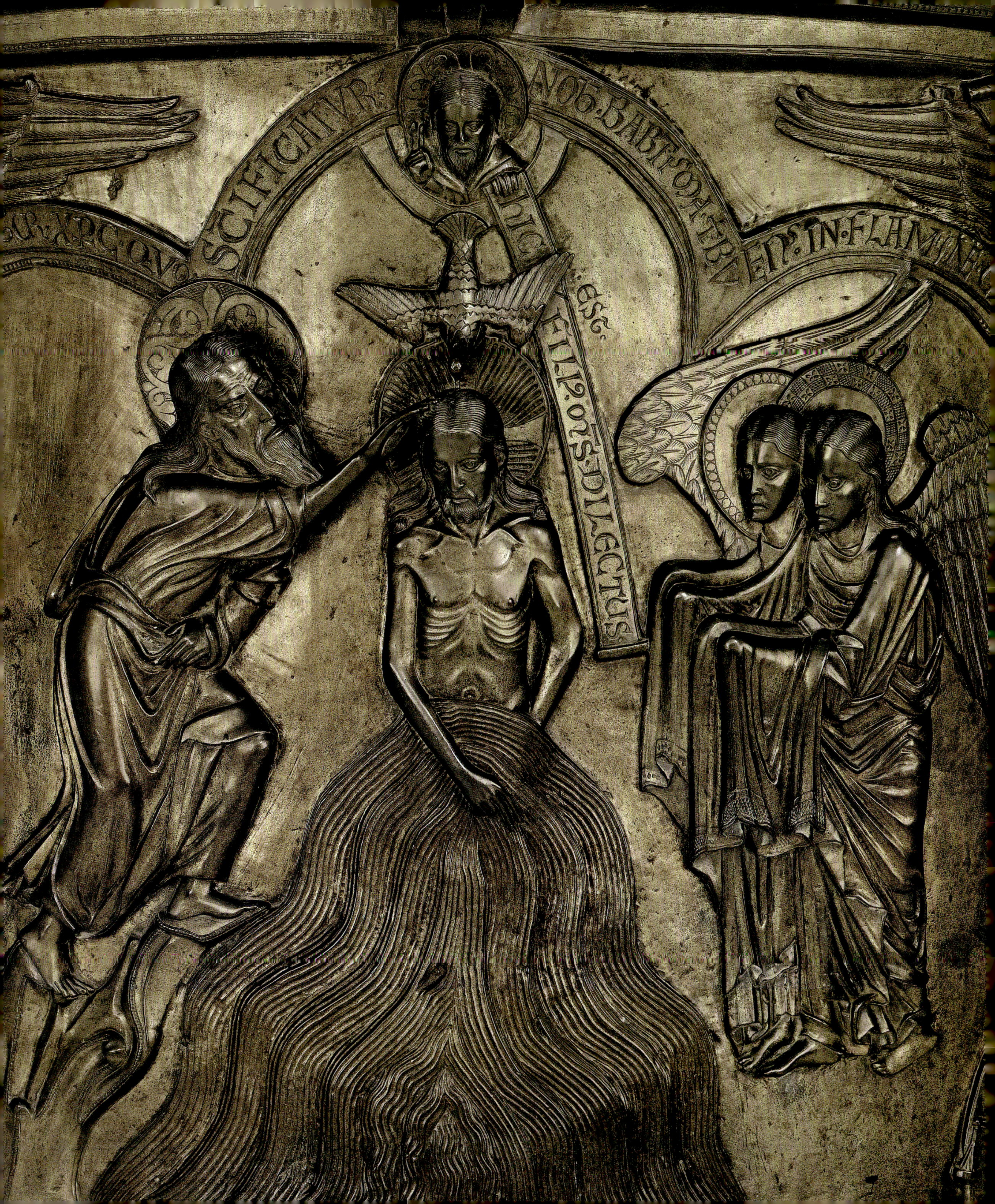

SCIFICATVR
HIC
EST
DILECTVS

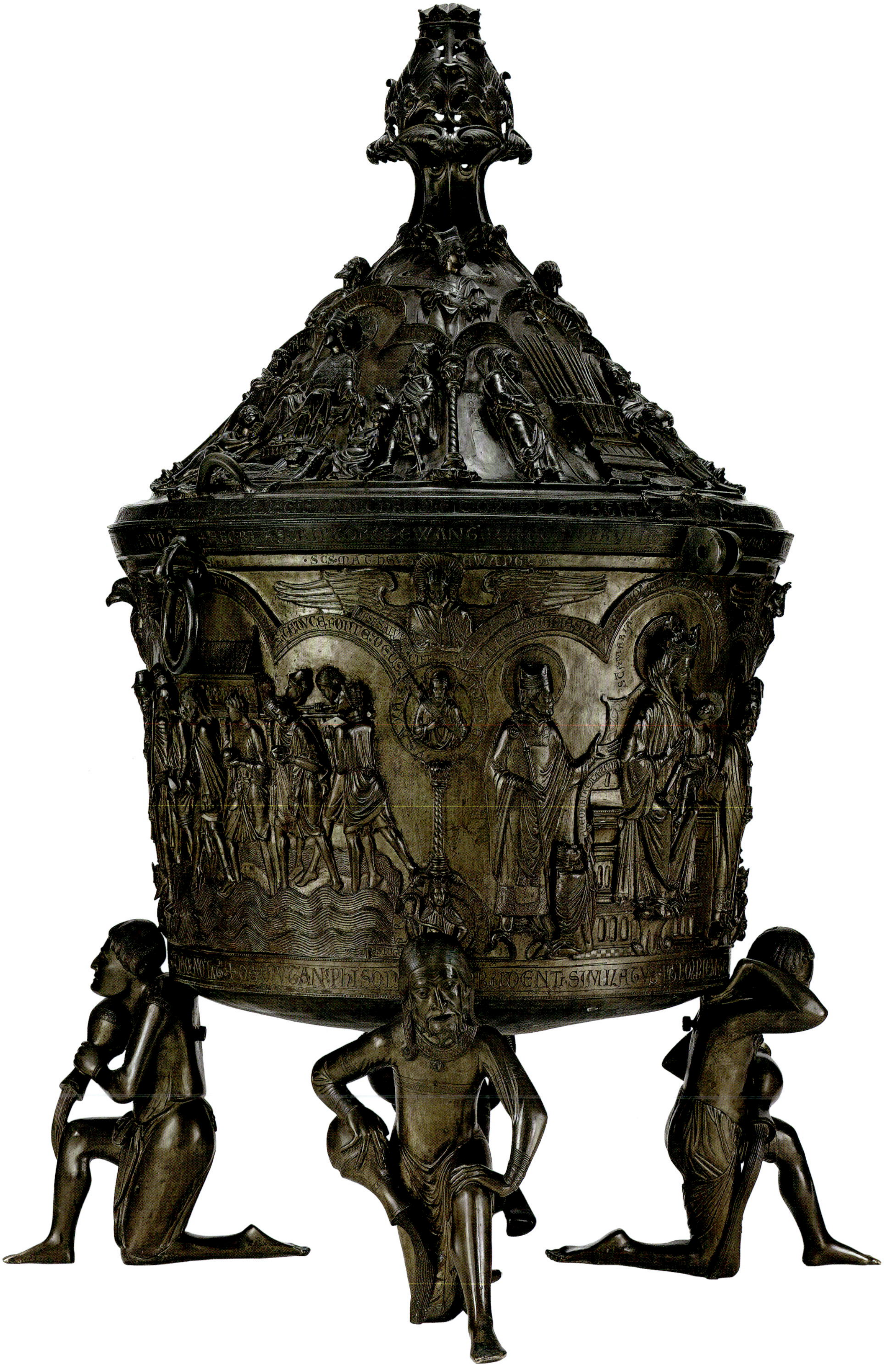

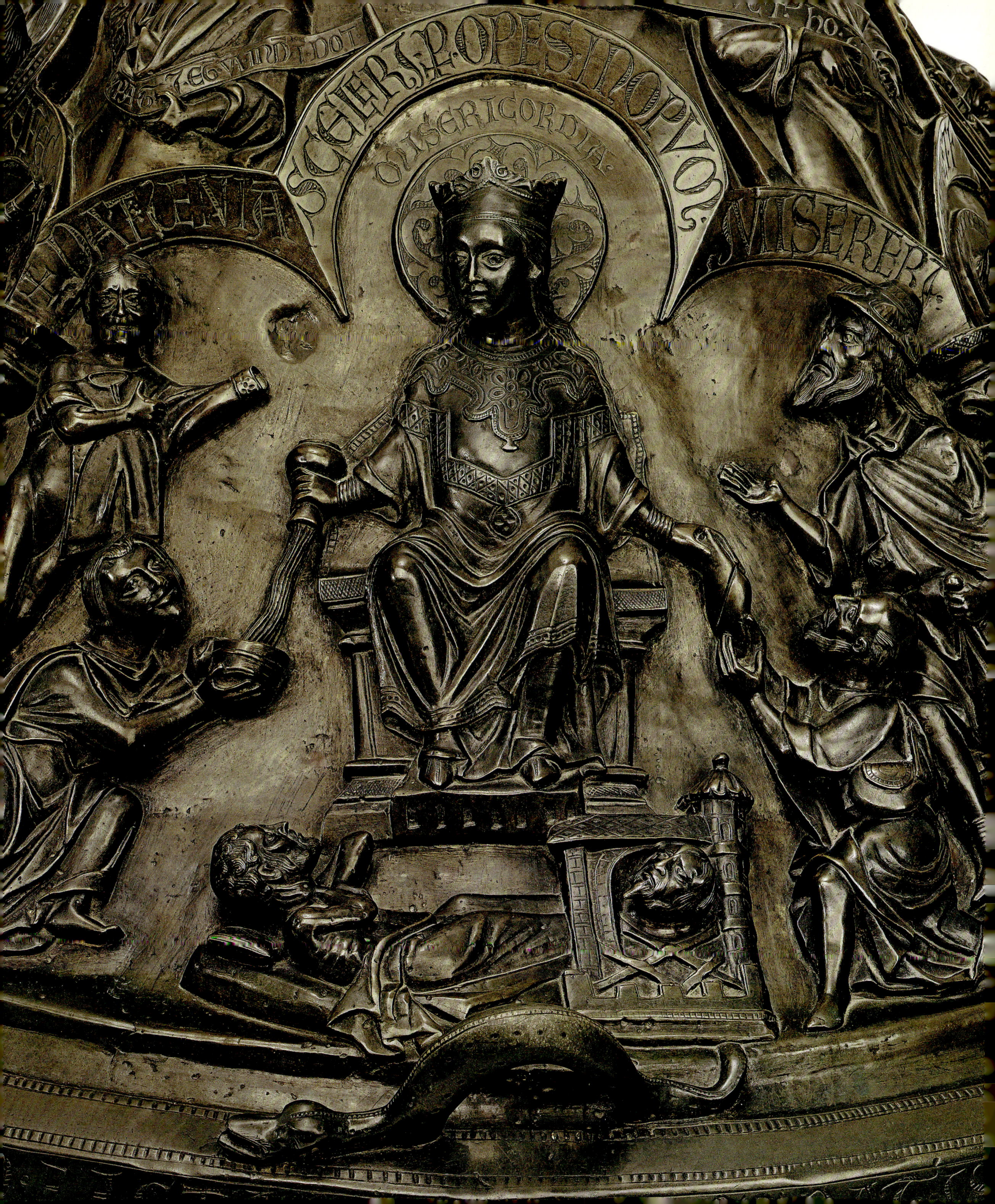
MISERICORDIA

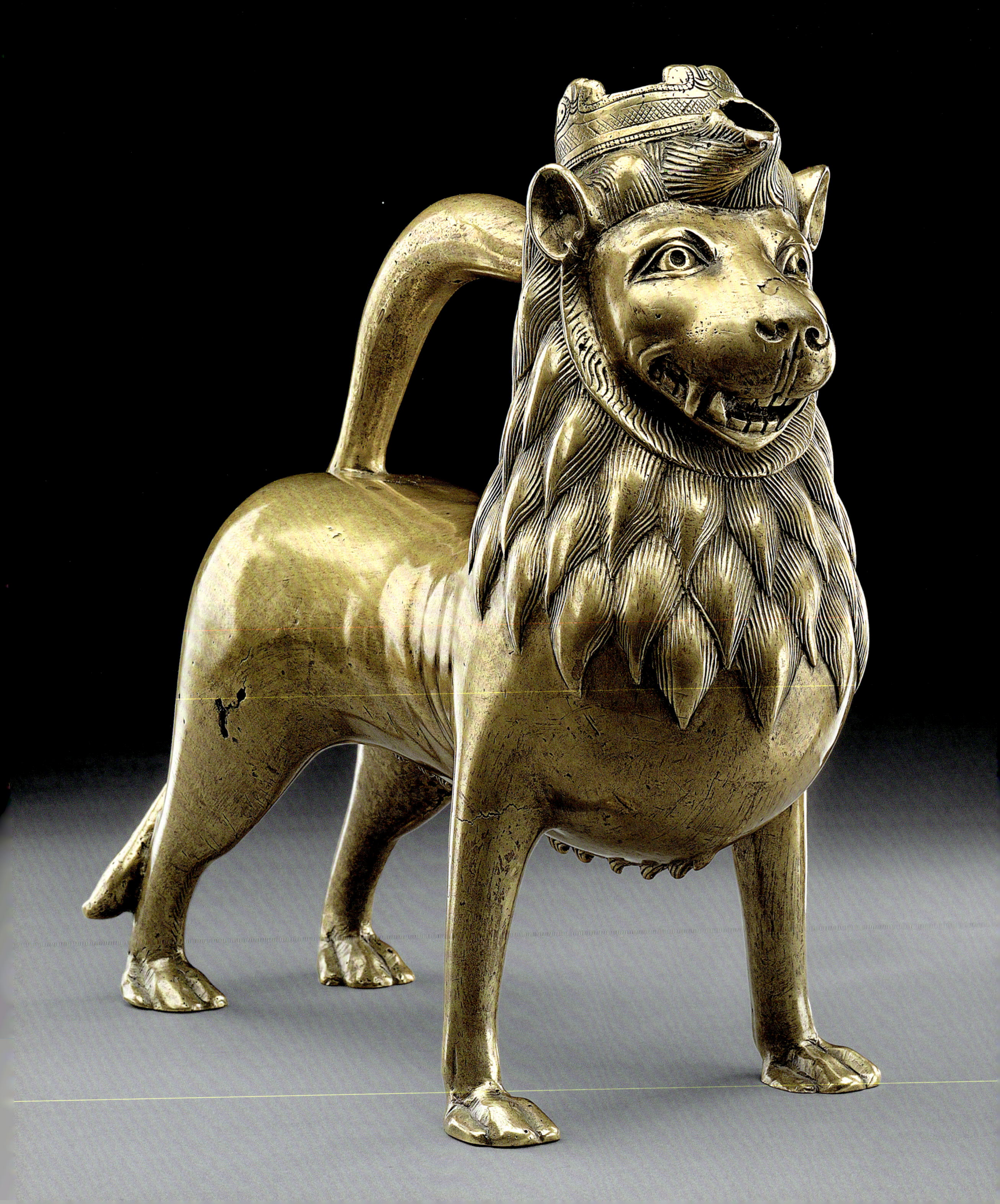

39 · Lion Aquamanile

German (Hildesheim), ca. 1220–30
Copper alloy
Overall 10 5/8 × 11 × 5 3/8 in. (27 × 28 × 13.5 cm)
Dom-Museum Hildesheim, joint ownership with the Stiftung Niedersachsen and the Ernst von Siemens Kunststiftung (2006-1)

Aquamanilia, from the Latin *aqua* (water) and *manus* (hand), are water vessels used for washing hands, for both liturgical and secular purposes. Aquamanilia in the shape of animals are among the most distinctive products of medieval craftsmen. They were the first hollow-cast vessels in copper alloy made in medieval Europe. The most commonly seen zoomorphic aquamanilia are lions, but dragons, griffins, and many other forms were also produced.

This example is a carefully observed naturalistic sculpture in the round. The energy of the lion is conveyed by his erect stance, with a swelling chest and extended hind legs. The mouth is not wide open to suggest a roar, but the sharp incisor teeth are bared, emphasizing the power of the beast. The mane is carefully articulated with a rich pattern of cast-in tufts of hair, enhanced by chased decoration. A row of tufts runs along the lion's belly, and his genitals are articulated between the hind legs. The crown is an unusual feature. The vessel was filled through an opening at the top of the head inside the crown, which is covered with a hinged flap. The water was poured though a spout in the forehead disguised as a tuft of hair. The handle takes the form of a serpent, its head behind the crown and its tail just above the lion's own.

The form of the Hildesheim aquamanile, like that of many other portable objects made in Lower Saxony, was inspired by the lion monument erected in Braunschweig's town square in about 1166 to honor Duke Henry the Lion. The lion aquamanile can be closely compared with details of the Hildesheim baptismal font (cat. 38) – for example, both works feature a serpent handle, and the lion's crown is very similar to the crown worn by the personification of Justice on the font – suggesting that it was made in Hildesheim at approximately the same date, possibly by the same workshop. Unlike the other works in this exhibition, the aquamanile entered the collection of the Dom-Museum recently (in 2005) through the art market.

P.B.

SELECTED REFERENCES: *Bild und Bestie*, 2008, pp. 374–77, no. 51 (Ursula Mende); *Schätze des Glaubens*, 2010, p. 102, no. 45 (Gerhard Lutz).

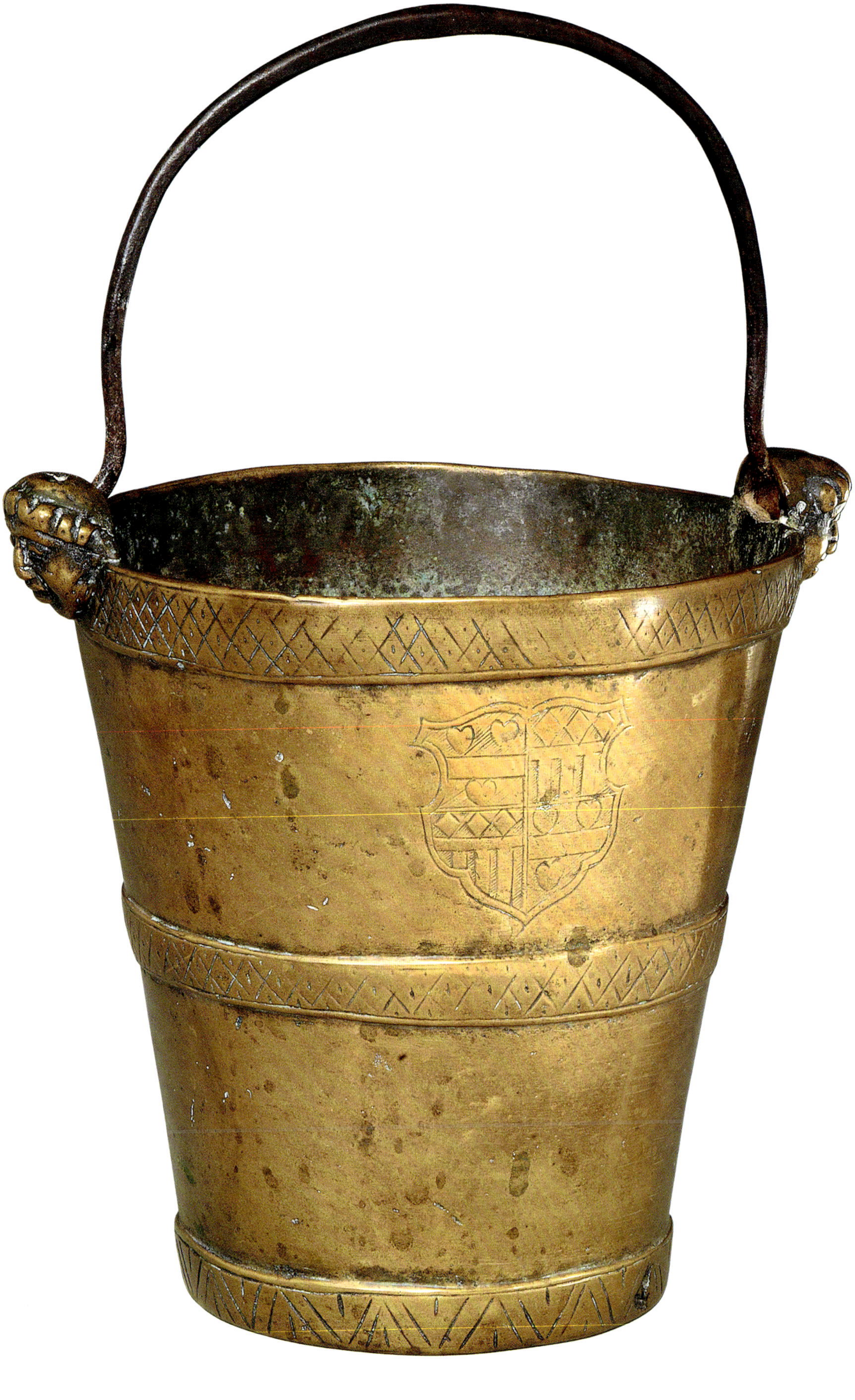

40 · Situla

German (Hildesheim), ca. 1220–30
Copper alloy with iron handle (probably restored)
H. without handle 7 in. *(17.7 cm)*; Diam. *(upper edge)* 6 ¼ in. *(15.7 cm)*
Dom-Museum Hildesheim, on loan from the parish church of St. Michael, Seesen-Bilderlahe (DEP 2005-3)

The situla served as a vessel for holy water. During Mass an aspergillum (a handled instrument) would be dipped into the vessel, and the water would be sprinkled on the congregation. Such vessels have a long history in the liturgy, but examples cast in copper alloy like this one are rare; fewer than twenty-five have survived from the period before about 1250. Most of them are conical, like the Hildesheim example, while a few are octagonal in shape. Like this one, several have human masks at the rim, where the handle attaches, and many have bands of cross-hatched engraving around the outside. This example is consistent with works cast in Hildesheim and was likely produced there in the same workshops that created aquamanilia, candlesticks, and other furnishings for the local churches. Some of the other surviving situlae were probably cast in Cologne.

This situla was until recently in use in the parish church of St. Michael in Seesen-Bilderlahe, in the diocese of Hildesheim, which was built in 1717. The post-medieval engraved coat of arms on the situla has not been identified, but it likely predates the construction of the parish church. When it was made, the situla was not a humble object, as it may now appear; the casting process was sophisticated and costly, and it probably originated in a church of some significance.

P.B.

SELECTED REFERENCES: *Bild und Bestie*, 2008, pp. 276–77, no. 17 (Michael Brandt).

41 · Lion Pricket Candlestick

German (Hildesheim), ca. 1250–75
Copper alloy
Overall 14 7/8 × 8 1/4 × 8 3/4 in. (37.8 × 20.8 × 22 cm);
H. without pricket 8 7/8 in. (22.4 cm)
Dom-Museum Hildesheim (DS 89)

This portable candelabrum for three candles in the form of a lion is unique, yet it stands firmly in the Lower Saxon tradition of leonine works cast in copper alloy. The great lion monument to Henry the Lion (ca. 1130–1195), duke of Saxony, in Braunschweig, from about 1166 is the seminal work. Its influence can be seen in another monumental work, the seven-branched candlestick of about 1170–80 in the cathedral of Braunschweig, which is nearly sixteen and a half feet (five meters) high and rests on four lion paws. It also can be seen on a smaller scale – for example, in the so-called Samson candlesticks (*Simsonleuchter*) that emerged in the twelfth century. These are pricket candlesticks, not confined to Lower Saxony, in the form of a lion with a human figure on its back. In that type, the pricket for the candle rises from the back of the human figure.

This lion candelabrum compares closely to a group of aquamanilia produced in Hildesheim. Following the Braunschweig monument, the works share features such as the prominent ruff-like collar and the upright rounded ears. An especially similar example to the one here is a lion aquamanile in the Cleveland Museum of Art (1972.167), which shares the facial characteristics as well as the rows of punched dots on the legs. The two must have been cast in the same workshop, and it is tempting to imagine a matched set of objects for an altar consisting of candlesticks, an aquamanile, and perhaps additional objects. The large pricket for the central candle that dominates this work is a modern restoration, and the ring on the underside of the animal is also a later addition, perhaps to allow it to be secured with a chain.

P.B.

SELECTED REFERENCES: Falke and Meyer, *Romanische Leuchter und Gefässe*, 1935, p. 27, fig. 417; Elbern and Reuther, *Der Hildesheimer Domschatz*, 1969, p. 78, no. 89; *Bild und Bestie*, 2008, pp. 264–67, no. 12 (Ursula Mende).

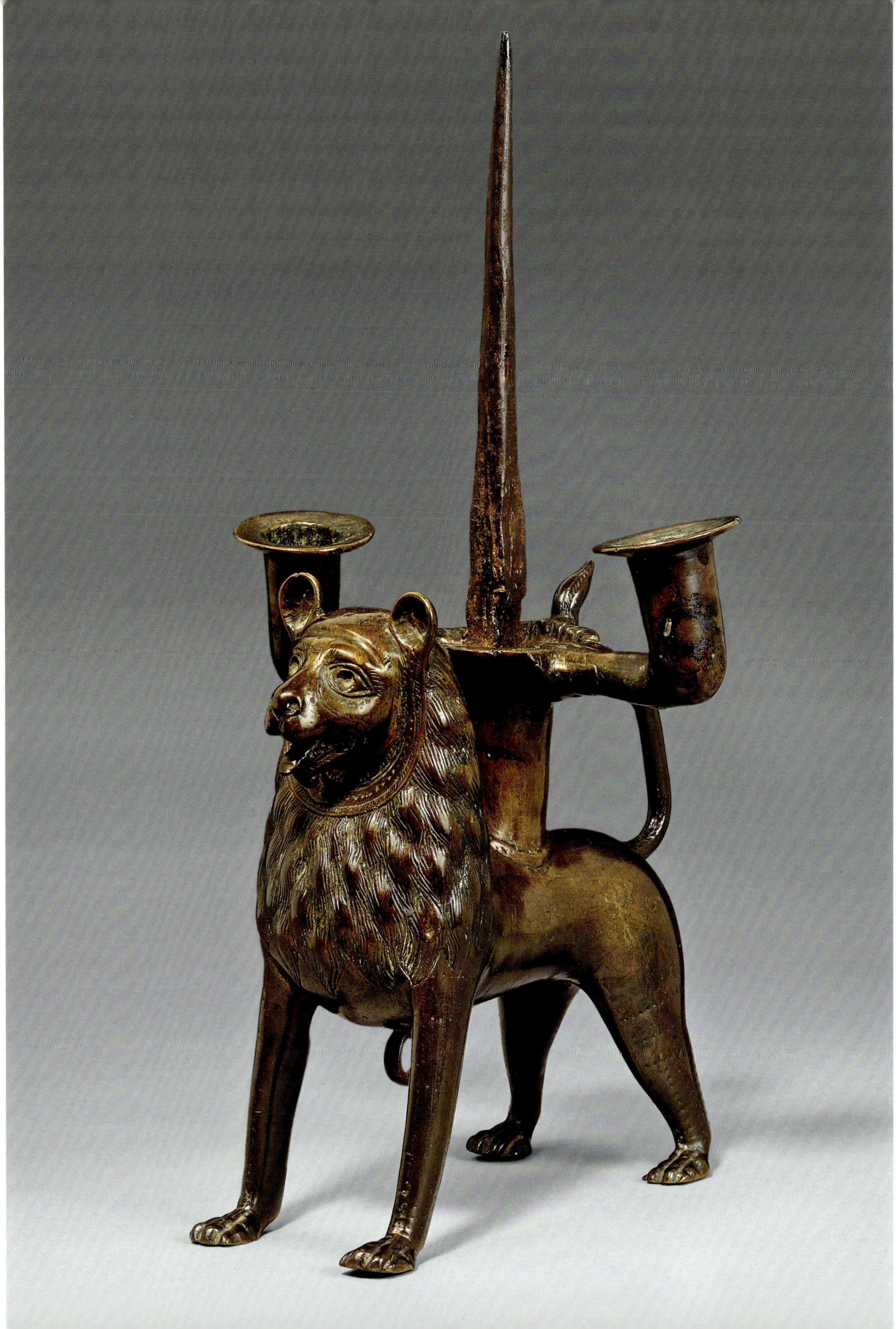

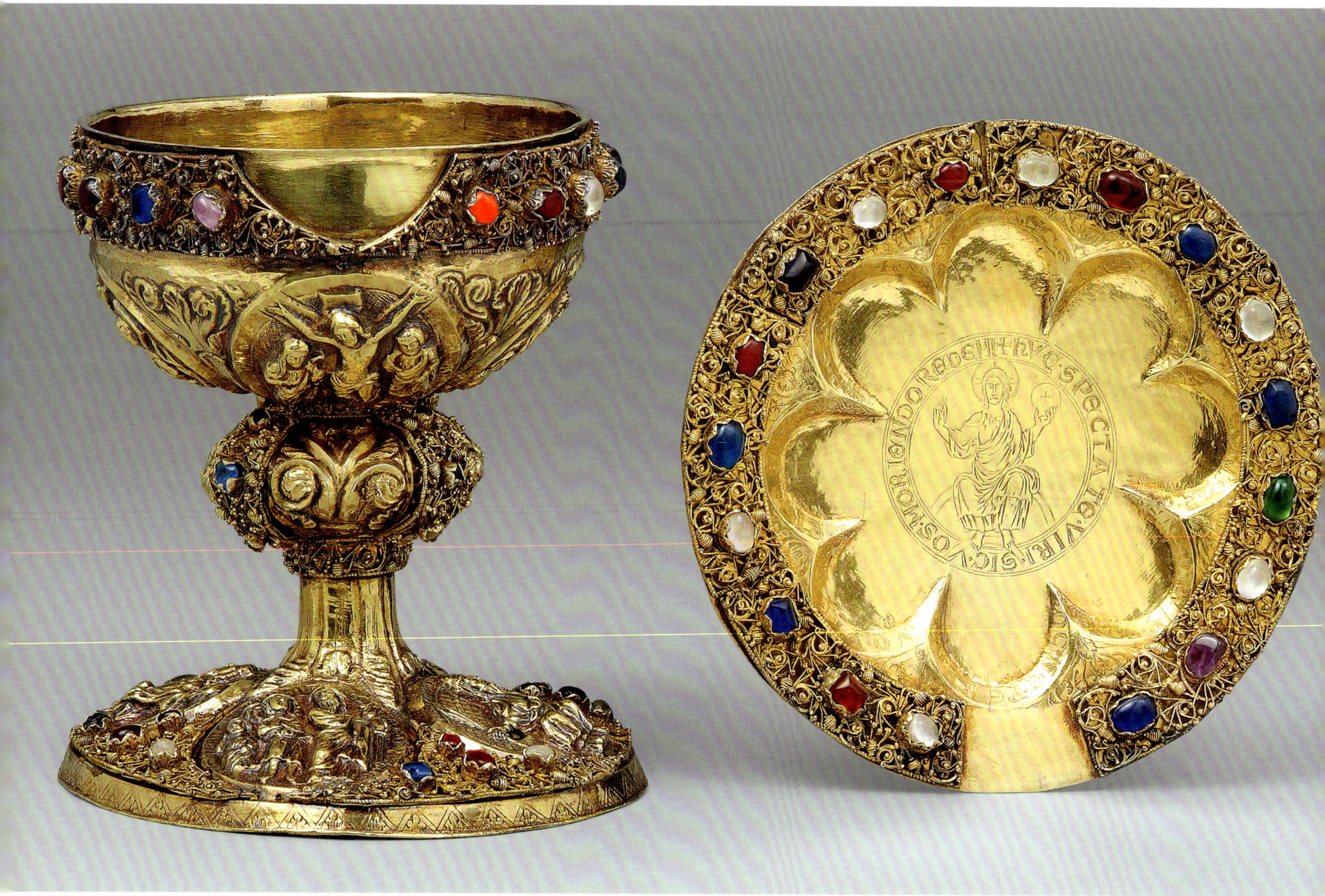
HVC·SPECTATO·VIRI·SIC·VOS·MORIENDO·REDEMI

42 · Chalice and Paten

German (Hildesheim), first third of 13th century
Silver, gilded silver, filigree, and semiprecious stones
CHALICE: *H. 6⅞ in. (17.5 cm); Diam. 5⅝ in. (14.1 cm);* PATEN: *Diam. 6⅞ in. (17.5 cm)*
Basilika St. Godehard, Hildesheim

The fine raised work on the cup and foot of this chalice (the so-called *Bernhardkelch* or Bernhard Chalice), the engraving of the paten, and the applied filigree openwork mounted with semiprecious stones distinguish this ensemble as one of the most luxurious examples of Romanesque goldsmiths' liturgical work. By tradition these objects were thought to be the gift of Bishop Bernhard (reigned 1130–53) to the church of St. Godehard, which he founded in 1133. However, an inventory entry suggests the objects may have come to St. Godehard's as a pledge from the cloister of St. Michael.

The four reliefs with Old Testament scenes on the foot of the chalice are typologically juxtaposed with four somewhat larger scenes from the life of Christ on the cup. Inscriptions around each medallion expound the iconographic program. For example, the Nativity represented on the cup is paired with an image of Melchisedech (the Old Testament king-priest) holding up a chalice and host, along with an inscription: ExEMPLO Xri VICTORIA CONGRVIT Isti (meaning that the Eucharist that Melchisedech holds foreshadows Christ's triumph through his sacrificial death). Between the roundels on the cup are raised palmette leaves; filigree openwork with semiprecious stones fills the interstices on the foot as well as between the raised foliate forms on the knob of the stem. A band of similar filigree encircles the lip of the cup, out of which a demilune has been cut to facilitate drinking.

The paten rim with eight raised lobes is centered on an engraved circle with Christ in Judgment seated on a rainbow, his right hand raised in benediction and his left holding the orb. The encircling inscription reads: HVC SPECTATE VIRI SIC VOS MORIENDO REDEMI (Behold here, mankind, for through my death I have redeemed you). The inscription on the vertical walls of the lobes declares that he who wishes to accept Christ must be pure of body and soul lest he be deemed corrupt and unworthy of reward. The rim is decorated with filigree mounted with precious stones, with a small section removed. The tight spiral twists of wire within the filigree work (*Schneckenfiligran*, or snail filigree) have been associated with the lower Rhineland, but current scholarship considers these exceptional altar vessels a local product of Hildesheim.

T.B.H.

SELECTED REFERENCES: *Die Zeit der Staufer*, 1977, vol. 1, pp. 453–54, no. 582, vol. 2, pl. 390 (Dietrich Kötzsche); *Bernward von Hildesheim und das Zeitalter der Ottonen*, 1993, vol. 2, pp. 632–33, no. IX-29 (Michael Brandt).

43 · Second Seal of the Cathedral Chapter

German (Hildesheim), ca. 1244
Brown wax
Diam. ca. 3 ¾ in. (9.3 cm)
Dom-Museum Hildesheim (S 311)

This wax seal shows the Virgin Mary and the Christ Child flanked by the patrons of the cathedral church, Saints Godehard and Epiphanius. Mary, seated frontally in the center of the seal on a throne of posts, points to the Child with her right hand. Jesus holds a book in his left hand and is blessing the viewer with his raised right hand.

The overall form follows that of the chapter's previous seal, which was in use from at least 1161. The artist of the later stamp modernized the seal, in terms of both style and the interpretation of the relationship of the Virgin and Child, favoring a more intense and direct affection. Whereas on the older seal Mary presents a flowering stem, she now points toward the Child, who turns his head toward his mother. The composition of their garments supports the unity of mother and son, as the rich draperies lapping both in rounded folds make it difficult to clearly distinguish the body of one from the other. This representation follows a broader trend since the second half of the twelfth century of depictions that increasingly focused on Christ's humanity.

The seal can be dated by its use in charters issued by the cathedral chapter: While its predecessor can last be found on documents dated July 1244, the new seal is attached to a charter of January 25, 1245. Thus the new seal was probably made during the second half of 1244 by a Hildesheim goldsmith. It served for legal documents until 1296.

Its style does not conform to the so-called Zackenstil, a regional "jagged style" (characteristically depicting angular robes and sharply folded drapery) that was particularly popular in Saxon manuscript illumination and painting in the second third of the thirteenth century. One example is on the painted ceiling of St. Michael's Church in Hildesheim (ca. 1230–40; see Introduction, fig. 8). While previous research detected a relationship between this seal and the so-called Muldenfaltenstil (a style depicting drapery with deep, troughlike folds, seen in works from the first third of the thirteenth century), the artist of the new seal was more immediately influenced by wooden sculptures from the 1230s and 1240s, such as the triumphal cross in the former collegiate church of Wechselburg in Saxony. There, Christ's loincloth shows a similar arrangement of lapping folds, a drapery that equally emphasizes sumptuous design and the body's plasticity.

G.L.

SELECTED REFERENCES: *Bernward von Hildesheim und das Zeitalter der Ottonen*, 1993, vol. 2, pp. 469–71, no. VII-17 (Rainer Kahsnitz); *Ego sum Hildensemensis*, 2000, p. 416, no. A8 (Sabine Wolfsbauer).

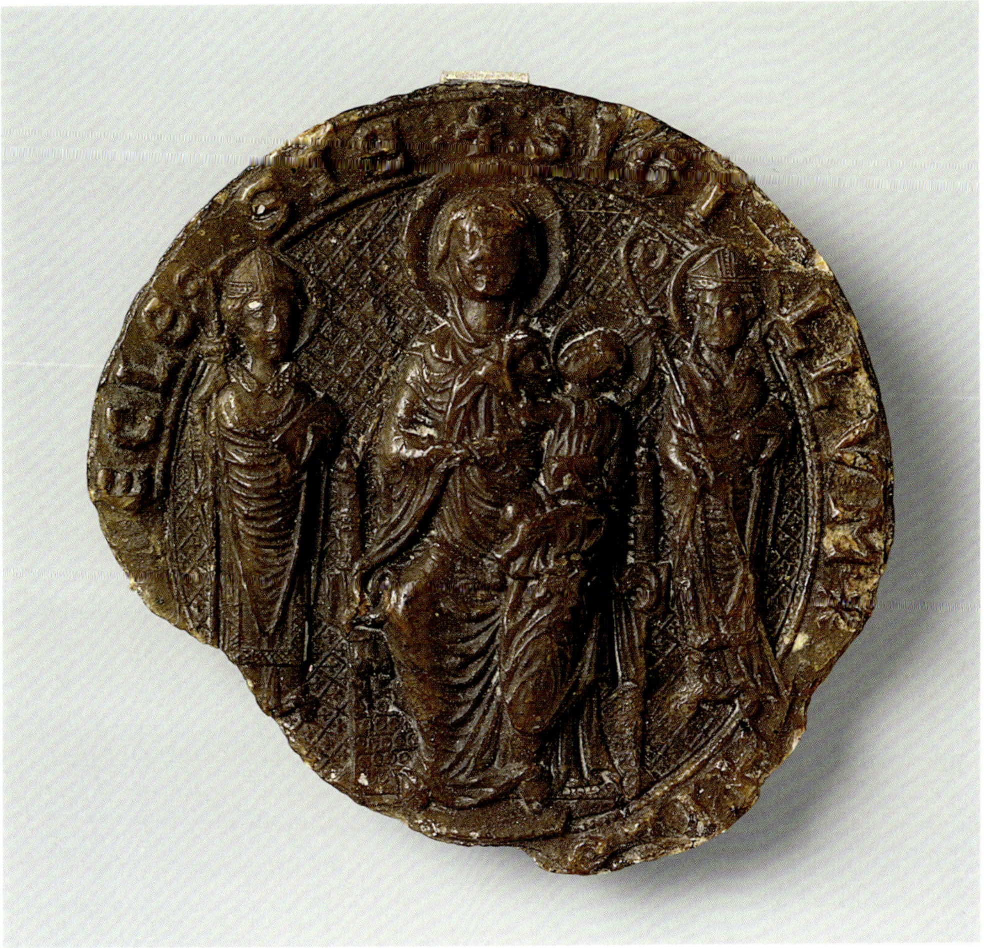

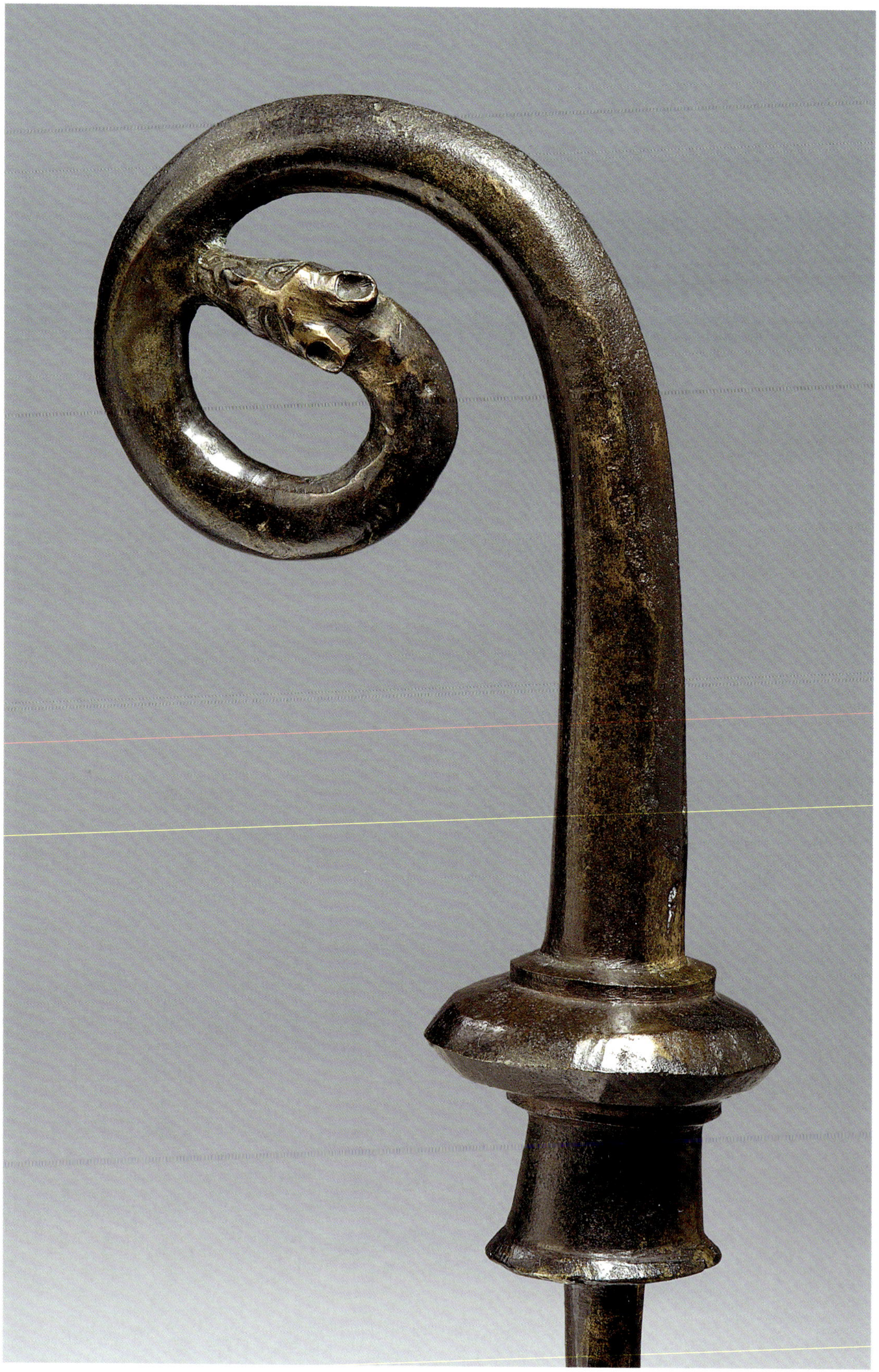

44 · Head of the Crosier of Bishop Johannes I

German (Hildesheim[?]), ca. 1257–60
Copper alloy
7 3/4 × 3 5/8 in. (19.5 × 9.2 cm) with tang
Dom-Museum Hildesheim (D 1978-44)

This crosier head in the form of a curled serpent was found in 1953 beneath the floor of the nave of Hildesheim Cathedral in the grave of Bishop Johannes I (Johann of Brakel, reigned 1257–60). The shaft, perhaps made of wood, has been lost. The serpentine form lends itself naturally to the crook of a crosier, the traditional insignia of office for bishops and abbots. Medieval examples were made of a range of materials, including ivory and various metals, many decorated with enamel. This example cast in copper alloy would surely have recalled the brazen serpent employed by Moses to heal the Israelites (Numbers 21:4–9). The stylistic details, including the compressed form of the knop (the stem's knob or decorative swelling) near the bottom, are consistent with mid-thirteenth-century metalwork in Hildesheim, suggesting that the crosier might have been commissioned for Bishop Johannes's consecration; he was ordained in 1257 after nearly forty years of service to the chapter.

P.B.

SELECTED REFERENCES: *Bild und Bestie*, 2008, pp. 274–75, no. 16 (Michael Brandt).

45 · Crosier of Bishop Otto I

IVORY: *southern Italy, mid-13th century or earlier*
INSCRIPTION BAND: *German (Braunschweig or Hildesheim), ca. 1260*
MOUNT: *German (Hildesheim), first half of 15th century*
Ivory, paint, silver, niello, and gilding
Overall 7⅞ × 6¾ in. (20 × 17 cm); H. with stem 66⅛ in. (168 cm)
Dom-Museum Hildesheim (DS 69)

The crosier's crook underscores the bishop's role as shepherd of his flock. Thus the inscription on the collar of this crosier is perfectly consonant with the bishop's responsibilities: + COLLIGE SVSTENTA STIMV / +LA VAGA MORBIDA LENTA + ATTRAHE PER PRIMVM ME / +DIO REGE PVNGE PER IMVM+ PASCE GREGE M NORMA DO / + CE SERVA CORRIGE FORMA (Pasture the flock well; teach [them], watch over [them], and set [them] right in the best way. Gather, support, and goad the confused, the sick, and the slow. Pull with the top; lead with the middle; prod with the bottom).

The crosier of Hildesheim's Bishop Otto I (reigned 1260–79) is strikingly like a series of others produced in southern Italy in the twelfth and thirteenth centuries, which were probably made as export products. A crosier head with a similar composition of the Lamb of God being threatened by a dragon is in the Ashmolean Museum, Oxford (AN1685 A 600). Usually ascribed to Siculo-Arabic workshops (where Muslim craftsmen produced objects in Norman-occupied Palermo for Christian clients), the ivory crosiers reflect the sharing of an artistic language among seemingly diverse cultures. The lamb within a volute formed by a threatening dragonlike creature derives from Islamic bronzes and carvings in wood and ivory; the stylized serpent's head and the gazelle-like lamb with bent forelegs echo painted Islamic hunting themes and Oriental motifs of animals' spirited combat. The works are usually embellished with paint and with mounts of silver, niello, and gilding, as seen here.

C.T.L.

SELECTED REFERENCES: Elbern and Reuther, *Der Hildesheimer Domschatz*, 1969, p. 68, no. 69; *Schätze des Glaubens*, 2010, p. 108, no. 49 (Michael Brandt).

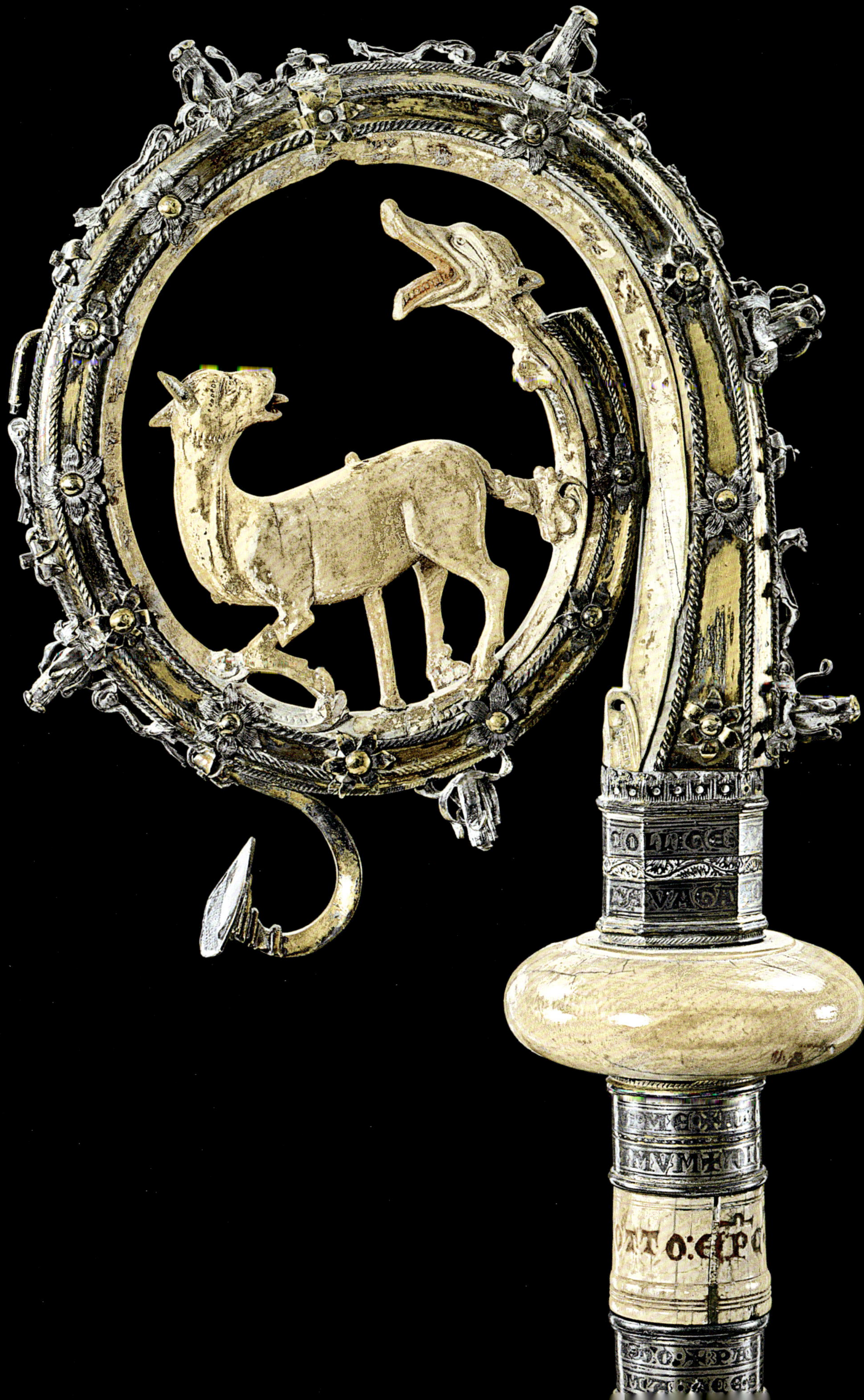

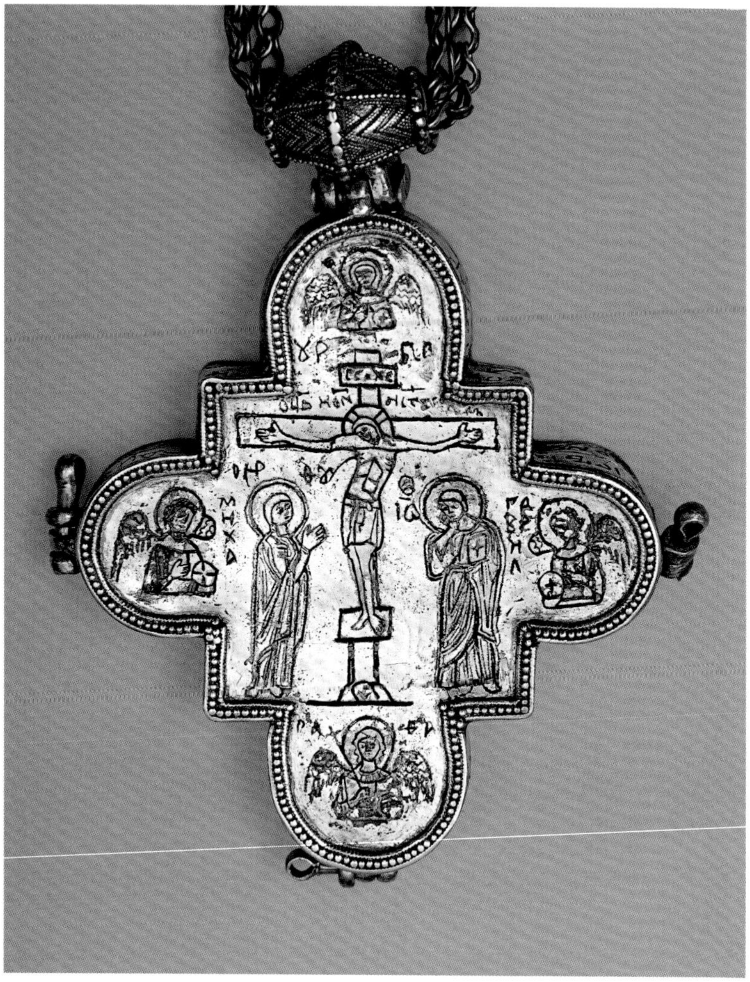

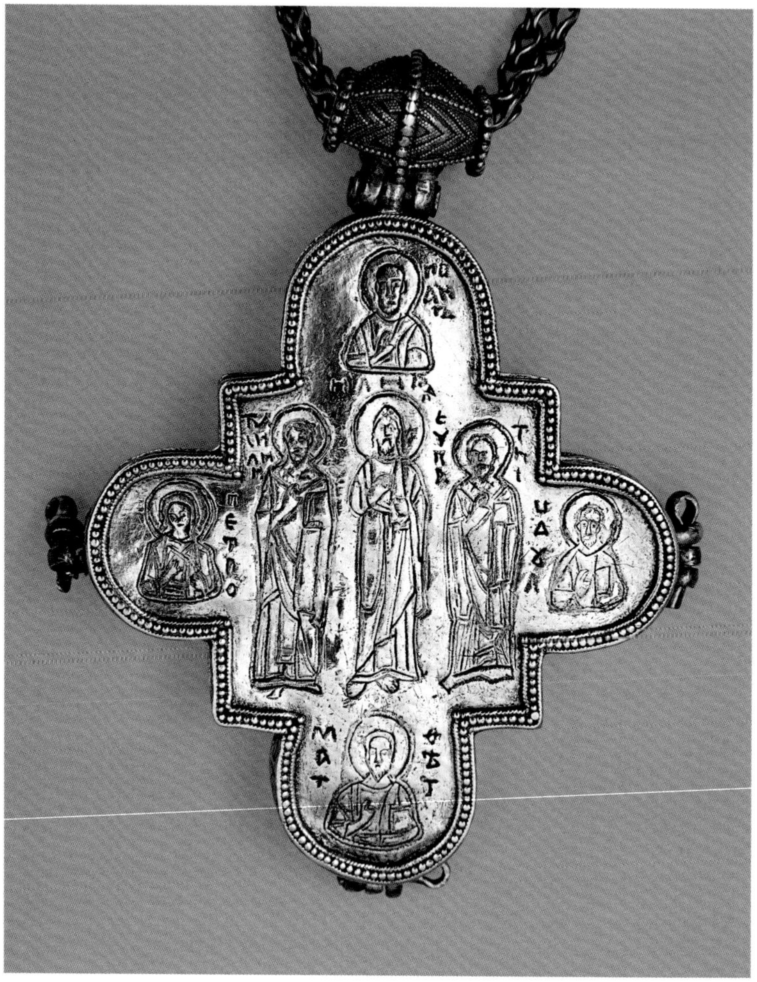

46 · Reliquary Cross

Byzantine or Russian, 13th century
Silver with traces of gilding, niello, granulated hinge, and a pearl
Overall (closed) 5 ½ × 4 × ¾ in. (14 × 10.2 × 1.7 cm)
Dom-Museum Hildesheim (DS 3)

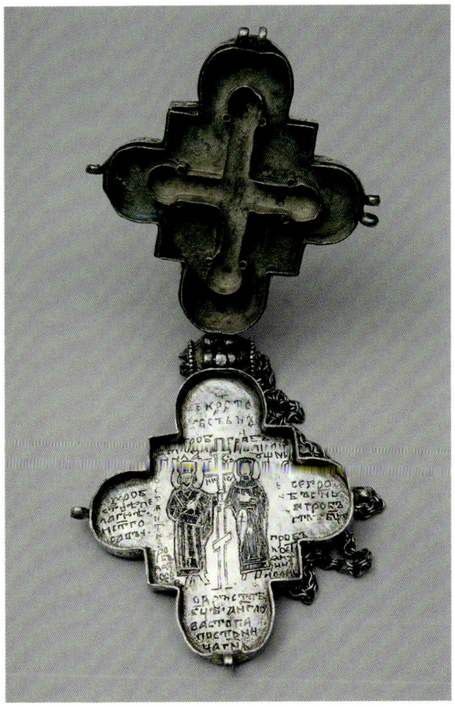

This richly decorated and inscribed cross is an encolpion, a work made to hold sacred relics and to be worn, hung from a chain, on the chest. On its face Christ on the cross is flanked by the Virgin Mary, hands raised in prayer, and Saint John the Evangelist, in a pose of grief; the skull of Adam is at the base of the cross. Busts of the archangels occupy the ends of the cross arms: Michael (left), Gabriel (right), Uriel (above), and Raphael (below). On the reverse, the prophet Elijah stands flanked by two saints – Basil the Great and, probably, Hypatius – in clerical dress. On the cross ends Saints Peter and Paul appear to the left and right, with John and Matthew above and below. Around the rim an inscription, "Lord, help your servant of God, Ilias, who has this Cross in this life and the life to come," names the owner, who has yet to be convincingly identified.

The cross opens like a locket to store relics, including one of the True Cross, now long gone. The interior surface depicts Saints Constantine and Helena, flanking the True Cross, in the formal, hieratic poses typical of icons used for the Orthodox Church's Feast of the Exultation of the Cross. Constantine was the first Christian emperor of Rome, and Helena, his mother, the discoverer of the True Cross in Jerusalem in the fourth century; their presence was intended to confirm the authenticity of the relic of the True Cross in the reliquary and may also associate the relic with Constantinople. The True Cross was taken from Jerusalem in the seventh century to the Byzantine capital, where containers for diplomatic gifts of relics of the True Cross often included images of the two saints, as found here.

The extensive inscriptions surrounding the True Cross image identify holy sites in Constantinople and in and near Jerusalem. Those in Constantinople are the tombs of Constantine and Helena, which were in the Church of the Holy Apostles, and the shrine of Saint John the Kalybites. Those in the Holy Land are the tombs of Christ, the Virgin, and Saints Lazarus, Pelagia, and Sava. The remaining site listed, the tomb of Saint Daniel, may refer to the prophet, whose tomb is near Jerusalem, or to Saint Daniel the Stylite, who is venerated in Constantinople.

The list of sites probably identifies the secondary relics that were in the encolpion and may be a record of the owner's pilgrimage to them. As the inscriptions are primarily in Slavonic, the cross has been attributed to medieval Russia, possibly Novgorod, the spiritual and political heart of the country. Paleographic study of the inscriptions questions the attribution to Novgorod while confirming a thirteenth-century date for the cross. There is no record of how the encolpion came into Hildesheim's treasury, but it has been suggested that it may have come through the trade routes of the Hanseatic League, a confederation of merchant guilds and market towns whose trade routes stretched along the coast of the Baltic Sea, connecting Russia with Germany.

H.C.E.

SELECTED REFERENCES: Elbern and Reuther, *Der Hildesheimer Domschatz*, 1969, pp. 16–17; Teteriatnikov, "True Cross Flanked by Constantine and Helena," 1995; Lehfeldt, "Die altrussischen Inschriften des Hildesheimer Enkolpions," 1999.

47 · Paten

German (Hildesheim[?]), before 1398
Gold
Diam. 7 3/8 in. (18.8 cm)
Dom-Museum Hildesheim (DS 14)

As late as the seventeenth century this paten was erroneously associated with Bishop Bernward (reigned 993–1022), as his *Vita* states he enriched the cathedral with expensive chalices. Entries in both the cathedral commemorative book and the treasury inventory of 1438 establish that this paten and the accompanying gold chalice (not exhibited) were presented to Hildesheim Cathedral by Bishop Gerhard vom Berge (reigned 1365–98). Moreover, another long-overlooked entry in the cathedral treasury inventory of 1409 describes the chalice in recognizable detail and clearly states that it and the golden paten were the donation of Bishop Gerhard.

The finely engraved design represents the apocalyptic image of the sacrificial lamb whose blood redeems mankind, as recounted in the Book of Revelation. In the center is the haloed Lamb of God supporting a banner as blood pours from its breast into a chalice. This symbol of Christ's redemptive sacrifice, encircled by a plain band, is flanked at cardinal points by the tetramorphs (the symbols of the Four Evangelists), similarly encircled. In between, against a stippled background, are censing angels.

Within the rim of the paten surrounding the imagery is a band inscribed: + victima que vicit•× septem signacula solvit / Vt comedas pascha × scandes cenacula celsa (the sacrifice that conquers breaks the seven seals; he who partakes of the sacrificial lamb will rise up to the Last Supper). The first verse alludes to Revelation 5:9: ". . . O Lord, to take the book, and to open the seals thereof; because thou wast slain, and hast redeemed us to God, in thy blood. . . ." The second verse addresses the officiating priest who, in celebrating Mass, represents the sacrifice of Christ anew. The style of the engraving accords generally with that of Westphalia–Lower Saxony and foreshadows that of Hildesheim masters of about 1415–20.

T.B.H.

SELECTED REFERENCES: *Bernward von Hildesheim und das Zeitalter der Ottonen*, 1993, vol. 2, pp. 633–34, no. IX-30 (Michael Wolfson); Wolfson, *Der große Goldkelch Bischof Gerhards*, 1996; *Schätze des Glaubens*, 2010, p. 122, no. 57 (Michael Brandt).

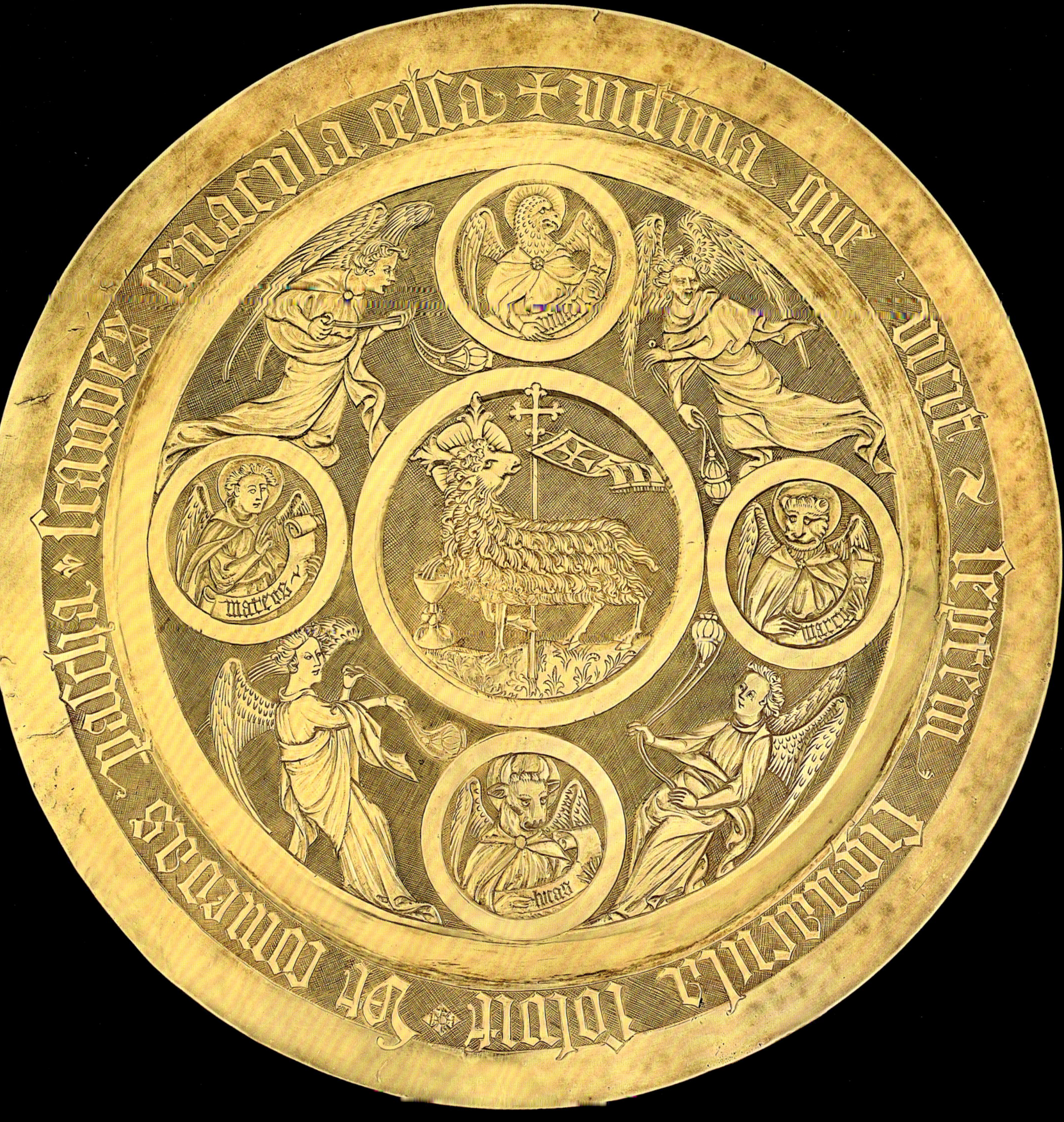

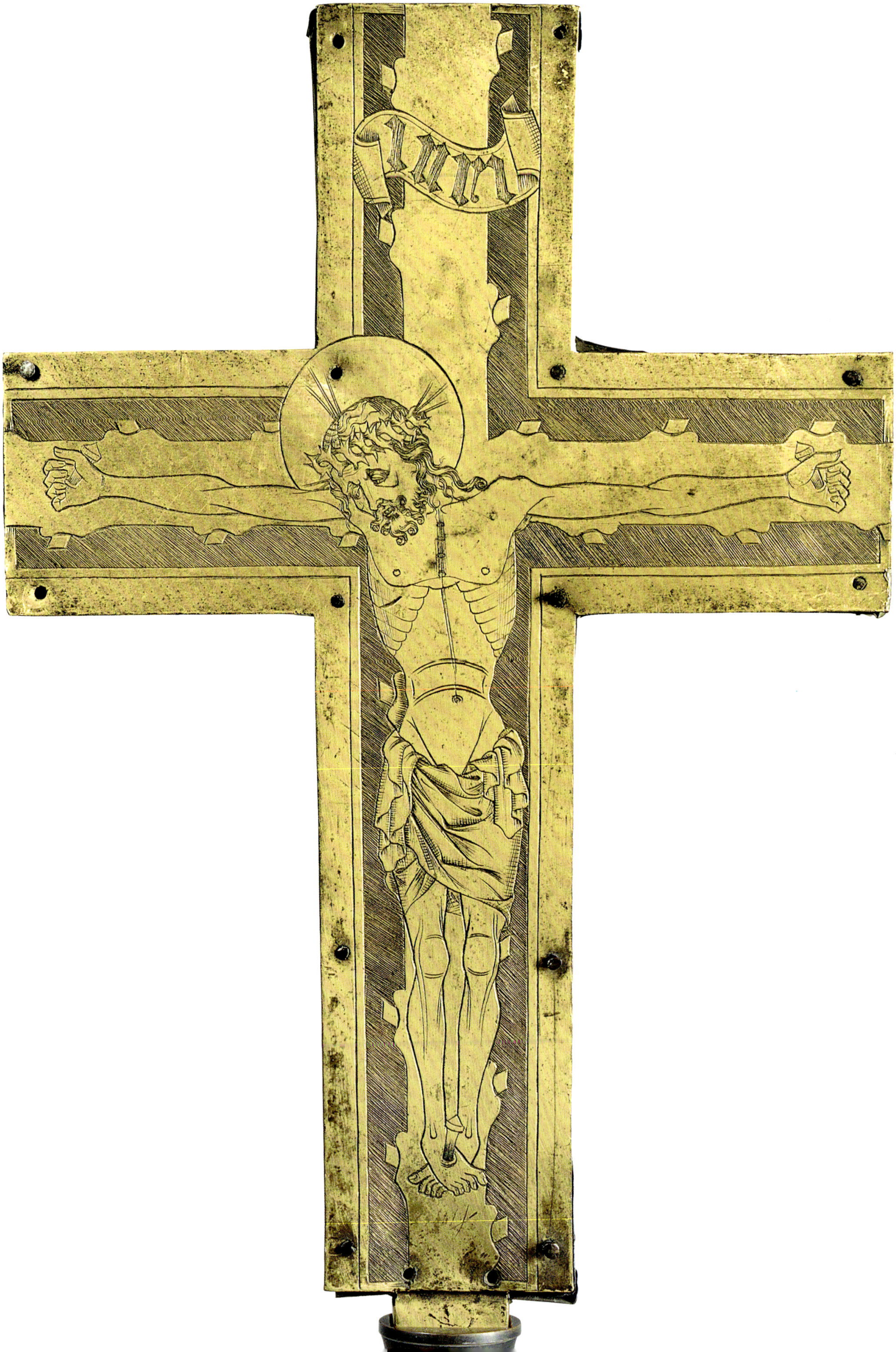
inri

48 · So-called Burial Cross

German (Hildesheim[?]), ca. 1400
Gilded copper alloy; wood core
13 ¼ × 9 ¼ × 1 in. (33.5 × 23.5 × 2.4 cm)
Dom-Museum Hildesheim (DS 90)

This processional cross in all probability came from the sacristy of Hildesheim Cathedral and became known as the Burial Cross because it was long employed for interment services. Highly unusual is the cross's plain profile with its straight-edged terminals, which in this period were almost always lobed or otherwise elaborated. Additionally, the expressive and technically accomplished engraving on the front plaque contrasts with the rather rude manner in which the copper plates are mounted on the wood core. This, along with the apparently trimmed terminals, suggests the front plate was reused from another work of art, perhaps a larger processional cross whose arms terminated with separate three-lobed plaques representing the symbols of the Four Evangelists.

The deeply furrowed face, downcast head, and wasted body all underscore the agony suffered by Christ. This type of representation, the *Crucifixus Dolorosus*, emerged as a popular devotional image in the first half of the fourteenth century, a time when the devout sought a deeper, more direct connection with God through the contemplation of Christ's redemptive suffering. He hangs from a knotty wooden cross with branch stubs, which was understood as the Tree of Life. Christ's triumph over death through his sacrifice on such a cross and his subsequent resurrection is a theme that would be appropriate for the interment of the faithful seeking everlasting life. The type was disseminated in different media throughout Europe; a similarly conceived image appears in the stained glass program of the choir of Halberstadt Cathedral, just east of Hildesheim.

T.B.H.

SELECTED REFERENCES: *Stadt im Wandel*, 1985, vol. 1, pp. 390–91, no. 313; *Schätze des Glaubens*, 2010, p. 124, no. 59 (Michael Brandt).

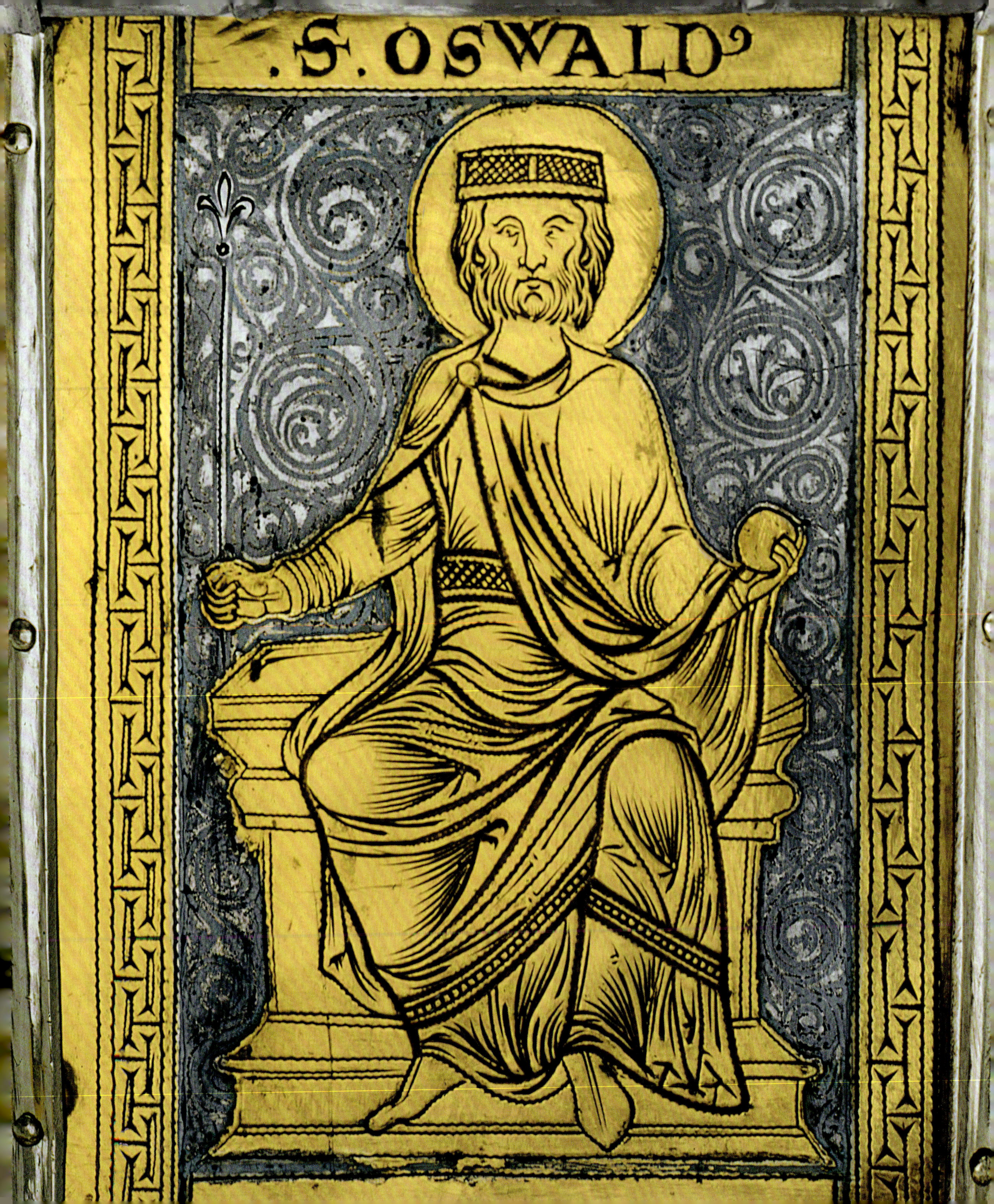
.S.OSWALD9

BIBLIOGRAPHY

Abglanz des Himmels: Romanik in Hildesheim. Edited by Michael Brandt. Exh. cat., Dom-Museum Hildesheim. Regensburg: Schnell + Steiner, 2001.

Beer, Manuela. "Orte und Wege: Überlegungen zur Aufstellung und Verwendung frühmittelalterlicher Marienfiguren." In *"Luft unter die Flügel . . .": Beiträge zur mittelalterlichen Kunst; Festschrift für Hiltrud Westermann-Angerhausen*, edited by Andrea von Hülsen-Esch and Dagmar Täube, pp. 99–121. Hildesheim and New York: Olms, 2010.

Bernward von Hildesheim und das Zeitalter der Ottonen. Edited by Michael Brandt and Arne Eggebrecht. 2 vols. Exh. cat., Dom-Museum Hildesheim; Roemer- und Pelizaeus-Museum, Hildesheim. Hildesheim: Bernward Verlag; Mainz am Rhein: Ph. von Zabern, 1993.

Bild und Bestie: Hildesheimer Bronzen der Stauferzeit. Edited by Michael Brandt. Exh. cat., Dom-Museum Hildesheim. Regensburg: Schnell + Steiner, 2008.

Binding, Günther. *Der früh- und hochmittelalterliche Bauherr als sapiens architectus.* 2nd ed. Darmstadt: Wissenschaftliche Buchgesellschaft, 1998.

Brandt, Michael. "Tragaltäre im Hochaltar: Ein Reliquienfund im Hildesheimer Dom." In *Ars et Ecclesia: Festschrift für Franz Ronig zum 60. Geburtstag*, edited by Hans-Walter Stork, Christoph Gerhardt, and Alois Thomas, pp. 69–77. Trier: Paulinus Verlag, 1989.

———. "Ein Hildesheimer Vortragekreuz mit Grubenschmelzen." *Aachener Kunstblätter* 60 (1994), pp. 223–36.

———. "Bernward und Byzanz." In *Buchkunst im Mittelalter und Kunst der Gegenwart: Scrinium Kilonense; Festschrift für Ulrich Kuder*, edited by Hans-Walter Stork, Babette Tewes, and Christian Waszak, pp. 43–54. Nordhausen: Bautz, 2008.

———. *Bernwards Säule.* Schätze aus dem Dom zu Hildesheim 1. Regensburg: Schnell + Steiner, 2009.

———. "Bernward d'Hildesheim et ses trésors." *Les Cahiers de Saint-Michel de Cuxa* 41 (2010), pp. 133–42.

———. *Bernwards Tür.* Schätze aus dem Dom zu Hildesheim 3. Regensburg: Schnell + Steiner, 2010.

Braun, Joseph. *Das christliche Altargerät in seinem Sein und in seiner Entwicklung.* Munich: M. Hueber, 1932.

Buch und Bild im Mittelalter. Edited by Ulrich Knapp. Exh. cat. Hildesheim: Dom-Museum Hildesheim, 1999.

Byzanz: Die Macht der Bilder. Edited by Michael Brandt and Arne Effenberger. Exh. cat. Hildesheim: Dom-Museum Hildesheim; Berlin: Staatliche Museen zu Berlin, Preussischer Kulturbesitz, 1998.

Canossa 1077: Erschütterung der Welt; Geschichte, Kunst und Kultur am Aufgang der Romanik. Edited by Christoph Stiegemann and Matthias Wemhoff. Exh. cat., Museum in der Kaiserpfalz, Erzbischöfliches Diözesanmuseum, and Städtische Galerie am Abdinghof, Paderborn. 2 vols. Munich: Hirmer, 2006.

Dolle, Josef, and Dennis Knochenhauer, eds. *Niedersächsisches Klosterbuch: Verzeichnis der Klöster, Stifte, Kommenden und Beginenhäuser in Niedersachsen und Bremen von den Anfängen bis 1810. Vol. 2, Gartow bis Mariental.* Veröffentlichungen des Instituts für Historische Landesforschung der Universität Göttingen 56, no. 2. Bielefeld: Verlag für Regionalgeschichte, 2012.

Ego sum Hildensemensis: Bischof, Domkapitel und Dom in Hildesheim 815 bis 1810. Edited by Ulrich Knapp. Exh. cat., Dom-Museum Hildesheim. Kataloge des Dom-Museums Hildesheim 3. Petersberg: M. Imhof, 2000.

Ehlers, Joachim, and Dietrich Kötzsche. *Der Welfenschatz und sein Umkreis.* Mainz am Rhein: Ph. von Zabern, 1998.

Elbern, Victor H., and Hans Reuther. *Der Hildesheimer Domschatz.* Hildesheim: Verlagsbuchhandlung August Lax, 1969.

Engel, Patricia, and Bernhard Gallistl. "Die Reichenauer Handschriften der Dombibliothek Hildesheim und der Herzog August Bibliothek Wolfenbüttel im Vergleich." *Wolfenbütteler Beiträge* 15 (2009), pp. 129–77.

Exner, Matthias. *Das Guntbald-Evangeliar: Ein ottonischer Bilderzyklus und sein Zeugniswert für die Rezeptionsgeschichte des Lorscher Evangeliars.* Quellen und Studien zur Geschichte und Kunst im Bistum Hildesheim 1. Regensburg: Schnell + Steiner, 2008.

Falke, Otto von, and Erich Meyer. *Romanische Leuchter und Gefässe: Giessgefässe der Gotik.* Bronzegeräte des Mittelalters 1. Berlin: Deutscher Verein für Kunstwissenschaft, 1935.

Forsyth, Ilene. *The Throne of Wisdom: Wood Sculptures of the Madonna in Romanesque France.* Princeton: Princeton University Press, 1972.

Für Königtum und Himmelreich: 1000 Jahre Bischof Meinwerk von Paderborn. Edited by Christoph Stiegemann and Martin Kroker. Exh. cat., Museum in der Kaiserpfalz and Erzbischöfliches Diözesanmuseum Paderborn. Regensburg: Schnell + Steiner, 2009.

Gallistl, Bernhard. *Epiphanius von Pavia: Schutzheiliger des Bistums Hildesheim.* Hildesheimer Chronik: Beiträge zur Geschichte des Bistums Hildesheim 7. Hildesheim: Verlag für Regionalgeschichte, 2000.

Giese, Martina. *Die Textfassungen der Lebensbeschreibung Bischof Bernwards von Hildesheim.* Monumenta Germaniæ Historica, Studien und Texte 40. Hannover: Hahnsche Buchhandlung, 2006.

———. "Die schriftliche Pflege des Bernward-Kultes im Wandel der Zeit vom 11. bis 18. Jahrhundert." In *Einen Platz im Himmel erwerben: Bücher und Bilder im Dienste mittelalterlicher Jenseitsfürsorge; Vorträge zur Ausstellung "Schätze im Himmel—Bücher auf Erden,"* edited by Monika E. Müller and Christian Heitzmann, pp. 15–54, 113–19. Wolfenbütteler Hefte 32. Wiesbaden: Harrassowitz, 2012.

The Glory of Byzantium: Art and Culture of the Middle Byzantine Era (A.D. 843–1261). Edited by Helen Evans and William D. Wixom. Exh. cat. New York: The Metropolitan Museum of Art, 1997.

Goetting, Hans. *Die Hildesheimer Bischöfe von 815 bis 1221 (1227).* Vol. 3 of *Die Bistümer der Kirchenprovinz Mainz: Das Bistum Hildesheim.* Germania Sacra, n.s., 20. Berlin and New York: De Gruyter, 1984.

Goldschmidt, Adolph. *Die Elfenbeinskulpturen aus der Zeit der karolingischen und sächsischen Kaiser.* 4 vols. Berlin: Bruno Cassirer, 1914–26.

Gosebruch, Martin, and Frank Neidhart Steigerwald, eds. *Bernwardinische Kunst. Bericht über ein wissenschaftliches Symposium in Hildesheim vom 10.10. bis 13.10.1984.* Schriftenreihe der Kommission für Niedersächsische Bau- und Kunstgeschichte bei der Braunschweigischen Wissenschaftlichen Gesellschaft 3. Göttingen: E. Goltze, 1988.

Grote, Rolf-Jürgen, and Vera Kellner, eds. *Die Bilderdecke der Hildesheimer Michaeliskirche. Erforschung eines Weltkulturerbes. Aktuelle Befunde der Denkmalpflege im Rahmen der interdisziplinären Bestandssicherung und Erhaltungsplanung der Deckenmalerei.* Munich and Berlin: Deutscher Kunstverlag, 2002.

Hahn, Cynthia. *Strange Beauty: Issues in the Making and Meaning of Reliquaries, 400–circa 1204.* University Park: Pennsylvania State University Press, 2012.

Heinrich der Löwe und seine Zeit: Herrschaft und Repräsentation der Welfen 1125–1235. Edited by Jochen Luckhardt and Franz Niehoff. Exh. cat., Herzog Anton Ulrich-Museum, Braunschweig. 3 vols. Munich: Hirmer, 1995.

Höhl, Claudia. *Das Taufbecken des Wilbernus.* Schätze aus dem Dom zu Hildesheim 2. Regensburg: Schnell + Steiner, 2009.

Hoogeweg, H[ermann], and Karl Janicke, eds. *Urkundenbuch des Hochstifts Hildesheim und seiner Bischöfe*, vol. 1, Bis 1221. Hannover and Leipzig: Hahn, 1896.

Jakobs, Hermann, ed. *Germania Pontificia.* Vol. 5.2, *Provincia Maguntinensis*, part 6, *Dioceses Hildesheimensis et Halberstadensis. Appendix: Saxonia.* Regesta Pontificum Romanorum 5.2.6. Göttingen: Vandenhoeck & Ruprecht, 2005.

Jülich, Theo. "Gemmenkreuze: Die Farbigkeit ihres Edelsteinbesatzes bis zum 12. Jahrhundert." *Aachener Kunstblätter* 54–55 (1986–87), pp. 99–258.

Kahsnitz, Rainer. "Coronas aureas in capite: Zum Allerheiligenbild des Reichenauer Kollektars in Hildesheim." In *Per assiduum studium scientiæ adipisci margaritam: Festgabe für Ursula Nilgen zum 65. Geburtstag*, edited by Annelies Amberger et al., pp. 61–97. St. Ottilien: EOS Verlag, 1997.

Kaiser Heinrich II., 1002–1024. Edited by Josef Kirmeier et al. Exh. cat., Bayerische Landesausstellung, Bamberg. Veröffentlichungen zur bayerischen Geschichte und Kultur 44. Stuttgart: Theiss, 2002.

Kingsley, Jennifer P. "Picturing the Treasury: The Power of Objects and the Art of Memory in the Bernward Gospels." *Gesta*, 2011, pp. 19–39.

———. "VT CERNIS and the Materiality of Bernwardian Art." In *1000 Jahre St. Michael in Hildesheim: Kirche—Kloster—Stifter*, edited by Gerhard Lutz and Angela Weyer, pp. 171–84. Schriften des Hornemann Instituts 14. Petersberg: Michael Imhof Verlag, 2012.

Kirchenkunst des Mittelalters: Erhalten und Erforschen. Edited by Michael Brandt. Exh. cat., Dom-Museum Hildesheim. Hildesheim: Bernward Verlag, 1989.

Das Kostbare Evangeliar des Heiligen Bernward. Edited by Michael Brandt. Munich: Prestel, 1993.

Kruppa, Nathalie, and Jürgen Wilke, eds. *Die Hildesheimer Bischöfe von 1221 bis 1398.* Vol. 4 of *Das Bistum Hildesheim.* Germania Sacra, n.s., 46. Berlin and New York: De Gruyter, 2006.

Lasko, Peter. *Ars Sacra, 800–1200.* Pelican History of Art. Harmondsworth and Baltimore: Penguin Books, 1972.

Leclercq-Marx, Jacqueline. "Monstruos en la escritura, monstruos en imágenes: La doble tradición medieval/Monstres écrits, monstres figurés: Une Double Tradition médiévale." *Quintana*, no. 4 (2005), pp. 13–53.

Lehfeldt, Werner. "Die altrussischen Inschriften des Hildesheimer Enkolpions." *Nachrichten der Akademie der Wissenschaften in Göttingen, I. Philologisch-Historische Klasse*, no. 1 (January 1999), pp. 3–54.

Lüntzel, H[ermann] A[dolf]. *Geschichte der Diöcese und Stadt Hildesheim*. 2 vols. Hildesheim: Gerstenberg, 1858.

Lutz, Gerhard, Marietta Cambareri, and Shirin Fozi, eds. *Striking Images: Christ on the Cross and the Emergence of Medieval Monumental Sculpture*. Turnhout: Brepols / Harvey Miller, forthcoming.

Lutz, Gerhard, and Angela Weyer, eds. *1000 Jahre St. Michael in Hildesheim: Kirche—Kloster—Stifter*. Schriften des Hornemann Instituts 14. Petersberg: Michael Imhof Verlag, 2012.

Mayr-Harting, Henry. *Ottonian Book Illumination: An Historical Study*. 2 vols. in 1. London: H. Miller, 1999.

Mende, Ursula. "Romanische Bronzen: Hildesheim und sein Umkreis." In *Abglanz des Himmels: Romanik in Hildesheim*, edited by Michael Brandt, pp. 199–209. Exh. cat., Dom-Museum Hildesheim. Regensburg: Schnell + Steiner, 2001.

Nees, Lawrence. "Aspects of Antiquarianism in the Art of Bernward and Its Contemporary Analogues." In *1000 Jahre St. Michael in Hildesheim: Kirche—Kloster—Stifter*, edited by Gerhard Lutz and Angela Weyer, pp. 153–70. Schriften des Hornemann Instituts 14. Petersberg: Michael Imhof Verlag, 2012.

Nørlund, Paul. "An Early Group of Enamelled Reliquaries: 1st Dating and Provenance." *Acta Archæologica* 4 (1933), pp. 1–32.

Ornamenta ecclesiæ: Kunst und Künstler der Romanik. Edited by Anton Legner. 3 vols. Exh. cat. Cologne: Schnütgen-Museum der Stadt Köln, 1985.

Pawlik, Anna. *Das Bildwerk als Reliquiar? Funktionen früher Großplastik im 9. bis 11. Jahrhundert*. Petersberg: Michael Imhof Verlag, 2013.

Peter, Michael. "Das sogenannte Kreuz Heinrichs des Löwen." *Jahrbuch für Geschichte und Kunst im Bistum Hildesheim* 75/76 (2007–8), pp. 291–318.

Petersen, Stefan. "Stadtentstehung im Schatten der Kirche: Bischof und Stadt in Hildesheim bis zum Beginn des 13. Jahrhunderts." In *Bischof und Bürger: Herrschaftsbeziehungen in den Kathedralstädten des Hoch- und Spätmittelalters*, edited by Uwe Grieme, Nathalie Kruppa, and Stefan Pätzold, pp. 143–63. Veröffentlichungen des Max-Planck-Instituts für Geschichte 206; Germania sacra 26. Göttingen: Vandenhoeck & Ruprecht, 2004.

Der Schatz von St. Godehard. Edited by Michael Brandt. Exh. cat. Hildesheim: Dom-Museum Hildesheim and Bernward Verlag, 1988.

Schätze des Glaubens: Meisterwerke aus dem Dom-Museum Hildesheim und dem Kunstgewerbemuseum Berlin. Edited by Lothar Lambacher. Exh. cat., Bode Museum, Berlin. Berlin: Kunstgewerbemuseum Staatliche Museen zu Berlin; Regensburg: Schnell + Steiner, 2010.

Schätze im Himmel—Bücher auf Erden: Mittelalterliche Handschriften aus Hildesheim. Edited by Monika E. Müller. Exh. cat., Herzog August Bibliothek Wolfenbüttel. Wiesbaden: Harrassowitz Verlag in Kommission, 2010.

Schatzkammer auf Zeit: Die Sammlungen des Bischofs Eduard Jakob Wedekin, 1796–1870. Edited by Michael Brandt. Exh. cat. Hildesheim: Dom-Museum Hildesheim, 1991.

Schulz-Mons, Christoph. *Das Michaeliskloster in Hildesheim: Untersuchungen zur Gründung durch Bischof Bernward (993–1022)*. 2 vols. Quellen und Dokumentationen zur Stadtgeschichte Hildesheims 20, nos. 1–2. Hildesheim: Gerstenberg, 2010.

Segers-Glocke, Christiane, ed. *St. Michaelis in Hildesheim: Forschungsergebnisse zur bauarchäologischen Untersuchung im Jahr 2006*. Arbeitshefte zur Denkmalpflege in Niedersachsen 34. Hameln: Niemeyer, 2008.

Springer, Peter. *Kreuzfüsse: Ikonographie und Typologie eines hochmittelalterlichen Gerätes*. Bronzegeräte des Mittelalters 3. Berlin: Deutscher Verein für Kunstwissenschaft, 1981.

Stadt im Wandel: Kunst und Kultur des Bürgertums in Norddeutschland, 1150–1650. 4 vols. Edited by Cord Meckseper. Exh. cat., Braunschweigisches Landesmuseum, Herzog Anton Ulrich-Museum, and the Dom am Burgplatz, Braunschweig. Stuttgart-Bad Cannstatt: Edition Cantz, 1985.

Stähli, Marlis. *Die Handschriften im Domschatz zu Hildesheim*. Edited by Helmar Härtel. Mittelalterliche Handschriften in Niedersachsen 7. Wiesbaden: In Kommission bei O. Harrassowitz, 1984.

Teteriatnikov, Natalia. "The True Cross Flanked by Constantine and Helena: A Study in the Light of the Post-Iconoclastic Re-evaluation of the Cross." *Deltion* (Christian Archaeological Society, Athens), ser. 4, 18 (1995), pp. 169–88.

Wilschewski, Frank. *Die karolingischen Bischofssitze des sächsischen Stammesgebietes bis 1200*. Studien der internationalen Architektur- und Kunstgeschichte 46. Petersberg: Imhof, 2007.

Wolfson, Michael. *Der große Goldkelch Bischof Gerhards: Geschichte, Frömmigkeit und Kunst um 1400*. Der Hildesheimer Dom: Studien und Quellen 1. Hildesheim, Zürich, and New York: Olms, 1996.

Wulf, Christine. *Die Inschriften der Stadt Hildesheim*. 2 vols. Die deutschen Inschriften 58, Göttinger Reihe 10. Wiesbaden: Reichert, 2003. Based on the work of Hans Jürgen Rieckenberg.

Die Zeit der Staufer: Geschichte, Kunst, Kultur. Edited by Reiner Haussherr. 5 vols. Exh. cat. Stuttgart: Württembergisches Landesmuseum, 1977–79.

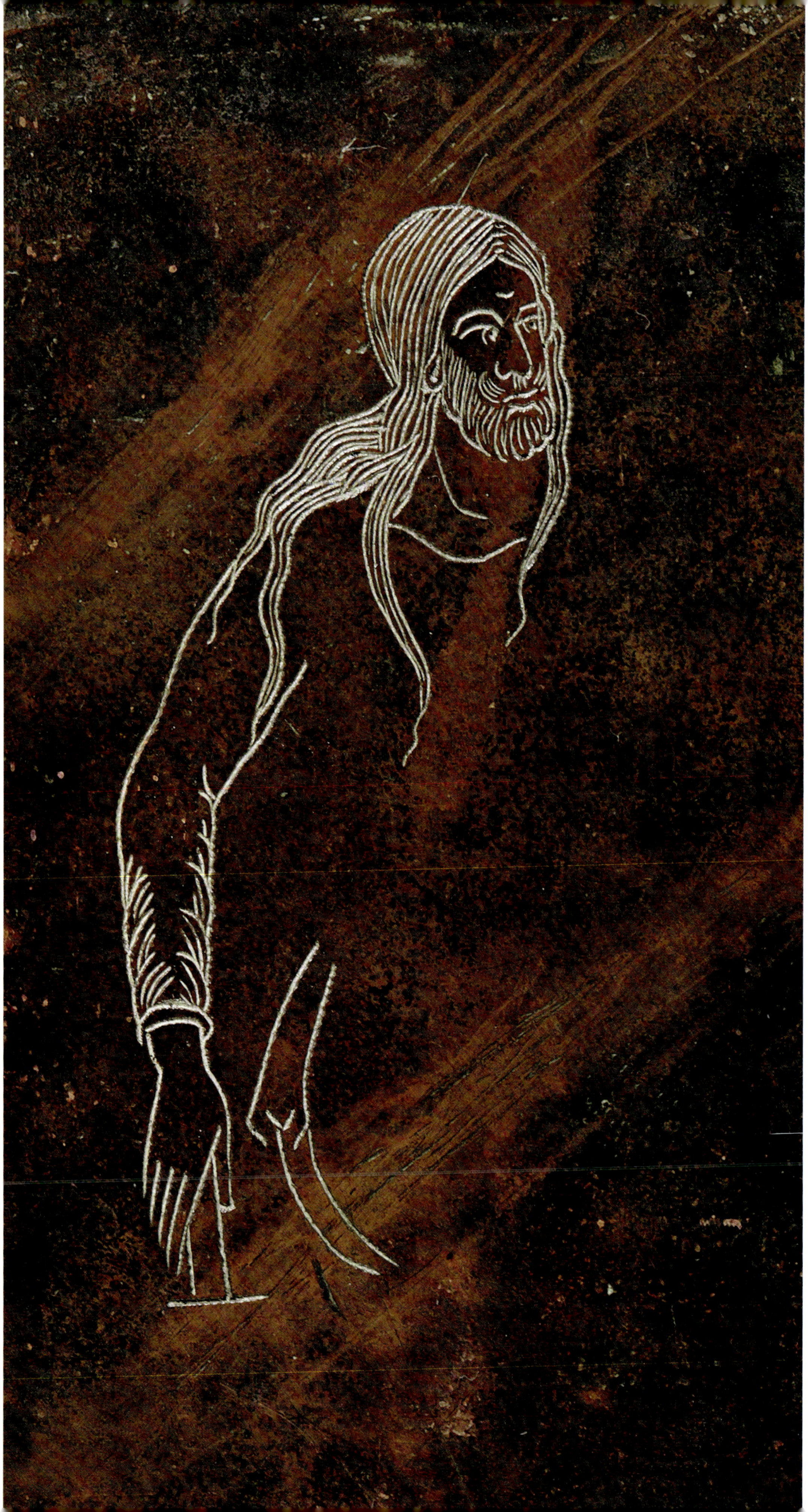

INDEX

Page numbers in **bold** *refer to illustrations.*

Adalbero II of Metz, 44, 48

Adoration of the Magi, **13** (fig. 14), 14

All Saints Day illuminations from lectionary and collectar (cat. 6), 38, **39**

allegorical figures, 68, **68–69**, 104, **107**

altar cross (cat. 24), 70, **72–73**, 73

Altfried (bishop of Hildesheim), 3, 4

apostles. *See* Twelve Apostles

aquamanilia, 18, **108**, 109, 112

arm reliquaries: of Bernward (cat. 33), 64, **94**, 95; Guelph Treasure, 98; inventoried at St. Michael's (1542), 95; of military saint (cat. 20), 64, **65**

Ascension / Assumption of the Virgin, 38, **40–41**

Azelin (bishop of Hildesheim), 4

ball, reliquary in form of (cat. 34), 96, **97**

Baptism of Christ, 14, 104, **105**

baptismal fonts: Hildesheim Cathedral (cat. 38), 103, 104, **105–7**; Osnabrück, 104

Basil the Great, Saint, on reliquary cross (cat. 46), **122**, 123

beaker of Saint Godehard (cat. 35), 16, 98, **99**

Berengar (caster of Willigis's bronze doors), 15

Bernhard (bishop of Hildesheim), 15–16, 70, 73, 98, 115

Bernhard Chalice (*Bernhardkelch*) and Paten (cat. 42), 70, 98, **114**, 115

Bernward (bishop of Hildesheim): altar cross (cat. 24) and, 73; arm reliquary (cat. 33), 64, **94**, 95; as artist and scribe, 17, 35, 48; Bernward Bible (cat. 5) and, 35; biographies of, 6–7, 48, 50; crosier of Abbot Erkanbald (cat. 12) and, 53; Descent from the Cross (cat. 15) and, 58; Golden Madonna (cat. 7) and, 42; Guntbald Gospels (cat. 3) and, 29; Guntbald Sacramentary (cat. 4) and, 31; head reliquary of, 95; Hezilo Gospels (cat. 2) and, 25; paten of Bishop Gerhard vom Berge (cat. 47) associated with, 18, 124; as patron of the arts, 4, 6–15, 104; on portable altar (cat. 28), 83, **83**; portable altar (cat. 9) and, 47; portrait of, Precious Gospels (fig. 10), 10, **11**, 47, 50, 90; possible portrait of, Bernward Bible (cat. 5), 35, **37**; in Ratmann Sacramentary (cat. 21), 66; Ringelheim Crucifix (cat. 8) and, 44; Small Bernward Cross (cat. 25), 73, 74, **74–75**; Small Bernward Gospel (cat. 1) of, 4, 6, **20**, 21, **22**, **23**, 58; tomb of (fig. 9), **10**, 19, 50; translation of remains, 50, 95; veneration and canonization of, 7, 21, 73, 74, 90, 95. *See also* Precious Gospels of Bernward

Bernward Bible (cat. 5), **34**, 35, **36**, **37**

Bernward Cross (cat. 10), 48, **48–49**, 74

Bernward Cross (fig. 20), 17, **18**, 74

Bernward's Candlesticks (cat. 11), **v**, 11, 50, **50–51**, 53

Bernward's Column (figs. 15–17), 14, **14–15**

Bernward's Doors (figs. 12–14), 11–14, **12–13**, 15

biblical scenes: baptismal font (cat. 38), 104, **106**; Bernward's Column (figs. 16–17), **15**; Bernward's Doors (figs. 12–14), 11, **12–13**, 14; crosier of Abbot Erkanbald (cat. 12), **52**, 53. *See also specific scenes*, e.g. Entry into Jerusalem

bishopric of Hildesheim, vii, 3–4, 6, 18–19

book covers. *See* manuscript covers

Braunschweig: Cathedral, 98, 112; Duke of, 18, 19; lion monument in town square of, 109, 112

burial cross (so-called; cat. 48), **126**, 127

Byzantine ivories, 6, **20**, 21, 58, **59**, 90, **91**

Byzantine or Russian reliquary cross (cat. 46), 18, **122–23**, 123

cameos, 88, **89**

candlesticks: altar candlesticks, pair of (cat. 22), 18, 68, **68–69**; Bernward's Candlesticks (cat. 11), **v**, 11, 50, **50–51**, 53; Braunschweig Cathedral seven-branched candlestick, 112; lion pricket candlestick (cat. 41), 112, **113**; Samson candlesticks (*Simsonleuchter*), 112; Trivulzio Candlestick, 104

canon tables, 21, 29, 35, **36**

canonization: Bernward, veneration and canonization of, 7, 17, 21, 73, 74, 90, 95; of Godehard, 15, 16, 57, 98

Carmen Paschale (Sedulius), **24**, 25, **26**

Carolingians and Carolingian era, 3, 4, 25, 29

cathedral school, Hildesheim, 3, 6, 16, 18

chalices. *See* communion vessels

champlevé enamel: domed reliquary (cat. 26), 76, **76–77**; enamel plaques (cat. 27), **i**, **1**, 17, 78, **79–81**; portable altar (cat. 16), **60**, 61; portable altar (cat. 28), **82–83**, 83; processional cross (cat. 36), 17, **100–101**, 101

Charlemagne, 3, 4, 11, 15, 29

Charles the Bald, sacramentary of, 31

choir screen, St. Michael's (fig. 7), 7, **9**, 98

Christ in Majesty / Judgment, **28**, 29, 38, **39**, 78, 90, **114**, 115

Christ trampling beasts, 66, **67**

Christopher, Saint, on portable altar (cat. 29), 84, **85**

cloisonné enamel, 58, 88, **89**

collectar and lectionary (cat. 6), 38, **39–41**

communion vessels: beaker of Saint Godehard (cat. 35), 16, 98, **99**; Bernhard Chalice and Paten (cat. 42), 70, 98, **114**, 115; chalice of Bishop Gerhard vom Berge, 18, 124; paten of Bishop Gerhard vom Berge (cat. 47), 18, 98, 124, **125**

Constantine the Great (Roman emperor), on reliquary cross (cat. 46), 123, **123**

Constantinople, 86, 90, 123
crosiers: Ashmolean Museum crosier head, 120; of Abbot Erkanbald (cat. 12), **52**, 53; of Saint Godehard (cat. 14), 16, **56–57**, 57; of Bishop Johannes I (cat. 44), **118**, 119; of Bishop Otto I (cat. 45), 120, **121**; of Abbot Theodoric, 57
crosses: Bernward Cross (fig. 20), 17, **18**, 74: Hezilo Cross (cat. 13), **54–55**, 55; Imperial Cross, 55; reliquary cross (cat. 30), 18, 86, **86–87**; reliquary cross (cat. 46), **122–23**, 123; Small Bernward Cross (cat. 25), 73, 74, **74–75**; Victoria and Albert gilded copper cross, 68
crucifixes and crucifixions: altar cross (cat. 24), 70, **72–73**, 73; Bernward Cross (cat. 10), 48, **48–49**, 74; Bernward's Doors, 14; burial cross (so called; cat. 48), **126**, 127; cross on a pyx (cat. 23), 70, **71**, 73; enamel plaques (cat. 27), 78, **81**; Gero Crucifix, 44; Guntbald Sacramentary (cat. 4), **30**, 31; ivory panel made for Adalbero II of Metz, 44, 48; portable altar (cat. 16), **60**, 61; processional cross (cat. 36), 17, 48, 74, **100–101**, 101; on reliquary cross (cat. 30), 86, **87**; Ringelheim Crucifix (cat. 8), 11, 44, **44–45**, 48; Small Bernward Gospel (cat. 1), **20**, 21, 58; Wechselburg triumphal cross, 116. *See also* Descent from the Cross; Virgin Mary and Saint John at the Cross
Crucifixus Dolorosus, 127

Deesis, Precious Gospels (cat. 32), 90, **91**
Descent from the Cross: enamel plaques (cat. 27), 78, **81**; ivory plaque (cat. 15), 58, **59**
Dinklar, Battle of (1367), 18–19
Diözesanmuseum cross base, 73
Dirking, Johannes (Jesuit monk), 98
domed reliquary (cat. 26), 76, **76–77**
doors, monumental bronze: of Bishop Bernward, Hildesheim (figs. 12–14), 11–14, **12–13**, 15; of Archbishop Willigis, Mainz, 11, 15
Dormition of the Virgin, 38, **41**
dragons: altar candlesticks, pair of (cat. 22), 68, **69**; altar cross (cat. 24), **72**, 73; aquamanilia in shape of, 109; Bernward's Candlesticks (cat. 11), 50, **51**; crosier of Bishop Otto I (cat. 45), 120, **121**; eagle lectern (cat. 37), **102–3**, 103; Ratmann Sacramentary (cat. 21), 66, **67**

eagle lectern (cat. 37), **102–3**, 103
Ecclesia plaque, on processional cross (cat. 36), **100**, 101
Elijah (prophet), on reliquary cross (cat. 46), **122**, 123
émail brun, 84
enamel: cloisonné, 58, 88, **89**; enamel plaques (cat. 27), **i**, **1**, 17, 78, **79–81**; Esztergom Reliquary, 58; Limoges enamels, 96. *See also* champlevé enamel
encolpion (reliquary cross; cat. 46), 18, **122–23**, 123
Entry into Jerusalem, 14, 78, **81**
Epiphanius of Pavia, Saint: on baptismal font (cat. 38), 104, **106**; Epiphanius Shrine, 16; as patron of Hildesheim, 3; on portable altar (cat. 28), 83, **83**; on second seal of cathedral chapter (cat. 43), 116, **117**
Erkanbald (abbot of Fulda and archbishop of Mainz), 53
Eucharist. *See* communion vessels; portable altars
Evangelists and Evangelist symbols: altar cross (cat. 24), **73**; baptismal font (cat. 38), 104, **106**; burial cross (so-called; cat. 48), 127; cross on a pyx (cat. 23), 70, **71**, 73; eagle lectern (cat. 37), **102–3**, 103; Guntbald Gospels (cat. 3), **29**; Hezilo Gospels (cat. 2), **24**, 25, **26**; paten of Bishop Gerhard vom Berge (cat. 47), 124, **125**; portable altar (cat. 9), 47; Precious Gospels (cat. 32), 86, 90, **91**, **92**; processional cross (cat. 36), 100, **101**; Ratmann Sacramentary (cat. 21), 66, **67**; reliquary of Saint Oswald (cat. 31), 88; Small Bernward Gospel (cat. 1), 21; Stavelot portable altar, 68; wood ceiling of St. Michael's, 10

fans, liturgical (cats. 17–19), **ii**, 17, **62–63**, 63, 70, 74
filigree: arm reliquary of Saint Bernward (cat. 33), 64, **94**, 95; Bernhard Chalice and Paten (cat. 42), 70, 98, **114**, 115; Bernward Cross (fig. 20), 17, **18**); Godehard (fig. 19) and Epiphanius shrines, 16–17, **17**; Golden Madonna (cat. 7), 11, 42, **43**; liturgical fans (cats. 17–19), **ii**, 17, **62–63**, 63, 70, 74; Precious Gospels (cat. 32), 6, 14, 86, 90, **91–93**; reliquary cross (cat. 30), 18, 86, **86–87**; reliquary of Saint Oswald (cat. 31), 18, 42, 88, **89**; *Schneckenfiligran* (snail filigree), 115; Small Bernward Cross (cat. 25), 73, 74, **74–75**
foundation reliquary (Shrine of Our Lady; fig. 2), 3, **4**, 19
Four Rivers of Paradise, 53, 88, 104, **106**
Franco-Saxon manuscript school, 21, 25
Frederick Barbarossa bust, Cappenberg Abbey, 70
Fundatio ecclesiæ Hildensemensis, 3

Gandersheim Abbey, 38, 53
gems. *See* rock crystal and precious and semiprecious stones
Gereon, Saint, 64
Gerhard vom Berge (bishop of Hildesheim), 18–19, 124
Gero (archbishop of Cologne), 11
Gero Crucifix, Cologne Cathedral, 44
Godehard (bishop of Hildesheim), 15–16: on baptismal font (cat. 38), 104, **106**; beaker of (cat. 35), 16, 98, **99**; canonization of, 14, 15, 16, 98; crosier of (cat. 14), 16, **56–57**, 57; on portable altar (cat. 28), 83, **83**; reliquary shrine of (fig. 19), 16, **17**, 70; on second seal of cathedral chapter (cat. 43), 116, **117**
Golden Madonna (Virgin and Child Enthroned; cat. 7), 11, 42, **43**
gospel books. *See* manuscripts
Guelph Treasure, vi, 98
Guntbald Gospels (cat. 3), **28–29**, 29, 31
Guntbald of Regensburg, 14, 29, 31
Guntbald Sacramentary (cat. 4), 29, **30**, 31, **32**, **33**, 35
Gunthar (bishop of Hildesheim), 3, 4

Heavenly Jerusalem, representations of, **5**, 6, 74
Helena, Saint, on reliquary cross (cat. 46), 123, **123**
Helmarshausen workshop and scriptorium, 17
Henry II (king of England), 88
Henry II (king of Germany), 48
Henry III (bishop of Hildesheim), 53
Henry III (Holy Roman emperor), 55
Henry the Lion (duke of Saxony and Bavaria), 17–18, 86, 88, 109, 112
Henry the Lion Gospel, 17–18
Hezilo (bishop of Hildesheim), 4, 6, 16, 25, 55
Hezilo Chandelier, Hildesheim Cathedral (fig. 3), **5**, 6
Hezilo Cross (cat. 13), **54–55**, 55
Hezilo Gospels (cat. 2), 21, **24**, 25, **26**, **27**
Hildesheim and Hildesheim treasures, vi, vii, 3–19: under Bernward, 4, 6–15, 104 (*see also*

Bernward); bishopric of Hildesheim, vii, 3–4, 6, 18–19; Cathedral (*see* St. Mary's Cathedral); cathedral school, 3, 6, 16, 18; Gandersheim Abbey, dispute between Hildesheim and Mainz over, 38, 53; under Godehard and Bernhard, 15–16; as metalwork center, 16–17, 50, 78, 104; organization and structure of town, 18; origins and history, 3–4; politics and society in medieval Hildesheim, 18–19; after Reformation, 19; secularization of church properties (1803) and collection of diocesan artworks, vii, 10, 19, 57, 70, 74, 76. *See also* specific Hildesheim monasteries and churches

Holy Cross relics. *See* True Cross relics

Hypatius, Saint, on reliquary cross (cat. 46), **122**, 123

Imperial Cross, 55

inscriptions: altar candlesticks, pair of (cat. 22), 68; altar cross (cat. 24), **73**; arm reliquary (cat. 20), 64; Bernhard Chalice and Paten (cat. 42), 115; of Bernward, 10–11, 29, 48; Bernward Cross (cat. 10), **48**; Bernward's Candlesticks (cat. 11), 50; Bernward's tomb, St. Michael's, 10; crosier of Abbot Erkanbald (cat. 12), 53; crosier of Saint Godehard (cat. 14), 57; crosier of Bishop Otto I (cat. 45), 120; Descent from the Cross (cat. 15), 58; domed reliquary (cat. 26), 76; in Guntbald Gospels (cat. 3), 29; Hezilo Cross (cat. 13), 55; paten of Bishop Gerhard vom Berge (cat. 47), 124, **125**; Precious Gospels (cat. 32), 90, **93**; Ratmann Sacramentary (cat. 21), 66; reliquary cross (cat. 46), 18, **122–23**, 123; reliquary of Saint Oswald (cat. 31), 88; Willigis, bronze doors of, 11

intaglios, 63, 86, 88, 90

ivory: Byzantine ivories, 6, **20**, 21, 58, **59**, 90, **91**; crosier of Saint Godehard (cat. 14), 16, **56–57**, 57; crosier of Bishop Otto I (cat. 45), 120, **121**; crucifixion panel made for Adalbero II of Metz, 44, 48; Descent from the Cross (cat. 15), 58, **59**; Mainz statuette of Virgin and Child Enthroned, 42; portable altar (cat. 28), **82–83**, 83, 84, portable altar (cat. 29), 84, **84–85**; Precious Gospels (cat. 32), 86, 90, **91**; Small Bernward Gospel (cat. 1), **20**, 21, 58

Johannes I of Brackel (Johann of Brackel; bishop of Hildesheim), 119

John, Saint: on Bernward's Column (fig. 16), **15**; on Precious Gospels (cat. 32), 90, **91**. *See also* Virgin Mary and Saint John at the Cross

John the Baptist, Saint, on portable altar (cat. 29), 84, **85**

Judith (sister of Bernward and abbess of Ringelheim), 44

Kratz, Johann Michael (historian), 74

Kunstgewerbemuseum Berlin cross base, 73

Lamb of God, 38, **39**, 48, 70, 73, **73**, 120, **121**, 124, **125**

Last Judgment, 38, **39**

Last Supper, **46**, 47, 78, **81**

lecterns: eagle lectern (cat. 37), **102–3**, 103; Villard de Honnecourt's drawing of, 103

lectionary and collectar (cat. 6), 38, **39–41**

Life of Saint Bernward (1540), 50

Limoges enamels, 96

lions: altar candlesticks, pair of (cat. 22), 68, **69**; altar cross (cat. 24), **72**, 73; aquamanile in shape of (cat. 39), **108**, 109; Braunschweig Cathedral seven-branched candlestick, 112; Cleveland Museum of Art aquamanile, 112; cross on a pyx (cat. 23), 70, **71**; pricket candlestick in shape of (cat. 41), 112, **113**; Ratmann Sacramentary (cat. 21), 66, **67**

liturgical fans (cats. 17–19), **ii**, 17, **62–63**, 63, 70, 74

Lorsch Gospels, 29

Louis the Pious, 3, 4

Lutheranism, Hildesheim's adoption of, 19

Mainz: Gandersheim Abbey, dispute with Hildesheim over, 38, 53; ivory statuette of Virgin and Child Enthroned, 42; monumental bronze doors of Bishop Willigis, 11, 15

manuscript covers: Descent from the Cross (cat. 15), 58, **59**; Precious Gospels of Bernward (cat. 32), 6, 14, 48, 86, 90, **91–93**; Ratmann Sacramentary (cat. 21), 17, 66, **67**, 73; from St. Godehard's, 74; Small Bernward Gospel (cat. 1), **20**, 21

manuscripts: Bernward Bible (cat. 5), **34**, 35, **36**, **37**; canon tables, 21, 29, 35, **36**; Guntbald Gospels (cat. 3), **28–29**, 29, 31; Guntbald Sacramentary (cat. 4), 29, **30**, 31, **32**, **33**; Henry the Lion Gospel, 17–18; Hezilo Gospels (cat. 2), 21, **24**, 25, **26**, **27**; lectionary and collectar (cat. 6), 38, **39–41**; Lorsch Gospels, 29; Nuremberg pericope book, 29; Ratmann Sacramentary (cat. 21), 17, 66, **67**, 73; sacramentary of Charles the Bald, 31; scriptorium, Helmarshausen, 17–18; Small Bernward Gospel (cat. 1), 4, 6, **20**, 21, **22**, **23**, 58; Stammheim Missal, 17; *Te Igitur* pages, **30**, 31; Wolfenbüttel psalter, 29. *See also* Precious Gospels

Matilda (daughter of Henry II of England and wife of Henry of Saxony), 88

Maurice, Saint, 64

metalwork: altar cross (cat. 24), 70, **72–73**, 73; arm reliquary of Saint Bernward (cat. 33), 64, **94**, 95; arm reliquary (cat. 20) for military saint, 64, **65**; baptismal font (cat. 38), 103, 104, **105–7**; beaker of Saint Godehard (cat. 35), 16, 98, **99**; Bernhard Chalice and Paten (cat. 42), 70, 98, **114**, 115; Bernward Cross (cat. 10), 48, **48–49**, 74; Bernward Cross (fig. 20), 17, **18**, 74; Bernward's Column (figs. 15–17), 14, **14–15**; Bernward's Doors (figs. 12–14), 11–14, **12–13**, 15; burial cross (so-called; cat. 48), **126**, 127; cross on a pyx (cat. 23), 70, **71**, 73; domed reliquary (cat. 26), 76, **76–77**; eagle lectern (cat. 37), **102–3**, 103; foundation reliquary (Shrine of Our Lady; fig. 2), 3, **4**, 19; Godehard Shrine (fig. 19), 16, **17**, 70; Golden Madonna (cat. 7), 11, 42, **43**; Hezilo Chandelier (fig. 3), **5**, 6; Hezilo Cross (cat. 13), **54–55**, 55; Hildesheim as center for, 16–17, 50, 78, 104; lion aquamanile (cat. 39), **108**, 109; liturgical fans (cats. 17–19), **ii**, 17, **62–63**, 63, 70, 74; in Mosan region, 68, 78; paten of Bishop Gerhard vom Berge (cat. 47), 18, 98, 124, **125**; processional cross (cat. 36), 17, 48, 74, **100–101**, 101; Ratmann Sacramentary (cat. 21), 17, 66, **67**, 73; reliquary cross (cat. 46), 18, **122–23**, 123; on reliquary cross (cat. 30), 18, 86, **86–87**; reliquary of Saint Oswald (cat. 31), 18, 42, 88, **89**, **128**; seal of city of Hildesheim (fig. 21), 18, **19**; Small Bernward Cross (cat. 25), 73, 74, **74–75**; Small Bernward Gospel (cat. 1), **20**, 21, 58; Victoria and Albert gilded copper cross, 68. *See also* candlesticks; crosiers; portable altars; Precious Gospels of Bernward

Meyer, Ernst Heinrich (goldsmith), 98

Milliken, William M., vi

Modoaldus of Trier (bishop), 17

Mosan region: altar candlesticks, pair of (cat. 22), 18, 68, **68–69**; enamelwork, 78; lectern sketched by Villard de Honnecourt, 103; metalwork from, 18, 68

Muldenfaltenstil, 116
Muslim craftsmen, 57, 120

Nativity scenes, **13** (fig. 14), 78, **80**, 115
Nicodemus (New Testament figure), 58, **59**
niello: altar candlesticks, pair of (cat. 22), 18, 68, **68–69**; Bernward's Candlesticks (cat. 11), **v**, 11, 50, **50–51**; crosier of Bishop Otto I (cat. 45), 120, **121**; portable altar (cat. 9), **46**, 47; Precious Gospels (cat. 32), 6, 14, 86, 90, **91–93**; reliquary cross (cat. 46), 18, **122–23**, 123; reliquary of Saint Oswald (cat. 31), 18, 42, 88, **89**, **128**
Nuremberg pericope book, 29

Old St. Peter's Basilica, Rome, 7, 14
Osnabrück baptismal font, 104
Oswald, Saint, reliquary of (cat. 31), 18, 42, 88, **89**, **128**
Othwin (bishop of Hildesheim), 3
Otto I (bishop of Hildesheim), 120
Otto II (Holy Roman emperor), 38
Otto III (Holy Roman emperor), 6, 21, 74, 90
Otto III Gospels, 38
Ottonians and Ottonian era, 3, 6, 7, 21, 25, 29, 31, 35, 38, 44, 48, 86

Passion of Christ: enamel plaques (cat. 27), 78, **81**; portable altar (cat. 9), 47, **48**; processional cross (cat. 36), 100, **101**. *See also* crucifixes and crucifixions; Descent from the Cross
patens. *See* communion vessels
portable altars: cat. 9, **46**, 47, 84; cat. 16, **60**, 61; cat. 28, **82–83**, 83, 84; cat. 29, 84, **84–85**; Stavelot portable altar, 68
post-Resurrection narratives: enamel plaques (cat. 27), 17, 78, **79–81**; portable altar (cat. 9), 47; processional cross (cat. 36), 100, **101**
Precious Gospels of Bernward (cat. 32), 90: back cover, 6, 14, 48, 90, **93**; front cover, 86, 90, **91**, **92**; Hezilo Gospels (cat. 2) and, 25; illuminations from (figs. 10, 11), 10, **11**, 42, 47, 50, 90; inscriptions commemorating Bernward's donation of, 90, **93**; portrait of Bishop Bernward (fig. 10), 10, **11**, 47, 50, 90; Virgin and Child Enthroned (fig. 11), 10, **11**, 42
precious stones. *See* rock crystal and precious and semiprecious stones
processional crosses: burial cross (so-called; cat. 48), 127; cross (cat. 36), 17, 48, 74, **100–101**, 101; Small Bernward Cross (cat. 25), 73, 74, **74–75**
Prudence statuette, Paris, 68
pyx, cross on (cat. 23), 70, **71**, 73

Rabanus Maurus (theologian), 50
Rainer of Huy, 104
Ratmann (monk), 66
Ratmann Sacramentary (cat. 21), 17, 66, **67**, 73
Reformation, 19, 70, 86, 95
relics and reliquaries: altar cross (cat. 24), 73; ball, reliquary in form of (cat. 34), 96, **97**; Bernward Cross (cat. 10), 48; cross on a pyx (cat. 23), 70; domed reliquary (cat. 26), 76, **76–77**; Epiphanius Shrine, 16; foundation reliquary (Shrine of Our Lady; fig. 2), 3, **4**, 19; Godehard Shrine (fig. 19), 16, **17**, 70; head reliquary of Saint Bernward, 95; Hezilo Cross (cat. 13), **54–55**, 55; from high altar of Hildesheim Cathedral (1833), 96; Hildesheim foundation story and, 3; portable altar (cat. 29) iconography, 84; reliquary cross (cat. 30), 86, **86–87**; reliquary cross (cat. 46), **122–23**, 123; reliquary of Saint Oswald (cat. 31), 18, 42, 88, **89**, **128**; reliquary of Saint Thomas Becket, 88; Ringelheim Crucifix (cat. 8), 44. *See also* arm reliquaries; True Cross relics
reliquary cross (cat. 46), Byzantine or Russian, 18, **122–23**, 123
reliquary cross (cat. 30), German, 18, 86, **86–87**
Ringelheim Crucifix (cat. 8), 11, 44, **44–45**, 48
Robert II (king of the Franks), 48
rock crystal and precious and semiprecious stones: altar cross (cat. 24), 70, **72–73**, 73; arm reliquary of Saint Bernward (cat. 33), 64, **94**, 95; Bernhard Chalice and Paten (cat. 42), 70, 98, **114**, 115; Bernward Cross (fig. 20), 17, **18**; domed reliquary (cat. 26), 76, **76–77**; foundation reliquary (Shrine of Our Lady; fig. 2), 3, **4**, 19; Godehard Shrine (fig. 19), 16, **17**, 70; Golden Madonna (cat. 7), 11, 42, **43**; Hezilo Cross (cat. 13), **54–55**, 55; liturgical fans (cats. 17–19), **ii**, 17, **62–63**, 63, 70, 74; portable altar (cat. 9), **46**, 47, 84; portable altar (cat. 28), **82–83**, 83, 84; Precious Gospels (cat. 32), 90, **91**, **92**; Ratmann Sacramentary (cat. 21), 17, 66, **67**, 73; reliquary cross (cat. 30), 18, 86, **86–87**; reliquary of Saint Oswald (cat. 31), 18, 42, 88, **89**; Small Bernward Cross (cat. 25), 73, 74, **74–75**; Small Bernward Gospel (cat. 1), **20**, 21
Roger of Helmarshausen (artist-monk), 17
Russian or Byzantine reliquary cross (cat. 46), 18, **122–23**, 123

St. Bartholomew's Monastery, Hildesheim, 15, 16
St. Godehard's, Hildesheim (fig. 18), 16, **16**, 17, 19, 48, 57, 70, 74, 98, 101, 115
St. Jacob's Church, Stendal, cross base from, 73
St. Mary's Cathedral, Hildesheim (figs. 1, 3), vi, vii, **2**, 3–6, **5**, 18, 19
St. Maurice's, Hildesheim, 16, 64
St. Michael's, Hildesheim (figs. 4–9), vii, 4, **6**, **7–10**, 14, 15, 16, 19, 116
St. Michael's Church, Seesen-Bilderlahe, 111
St. Simon and St. Jude Collegiate Church, Goslar, 55
Samson candlesticks (*Simsonleuchter*), 112
Schedula diversarum artium (attrib. Roger of Helmarshausen), 17, 86
Schneckenfiligran (snail filigree), 115
scriptorium, Helmarshausen, 17
seals: city of Hildesheim (fig. 21), 18, **19**; second seal of cathedral chapter (cat. 43), 116, **117**
secularization of church properties (1803), vii, 10, 19, 57, 70, 74, 76
Sedulius (poet), 25, 50
semiprecious stones. *See* rock crystal and precious and semiprecious stones
Shrine of Our Lady (foundation reliquary; fig. 2), 3, **4**, 19
Siculo-Arabic workshops, 57, 120
Simsonleuchter (Samson candlesticks), 112
situla (holy water vessel; cat. 40), **110**, 111
sketch engraved on reverse of enamel plaque (cat. 27), 78, **132**
Small Bernward Cross (cat. 25), 73, 74, **74–75**
Small Bernward Gospel (cat. 1), 4, 6, **20**, 21, **22**, **23**
snail filigree (*Schneckenfiligran*), 115
Sophia (sister of Emperor Otto II), 38
Stammheim Missal, 17
Stavelot Abbey (Liège, Belgium), 17
Stavelot portable altar, 68

Te Igitur pages, **30**, 31
tetramorphs. *See* Evangelists and Evangelist symbols
Thangmar of Hildesheim (author, *Vita Bernwardi*), 7, 48
Theban Legion, 64
Theodoric (abbot of St. Godehard's), 57

Theophano (Byzantine princess), 21
Thidericus (abbot of St. Godehard's), 98
Thietmar (bishop of Hildesheim), 6
Thietmar Chandelier, Hildesheim Cathedral, 6
Thietmar of Merseburg, 44
Thomas Becket, Saint, reliquary of, 88
Tree of Jesse wood ceiling, St. Michael's (figs. 6, 8), **8–9**, 10, 116
Tree of Life motif, 55, 74, 127
triumphal cross, collegiate church of Wechselburg, 116
Trivulzio Candlestick, Milan Cathedral, 104
True Cross relics: Bernward Cross (cat. 10), 48, **48–49**, 74; Bernward Cross (fig. 20), 17, **18**, 74; discovery of, 123; Esztergom Reliquary, 58; Imperial Cross, 55; reliquary cross (cat. 30), 18, 86, **86–87**; reliquary cross (cat. 46), 18, **122–23**, 123
Tuotilo (artist-monk), 42
Twelve Apostles: ball, reliquary in form of (cat. 34), 96; domed reliquary (cat. 26), 76, **76–77**; portable altar (cat. 9), **46**, 47, 84; portable altar (cat. 16), **60**, 61; portable altar (cat. 29), 84, **84–85**

vernis brun, **5**, 21, **23**, 63, 64, 101
Victoria and Albert gilded copper cross, 68
Villard de Honnecourt, 103
Virgin and Child: on baptismal font (cat. 38), 104, **106**; Golden Madonna (cat. 7), 11, 42, **43**; Mainz ivory statuette, 42; Precious Gospels (cat. 32), 6, 14, 48, 90, **93**; Precious Gospels (fig. 11), 10, **11**, 42; second seal of cathedral chapter (cat. 43), 116, **117**
Virgin Mary: Ascension/Assumption/Dormition illuminations from lectionary and collectar (cat. 6), 38, **40–41**; Deesis, Precious Gospels (cat. 32), 90, **91**; foundation reliquary (Shrine of Our Lady; fig. 2), 3, **4**, 19; as patron of Hildesheim, 3, 19; on portable altar (cat. 28), 83, **83**; Tree of Jesse wood ceiling, St. Michael's (fig. 8), **9**
Virgin Mary and Saint John at the Cross: Descent from the Cross (cat. 15), 58, **59**; Guntbald Sacramentary (cat. 4), **30**, 31; reliquary cross (cat. 46), **122**, 123; Small Bernward Gospel cover (cat. 1), **20**, 21
Vita Bernwardi, Thangmar of Hildesheim's, 7, 48

wax second seal of cathedral chapter (cat. 43), 116, **117**
Wedekin, Eduard J. (bishop of Hildesheim), vii, 19, 68, 70, 76, 96
Wilbrandus of Oldenburg-Wildeshausen, 104, **106**
Willigis (archbishop of Mainz), 11, 15
Wolfenbüttel psalter, 29
wood: ball, reliquary in form of (cat. 34), 96, 97; beaker of Saint Godehard (cat. 35), 16, 98, **99**; panel, probably original mount for enamel plaques, 78, **78**; Ringelheim Crucifix (cat. 8), 11, 44, **44–45**, 48; Tree of Jesse ceiling, St. Michael's (figs. 6, 8), 7–10, **8–9**, 116; triumphal cross, collegiate church of Wechselburg, 116

Zackenstil, 116
Zum Heiligen Kreuz, Hildesheim, 55

PHOTOGRAPHY CREDITS

Numerals refer to page numbers.

BILDARCHIV FOTO MARBURG: 5

DOMBIBLIOTHEK HILDESHEIM: 39 41 (photographs by Lutz Engelhardt)

DOM-MUSEUM HILDESHEIM: i, 1, 7, 45, 78–81; 11 (Bayerische Staatsbibliothek, Munich); 121 (photograph by Jutta Brüdern); 20 (photograph by Erika Dufour, courtesy of the Art Institute of Chicago); 22, 24, 26, 27, 57, 60, 74, 75, 89, 97, 128 (photographs by Lutz Engelhardt); 122–23 (photographs by Rudolf A. Hillebrecht); 24, 34, 36, 54, 55, 62, 63, 73, 76, 84, 98, 99, 100, 101, 110, 113, 114, 117, 118, 132 (photographs by Ansgar Hoffmann); 37 (photograph by Renate von Issen); 28–30, 32, 33, 82, 83, 126 (photographs by Ulrich Knapp); ii, 17, 44, 65, 71, 72, 77, 85, 94 (photographs by Jürgen Liepe); 2, 16 (photographs by Gerhard Lutz); 86, 87 (photographs by Torsten Schoepe); v, 4, 12, 13, 18, 23, 43, 46, 48–52, 59, 67, 91, 93 (photographs by Frank Tomio); 56, 68, 69, 102–3, 108, 125 (Staatliche Museen zu Berlin—Preußischer Kulturbesitz, photographs by Antje Voigt); 104–7 (photographs by Manfred Zimmermann)

EVANGELISCH-LUTHERISCHE KIRCHENGEMEINDE ST. MICHAELIS HILDESHEIM: 6, 8, 9 top, 10, 14, 15 top (photographs by Andreas Lechtape)

STADTARCHIV HILDESHEIM: 19 (photograph by Rudolf A. Hillebrecht)

UNIVERSITY OF APPLIED SCIENCES AND ARTS HILDESHEIM / HOLZMINDEN / GÖTTINGEN: 9 bottom, 15 bottom (photographs by Clemens Kappen)